FIRST AID

SAFETY ORIENTED

Third Edition – 1990

St. John Ambulance
312 Laurier Avenue East
Ottawa, Canada K1N 6P6

First Edition	–	*1983*
Second Edition	–	*1988*
Third Edition	–	*1990*
First Impression (1990)	–	*192,000*

Canadian Cataloguing in Publication Data

Main entry under title:
    First Aid: Safety Oriented

Third Edition 1990

Issued also in French under title: Secourisme
    orienté vers la sécurité.
ISBN 0-929006-09-7
(ISBN: 0-919434-80-0. 3ʳᵈ edition, 1988)

1. First aid in illness and injury -- Handbooks,
manuals, etc. I. St. John Ambulance.

RC86.F57 1990   616.02'52   C90-090386-4

This publication has been adopted by the Canadian
Forces and has been assigned NDID number:
A-MD-050-073/PT-001

Printed in Canada   Stock number: 3470

CONTENTS

FOREWORD TO THE FIRST EDITION

From the time of its founding, almost one thousand years ago, the Most Venerable Order of the Hospital of St. John of Jerusalem has been fortunate in those who established it and built upon its founding principles. The "Blesssed Gerard" was outstanding among early rectors. He was the first to consolidate and strengthen the small local hospital and establish a new Order of Hospitallers. He was succeeded by Raymond du Puy who became rector in the year 1120, beginning a stewardship of forty years. He has been called the second founder of the Order because he not only changed it to a military organization but laid the foundations of the greatest Order of Chivalry the world has ever known. He gave the members their first written rules – The Rule of Raymond du Puy. How interesting it would be if he had also laid down a guide to first aid. We may be sure it would have contained the most up-to-date methods then available, for the reputation of the hospital in Jerusalem was spread throughout Christendom by crusaders who returned to their homes in Western Europe after receiving treatment there.

A review of the various handbooks prepared by the Order of St. John shows how methods have improved progressively as new knowledge made change desirable. The flexibility of the Order in adopting new advances has been one of its great strengths. For example, a review of changes in artificial respiration clearly indicates this policy of change.

This writer received his first course in first aid in 1928 when he was a first year medical student. It followed the St. John Ambulance plan. The course included the Schaefer method of artificial respiration. This method was still in use seven or eight years later when I was teaching it to recruits of the Royal Canadian Army Medical Corps. About 1950, the Schaefer method was replaced by the Holger Nielsen. By the 1960s, mouth-to-mouth artificial respiration was being taught in St. John First Aid courses and this was soon supplemented by "external cardiac massage". Today, St. John Ambulance teaches cardiopulmonary resuscitation as a combined technique to maintain respiration and circulation.

The ever increasing number of St. John trained citizens has made a great impact on death rates and disabling injury statistics, especially in industry. What may not be so readily apparent is an equally significant decrease in accident rates, resulting from increased safety awareness. In keeping with the progessive outlook of the Order, First Aid Safety Oriented *lays stress on prevention and safety measures as they relate to each area of illness or injury. First aid, taught in this context, has been proved to reduce the number of accidents and to minimize injury, greatly increasing the effectiveness of St. John First Aid programmes.*

If Raymond du Puy and the other men and women of the early Order could see the skills which St. John-trained people bring to the aid of the sick and injured today, they would be amazed at the scope and sophistication of its techniques and at the emphasis given to prevention and safety. They could take pride and great satisfaction in the results of their early building and in the traditions which have been and will be maintained.

Robert C. Dickson,
OC, OBE, CStJ, CD, QHP,
January, 1983 MD(Tor), LLD(Dal), MACP, FRCP(Lond), FRCP(C)

PREFACE TO THE SECOND EDITION

First Aid, as in all fields of learning, needs to be kept up-to-date as new information becomes available through experience and research. St. John Ambulance conducts periodic reviews of all teaching materials to ensure that First Aiders are equipped with the latest knowledge and skills when they are called upon to give emergency care to the sick and injured.

The St. John Ambulance National Medical Advisory Committee met in 1984 and again in 1986 to consider changes to a number of first aid procedures, including snakebite, poisoning and spinal injuries. This Committee also considered the new standards recommended by the American Heart Association and the Canadian Heart Foundation (Heart and Stroke Foundation of Canada) for training in cardiopulmonary resuscitation. This Second Edition of First Aid Safety Oriented *reflects the new standards for basic life support in their entirety. The Committee recognized that the techniques that were previously taught were not harmful, but that the new standards are based on techniques that are considered better, easier to learn, and that should result in a longer retention of knowledge and skills.*

The key to becoming a good First Aider is training and experience, but retraining is the only way to keep first aid knowledge and skills current. The aim of this second edition is to provide the latest information on which to base the training of new First Aiders and the refresher training of those already in the field.

W. Roy Coleman, CStJ, CD, MD, FRCP(C)
January 1988   Chief Medical Officer

Note: *This third edition of First Aid Safety Oriented was prepared as a result of changes in the medical recommendations for certain first aid procedures. Consequently, the first aid for poisonings, eye injuries, snake and insect bites and a variety of other medical emergencies has been completely updated and included in this third edition.*

R.L. Rowlatt
August 1990   National Director of Training—St. John Ambulance

ACKNOWLEDGEMENTS

*St. John Ambulance, the Priory of Canada, records
grateful acknowledgement to those organizations
which granted permission to use certain material
or otherwise contributed to the production of
this manual, in particular the following:*

*The American Academy of Orthopaedic Surgeons,
American Heart Association, The Heart and Stroke Foundation of
Canada, Industrial Accident Prevention Association Ontario.*

EDITORIAL BOARD
for the First Edition

Table of Figures

CHAPTER 1

PRINCIPLES AND PRACTICES OF SAFETY ORIENTED FIRST AID

PRINCIPLES OF SAFETY

There are risks in most activities of daily living, but these risks can be eliminated or considerably reduced if you know what they are and if you take appropriate actions and safeguards. As a First Aider, you will know the terrible consequences of injury. This will motivate you to recognize hazards and to apply the principles of safety to avoid such injuries.

Applying the principles of safety means that you will:

- **assess risks** and report accident potentials. Learn the risks of working with hazardous materials as detailed on product labels and in the *Workplace Hazardous Materials Information System (WHMIS).* You should acquaint yourself also with the *Dangerous Goods Placards and Labels* used to identify hazardous materials during transportation.

- **plan the activity** so that the job can be performed safely and so that dangerous situations can be controlled as they arise. Take the precautions recommended on label instructions and *Material Safety Data Sheets (MSDS).*

- **train for the job** so that you can work safely with equipment and materials, recognize unsafe conditions and take appropriate steps to eliminate the accident potential.

- **using personal protective equipment** recommended for the job or activity, which includes proper headgear, safety footwear, eyeshields, breathing apparatus, safety harnesses, nets, gloves to assist in preventing injury and illness.

- **making a personal commitment to safety** at work, at home and in leisure activities, not only for yourself, but to set an example for others. It also means making an effort to determine the causes of accidents and planning safety measures to prevent them.

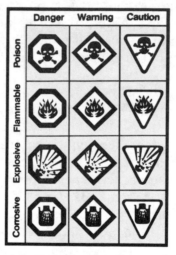

Fig. 1-1. Hazardous product symbols.

Learn to recognize the symbols that indicate hazards from products and take the precautions indicated to avoid injury. For information regarding hazardous materials in the work-place, see page 14.

SAFETY OF THE FIRST AIDER

As a First Aider, you may be exposed to hazardous situations in which you are required to act quickly. Take time to assess risks, and do not neglect safety precautions. Failing to do so could make you a casualty as well, and result in the loss of emergency care to the original victims of the accident. Therefore, carefully assess the situation and plan the rescue and first aid procedures. Take only assessed and calculated risks to help accident victims.

Three aspects of an accident may endanger the First Aider:

- **the energy source or factor that caused the original injury.** Energy applied to the human body at levels that exceed the body's tolerance causes injuries. Therefore, you must assess the degree of risk presented by an energy source, such as electricity or machinery, and eliminate, reduce or redirect that energy, or take appropriate precautions during rescue and first aid procedures.

- **the hazards from secondary or external factors.** There may be danger from factors other than that which caused the accident itself. A motor vehicle accident, for example, may be complicated by a subsequent fire or explosion. Roadside accidents frequently cause traffic slowdowns that increase the chance of collisions between the vehicles of curious onlookers. Therefore, you must take precautions to protect yourself and the casualties at the scene of an accident.

- **the hazards of rescue or first aid procedures.** Knowing the dangers of specific accident situations will help you to avoid injury during rescue or while giving first aid. For example, you must use a lifeline and self-contained breathing apparatus to rescue a victim overcome by gas in a silo. You can avoid back injuries by learning proper lifting techniques for rescue and transportation (see chap. 17). Take all necessary hygienic precautions in giving first aid, particularly if there may be contact with the casualty's body fluids — saliva, blood, vomitus, urine or feces. These fluids may carry disease organisms that can be transmitted through any breaks in your skin — (abrasions, minor cuts or chapped areas) — and through contact with mucous membrane. Wash your hands and other contaminated skin areas thoroughly as soon after the incident as possible.

FIRST AID

DEFINITION & OBJECTIVES

First aid is the emergency care given to the injured or suddenly ill person at the scene, using readily available materials. The objectives of first aid are to:

● preserve life;

● prevent the injury or illness from becoming worse;

● promote recovery.

Good safety practices prevent accidents. Good first aid prevents accidents from becoming tragedies.

Medical aid is the treatment given by or under the supervision of a physician at a medical facility or in transit to such a facility.

RESPONSIBILITIES OF A FIRST AIDER

The Legal Implications

Not all jurisdictions have "Good Samaritan" statutes, but the principles of "the Good Samaritan laws" are accepted throughout North America. These laws hold that "a Good Samaritan" [1] who goes to the aid of someone in need of emergency medical care shall not be held liable for negligence for what he does or fails to do, unless there is gross negligence, indicating wanton and willful misconduct. [2] Therefore, there is no need to hesitate nor to be concerned about legal liability provided that:

---

1. *Luke 10:30-36*
2. *Rozovsky, Lorne Elkin,* The Canadian Patient's Book of Rights *(Doubleday Canada Limited, Toronto 1980) p.61.*

- first aid is not forced on a conscious adult or older child who refuses such help. It is assumed that an infant, a younger child or an unconscious person wants help and that they would consent if they could. This is called an **implied consent.** If there are responsible adults accompanying the infant or child, they should be asked to give **verbal consent.**

- a casualty is not abandoned. When the offer of help is accepted, it must be given and continued until the casualty can be handed over to a more qualified person. If help is refused, remain with the person until help arrives.

- a common sense approach is adopted in giving first aid. If the casualty's life is not in danger and you do not know what to do, stay with him and send for help.

- you use caution in giving first aid so that you do not aggravate or increase injury.

- you give the help you would hope to receive if you were in similar circumstances.

Suspected Child Abuse

Be on the alert for signs of child abuse when giving first aid to children. Bruises, burns and fractures in infants and children, where the cause is not readily apparent or is suspicious in nature, should alert you to look for other signs. The child's apparent fear of a parent or babysitter should reinforce suspicions of child abuse.

Insist on medical attention for the child's injuries, no matter how minor they may be, to permit a full medical assessment. If the parent or babysitter refuses medical aid, you have a duty to notify the local child welfare agency or other authorities. **Do not accuse a parent or babysitter of child abuse, but for the child's welfare, do not hesitate to report suspected cases.**

PRIORITY ACTION APPROACH

Priority action approach (PAA) is the sequence of actions followed by a First Aider on arrival at an accident scene or when dealing with a person who has become suddenly ill to ensure that first aid for life-threatening conditions is given safely and in the proper sequence. Although circumstances may dictate that the order of the steps in PAA be changed, they should usually be performed in the following sequence:

1. Take charge of the situation.

2. Call to attract the attention of bystanders to assist you.

3. Assess the hazards at the scene.

4. Make the area safe for yourself and others.

5. Identify yourself to the casualties as a First Aider and offer to help.

6. Quickly assess the casualties for life-threatening conditions.

7. Give first aid for life-threatening conditions.

8. Send someone to call for help — ambulance, police, etc.

CONTROLLING THE SCENE

If emergency services have been called but are not yet at the scene, take charge of the situation to prevent further injury to those involved. Take appropriate precautions according to the type of damage and the cause of the accident. Examples are:

- **vehicle accidents.** Switch off the vehicle's ignition and warn people not to smoke. Make use of bystanders to control traffic or crowds, to call for help and, if they are capable, to assist with first aid.

● **electrical accidents.** Switch off the current or break contact between the injured person and the power source. Use nonconducting material, such as a dry stick, to remove housewires from the casualty. Ensure that the current is turned off or that loose wires are kept at a safe distance until the casualty is removed to safety. **Do not approach fallen high tension power lines until a power company official gives permission. Current discharging into the ground can kill!**

● **gas, smoke and poisonous fumes.** Shut off the source and remove the casualty to fresh air.

● **fires and collapsing buildings.** Move the casualty to safety away from fire, smoke or falling debris (see chap. 28).

CASUALTY ASSESSMENT

To determine the need for first aid, collect and interpret information in three categories: history of the case, signs and symptoms.

History of the case is information about the circumstances leading to or surrounding the incident. The state of the person's health, a record of previous illnesses, details of the incident given by witnesses, evidence of physical violence, the odour of gas and the presence of drug or poison containers all form part of the history of the case.

Signs are conditions you observe that indicate disease or injury. Three of these, temperature, pulse and respiration, are called vital signs. The significance of abnormal variations in these and other signs is specified for various illnesses and injuries and is discussed in later chapters.

Symptoms are sensations that a person feels and describes. These usually are feelings of discomfort due to heat and cold, pain, nausea, or other abnormal sensations. Numbness or the lack of sensation is also a symptom.

Make full use of your senses and learn the significance of changes in the body's vital signs so that you can interpret the history, signs and symptoms of a case.

Examining The Casualty

In many instances, the nature and extent of an injury or illness can be readily seen and a detailed examination of the casualty is not needed. A burn or laceration, for example, may have obvious causes. However, in some circumstances, the history, signs and symptoms may suggest that a systematic and detailed examination of the injured person's whole body be made. For example, an unconscious person with ill-defined injuries or an unknown medical condition might need to be examined thoroughly.

Conduct the examination of a casualty in two stages:

- **a primary examination** to determine life-threatening conditions;

- **a secondary examination** to determine injuries or illnesses which normally would not be an immediate threat to life.

Primary Examination

During a primary examination, identify life-threatening conditions and give first aid according to the following priorities.

- **breathing.** Ensure that the casualty is breathing. If not breathing, open the airway and start artificial respiration immediately (see chap. 7).

- **bleeding.** Control severe external bleeding (see chap. 13).

- **unconsciousness.** Care for unconsciousness is a priority because it may lead to breathing problems. An unconscious person may suffocate if left lying on his back. Unconscious persons who must be left unattended should be placed in the **recovery position** if injuries permit (see chap. 11).

Identify and give first aid for life-threatening conditions in all casualties before conducting a secondary examination. For any casualty with a suspected head or neck injury, steady and support the head and neck area before assessing responsiveness; once life-threatening conditions have been identified, and first aid has been given, apply a cervical collar before conducting a secondary examination.

Secondary Examination

When the casualty's life is no longer in danger, conduct a secondary examination if needed. This head-to-toe systematic examination should be conducted without repositioning the casualty. Each person should be examined for injuries that, while not life-threatening, would benefit from first aid. Be alert for changes in a casualty that may indicate his condition is deteriorating. The First Aider should search for medical information (eg: Medic-Alert device) that may give information about the person's condition.

The Conscious Casualty

When the casualty is conscious, do not examine for unlikely injuries. You should:

- ask where the injury or pain is located and examine that area first.

- ask if anything else is wrong and make sure there are no injuries that are masked by pain, numbness or drugs.

The extent of any additional examination will depend on the circumstances of the accident or illness. When it is obvious that only one part of the body is affected and the person complains of no other problems, a complete body examination should not be conducted.

When a complete body examination is indicated, carefully and methodically examine the injured person by feeling all parts of the body gently but firmly to check for abnormal conditions:

- assess vital signs — temperature, pulse and respiration — as a basis for subsequent assessments. Feel the forehead and neck for an abnormally high or low temperature; assess the radial or carotid pulse — noting its rhythm and strength; note the quality of breathing, its rate, rhythm and breathing sounds.

- start with the head and examine the eyes for reaction to light. The pupils may be abnormally large, small or unequal. Examine the skull for bleeding, bumps or depressions; check the ears, nose and mouth for discharge of fluids.

- examine the neck and feel gently for any deformity. Any tenderness in this region may indicate injury.

- examine the back and check carefully for irregularities in the spine. Feel gently underneath the back for indications of bleeding.

- examine the chest for unnatural movement; look for wounds and feel gently for fractures.

- examine the abdomen for bruises, abrasions or open wounds. Tenderness or rigidity in the abdomen may indicate internal injuries.

- examine the pelvic area for signs of crushed or fractured bones. Check for any abnormal turning outward of the lower legs which may indicate a fracture of the upper part of the femur.

- examine the lower extremities for pain or tenderness and for abnormal features such as swelling, bruises, unnatural angles and other bone irregularities. Loss of muscle power or numbness needs special attention.

- check for injuries, loss of muscle power and lack of feeling in the upper extremities.

Loss of sensation or inability to move the upper or lower limbs may indicate a neck or back injury. Check circulation in the limbs and compare with the opposite side.

The Unconscious Casualty

Assessing an unconscious casualty is more difficult because the person cannot relate symptoms. For this reason, you must rely on the history and a proper interpretation of all physical signs to determine the required first aid.

PRIORITIES IN FIRST AID – MULTIPLE INJURIES

When a casualty has more than one injury or when there is more than one casualty with injuries, you must decide in which order these injuries should receive first aid and which casualty should be evacuated first to medical aid. The sorting and assigning of priorities should be done as soon as you can safely do so. The assigned priorities should be reviewed frequently and changed if the casualties' conditions indicate a need for more urgent care.

The **highest priority must be given to** those persons requiring immediate first aid and transportation because of such conditions as:

- asphyxia and breathing difficulties;

- severe bleeding;

- unconsciousness;

- shock;

- other immediate life-threatening medical emergencies.

Next in priority are those casualties for whom first aid and transportation can be deferred. These include casualties with:

- burns;

- fractures;

- back injuries.

The **lowest priority** is given to those who may receive first aid and transportation last. These include conditions such as:

- minor fractures;

- minor bleeding;

- behavioural problems.

Provide first aid in the order of priority for all injuries and illnesses to the extent necessary to save life and to stabilize the casualty for transportation. Do not delay transportation to medical aid in order to provide first aid for minor conditions.

Continue to monitor the casualties for changes in their condition and change the priority for first aid and transportation accordingly. Stay with the casualties until responsibility for further care can be turned over to qualified persons, such as a more highly qualified First Aider, a qualified ambulance attendant, a nurse or a physician.

FIRST AID — FOLLOW-UP CARE

After immediate first aid is given:

- call emergency services if someone else has not already done so;

- monitor the casualties continuously;

- protect and shelter the casualty while awaiting the arrival of medical aid;

- safeguard the casualty's personal belongings;

- assist in the evacuation of the casualty by ambulance;

- ensure that casualties who do not require medical aid are placed in the care of friends or relatives;

- make notes of the names of the casualties and bystanders and record the first aid given.

Calling Emergency Services

When calling emergency services, be sure to give the dispatcher all the information needed to send appropriate help for the right number of casualties to the right place. Relay the following information (the mnemonic CHANT may help to remember):

C – Circumstances of the incident and condition of the casualties.

H – Help that has been given or is being given.

A – Address or location of the incident, giving cross-streets if applicable.

N – Number of casualties involved.

T – Telephone number from which the call is being placed.

Answer any questions the dispatcher may have and do not hang up until the call is completed. BE THE LAST TO HANG UP.

When handing over casualties to more qualified persons, be prepared to give a full report on the condition of each one and what first aid was given.

HAZARDOUS MATERIALS IN THE WORKPLACE

Hazardous products in the workplace display one of the following WHMIS symbols that include warnings on flammability, reactivity, and health risk, and indicate the personal protection required. An associated MSDS includes first aid instructions in the event of an accident. Familiarize yourself with these instructions.

Class	Symbol	Division
A		COMPRESSED GAS
B		FLAMMABLE AND COMBUSTIBLE MATERIAL
C		OXIDIZING MATERIAL
D		POISONOUS AND INFECTIOUS MATERIALS
D-1		Materials causing immediate and serious toxic effect.
D-2		Material causing other toxic effects.
D-3		Biohazardous infectious material.
E		CORROSIVE MATERIAL
F		DANGEROUS REACTIVE MATERIAL

Extracted from *Canada Gazette*, Part II, Vol. 122, No. 2, January 20, 1988

Fig. 1-2. Workplace hazardous materials symbols.

CHAPTER 2

I. INTRODUCTION TO ANATOMY AND PHYSIOLOGY

II. THE SKIN

III. THE MUSCULOSKELETAL SYSTEM

I. INTRODUCTION TO ANATOMY & PHYSIOLOGY

As a First Aider, you do not need a comprehensive knowledge of anatomy and physiology. However, you should know the basic structure of the human body and how it functions normally. This and subsequent chapters will describe the major organs and functions of the skin, the musculoskeletal system, the nervous system, the digestive and urinary systems, the circulatory system and the respiratory system. This should give you a better understanding of malfunctions and injuries, of the interrelationship of all body systems, and it should help you to determine the appropriate first aid for an injury or illness.

ANATOMIC TERMS

There are many anatomic terms to describe planes of the body, positions of organs and degrees of movement. Other terms describe regions of the body and surface areas. The following terms, most commonly used in first aid, will help you to be more precise when giving information about a person's condition:

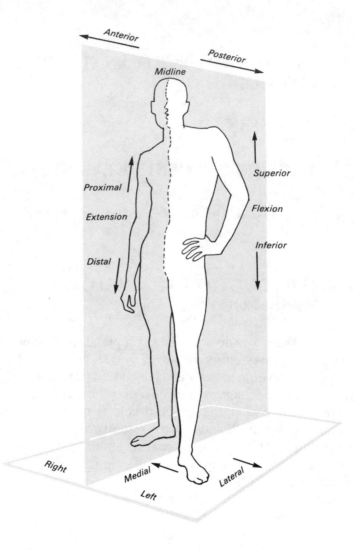

Fig. 2-1. Topographic anatomy.

- **anterior:** front part or front surface.

- **posterior:** back part or back surface.

● **distal:** the part of an extremity farther away from the attached end.

● **proximal:** the part of an extremity nearer its point of attachment to the body.

● **extension:** straightening; increasing the angle between two parts of a joint.

● **flexion:** bending; decreasing the angle between two parts of a joint.

● **inferior:** away from the head or upper body.

● **superior:** nearer the head or upper body.

● **midline:** an imaginary vertical line that divides the body into right and left halves.

● **medial:** near the midline.

● **lateral:** away from the midline of the body.

● **right** and **left:** the anatomic right and left side of the midline.

II. THE SKIN

The skin is one of the most important organs of the body. Its primary functions are to protect the body from environmental hazards and infection, to eliminate waste in the form of perspiration and to help adjust to temperature changes.

Environmental control. A rich supply of nerves in the skin keeps the brain aware of environmental changes. These nerves are sensitive to heat, cold, pain and touch, and they transmit these sensations to the brain. The skin helps the body adjust to its environment and protects it from extreme temperatures. Blood vessels constrict in cold temperatures, preventing loss of heat from the body core. Fatty layers under the skin act as insulators to retain body heat. In extreme heat, the evaporation of perspiration on the skin cools the body.

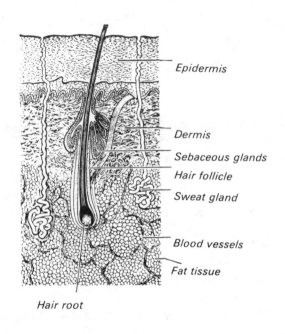

Fig. 2-2. Skin and underlying tissues.

III. THE MUSCULOSKELETAL SYSTEM

The musculoskeletal system is the framework of the human body within which organs and systems function. The framework includes muscles, tendons, bones and joints. It protects the organs, supports the body and provides for its movement. All parts of the musculoskeletal system are interrelated so that injury to one part usually affects the function of others.

THE MUSCLES

Muscles are a special kind of tissue that contracts (shortens) as a result of nerve stimulation. Generally, movement of parts of the body is caused by the action of several muscles contracting and relaxing in combination. Muscles are classified as voluntary or involuntary. Each is defined as follows:

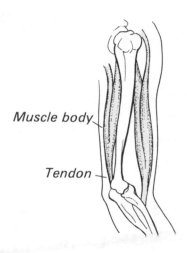

Fig. 2-3. Voluntary muscles.

- **voluntary** muscles are directly controlled by the brain, that is, they can be contracted or relaxed at the will of the individual. Skeletal muscles are voluntary. They are attached to the skeleton by strong **tendons.** When muscles contract, the attached tendons create coordinated movement of the bones to which they are connected.

- **involuntary** muscles contract and relax rhythmically without any conscious effort on the part of the individual. The cardiac muscle, which has its own regulating system, is a good example of an involuntary muscle.

The **diaphragm,** a large dome-shaped muscle separating the thoracic and abdominal cavities, has characteristics of both voluntary and involuntary muscles. As a person breathes, the diaphragm automatically contracts to a flat shape and relaxes to a dome shape, in rhythm with breathing. The contraction of this muscle and the rate of breathing can be changed at will for short periods of time.

Muscles are supplied with oxygen and nutrients from arterial blood and the veins carry away the waste products of muscular activity. Muscles have a nerve supply which carries impulses to and from the brain.

THE SKELETON

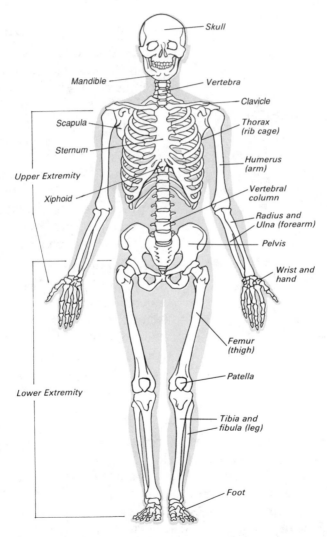

Fig. 2-4. The human skeleton.

The skeleton forms the supporting bony framework of the human body, giving the body its shape and firmness. The skeleton also protects vital organs. The brain is protected by the skull; the heart and lungs, by the ribs; the liver, spleen and kidneys, in part, by the lower ribs; and the spinal cord, by the vertebrae that form the spinal canal.

The Joints

The bones of the skeleton allow for body movement by serving as rigid levers for tendons and muscles. Joints are formed by the junction of two or more bones. **Immovable** joints are those in which the edges of the bones are fitted firmly into each other so that there is no movement, as in the bones of the adult skull. The bones of **movable** joints are constructed to allow movement in one or more directions. There are three types of movable joints:

- **hinge** joints are those in which the surfaces of the bones are moulded to each other, allowing free movement in one plane only. Examples of hinge joints are those of the lower jaw, elbows, knees and fingers.

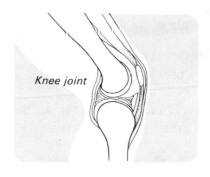

Fig. 2-5.
Hinge joint.

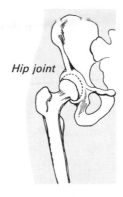

Fig. 2-6.
Ball-and-socket joint.

- **ball-and-socket** joints, formed by the round head of one bone fitting into a cup-shaped cavity of another bone. This allows movement in more than one direction. The hip and shoulder are examples of ball-and-socket joints.

- **slightly movable** joints allow only limited movement. Examples are the joints between the vertebrae, and between the ribs and spine.

The ends of the bones of movable joints are covered with smooth **cartilage** to minimize friction, and are held together by bands of strong tissue called **ligaments.** The entire joint is encased in a capsule of strong tissue. The synovial membrane (inner lining of the joint) produces a lubricating fluid for the joint.

The Vertebral Column

The **vertebral column** (spine) is composed of 33 bones called the vertebrae. The front part of each vertebra consists of a rounded bony area. Three bony projections at the back of each vertebra unite to form a tunnel along the spine. This is called the spinal canal.

The spinal canal encloses the spinal cord and provides openings for nerves to branch off to all parts of the body. The spine is divided into five regions:

- the first 7 vertebrae form the **cervical spine** (neck);

- the next 12 vertebrae, to which 12 pairs of ribs are attached, form the **thoracic** or **dorsal spine** (upper back);

- the next 5 vertebrae form the **lumbar spine** (lower back);

- the next 5 vertebrae are fused and form the **sacral spine** (sacrum) and part of the pelvis;

- the last 4 vertebrae are also fused and form the **coccygeal spine** (coccyx, or tailbone).

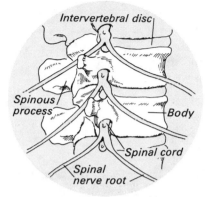

Fig. 2-7. *Vertebrae.*

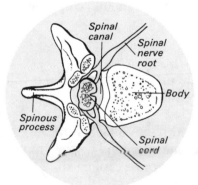

Fig. 2-8. *Spinal canal.*

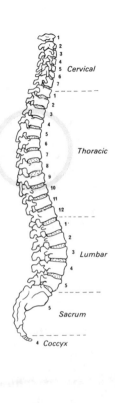

Fig. 2-9. *Spinal column.*

The vertebrae are connected to each other by ligaments. The cervical, thoracic and lumbar vertebrae are separated by thick pads of cartilage called **intervertebral discs.** The discs and ligaments allow for the normal turning and bending motions of the trunk, but prevent excessive movement which could injure the spinal cord.

The Skull

The bones of the skull, forming the framework of the head,
are divided into the cranium
and the face. The bones of the
cranium are fused to form a
rigid vault for the brain. The
bones of the face are united
with the bones of the cranium
to form the eye and nose cavities and to protect the vul-

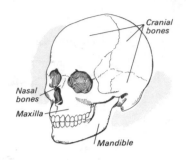

Fig. 2-10. The skull.

nerable organs of sight and smell. The jaw is in two parts. The
maxilla (upper jaw) is part of the facial bone structure and is
immovable; the **mandible** (lower jaw) is attached to the skull by
a hinge joint on each side, allowing the mouth to open and close.

The Thorax

The **thorax** (ribcage) is made up of the **ribs,** 12 thoracic vertebrae, and the **sternum** (breastbone).

The ribs are 12 pairs of curved bones attached to the thoracic
vertebrae, extending on both sides around to the front of the
body. Ten pairs are attached in front as follows:

● the upper 7 pairs are attached to the sternum by
  cartilage;

● the next 3 pairs are attached to each other and
  to the ribs above them by
  cartilage;

The last 2 pairs are unattached
in front and are described as
floating ribs.

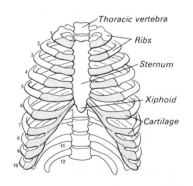

Fig. 2-11. The thorax.

The sternum, which forms the middle part of the front of the thoracic cage, is dagger-shaped with the point downward. The **xiphoid process** is the small prominent tip at the lower end of the sternum. It is an important landmark in certain first aid procedures.

The thorax encloses and protects the trachea, lungs, heart, major blood vessels and oesophagus. It also gives some protection to the liver, stomach, pancreas, spleen and kidneys.

The Shoulder and Upper Extremity

The shoulder is the base of attachment for the upper extremity. The bones of the shoulder are the **clavicle** (the collarbone), the **scapula** (shoulderblade), and the **humerus** (upper arm).

The clavicle is a narrow, slightly curved bone between the upper end of the sternum and the shoulder joint. One end of the clavicle is attached to the top and sides of the sternum by ligaments; the other end is attached to the scapula near the shoulder joint. The clavicle acts as a structural support for the shoulder.

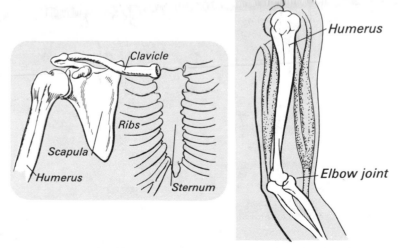

Fig. 2-12. Shoulder joint.   *Fig. 2-13. Upper arm.*

The scapula is at the upper end and outer part of the back and forms the socket for the ball of the humerus.

The upper extremity includes the humerus, the radius and ulna, carpals, metacarpals and phalanges forming the wrist and hand. The humerus, extends from the shoulder to the elbow. Its upper, rounded head fits into a shallow socket in the scapula. At its lower end, the humerus is connected with the bones of the radius and ulna to form the elbow joint.

The two bones of the forearm are the **radius** on the thumb side and the **ulna** on the little finger side. These bones rotate on each other to allow the forearm and hand to turn. The radius and ulna, with the eight **carpal** bones of the wrist, form the wrist joint. The carpal bones are arranged in two rows of four.

The palm of the hand contains five long **metacarpal** bones. Each of the four fingers has three short bones, the **phalanges;** the thumb has two phalanges.

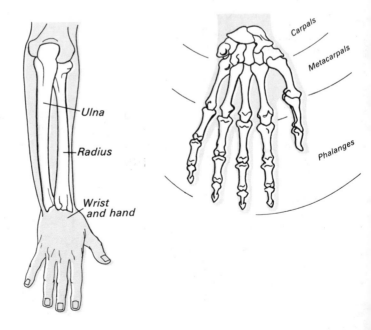

Fig. 2-14. Lower arm.   Fig. 2-15. Wrist and hand.

The Pelvis and Lower Extremity

The **pelvis** is a bowl-shaped bony ring attached to the lower part of the spine. It is formed by the **sacrum** and the two large pelvic bones or hip bones. The pelvis contains the sockets of the two hip joints. The entire weight of the upper body is transmitted through the pelvis to the lower extremities.

The pelvis forms the pelvic cavity and supports the organs of the lower abdomen. It provides protection for the bladder, the **urethra** (urinary passage), the lower part of the intestine, the **rectum,** and reproductive organs.

The lower extremity consists of the **femur** (thigh bone), the **patella** (kneecap), the **tibia** and **fibula** (leg bones), and the **tarsals, metatarsals** and **phalanges** (bones of the foot). The

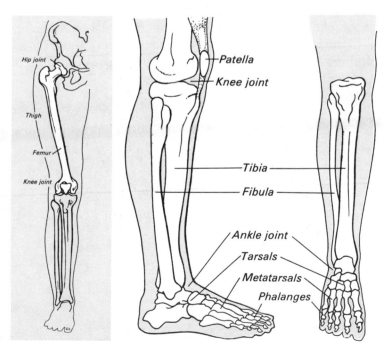

Fig. 2-16. Upper leg.　　　*Fig. 2-17. Lower leg and foot.*

femur is the longest and strongest bone in the body. It extends from the socket of the pelvis to the knee. It connects with the upper end of the tibia to form the knee joint.

The knee joint is the largest hinge joint in the body. The ligaments that give it stability are complex and susceptible to injury, particularly from sports activities. The patella lies in front of, and gives protection to, the knee joint.

The tibia extends from the knee to the ankle and forms part of the knee and ankle joints. Its sharp edge can be felt just below the skin on the front of the leg. The fibula is on the outer side of the tibia. It does not form a part of the knee joint, but its lower end forms the outer part of the ankle joint.

The foot is similar to the hand in many ways. It includes 7 irregular **tarsal** bones that form the instep and support the entire weight of the body; 5 long **metatarsal** bones that are distal to the tarsals and connect with the bones of the toes; and 14 **phalanges** that form the toes; 2 short phalanges in the big toe and 3 phalanges in each of the other toes.

CHAPTER 3

THE NERVOUS SYSTEM

The nervous system is composed of the brain, spinal cord and nerves. The brain and spinal cord are called the **central nervous system** and the nerves that spread out to all parts of the body are called **peripheral nerves.** The nervous system is subdivided by function into the voluntary nervous system and the autonomic nervous system. The **voluntary nervous system** controls conscious functions at the will of the individual and the **autonomic nervous system** controls involuntary functions, such as heart action, without any conscious effort on the part of the individual.

THE CENTRAL NERVOUS SYSTEM

The **brain,** the controlling organ of the body, occupies almost all the space in the cranium. It is the centre of consciousness and has many functions such as memory and thought processes. It also receives information and transmits impulses to all parts of the body for voluntary and involuntary activities. Those impulses are transmitted through the **spinal cord** and **peripheral nerves.**

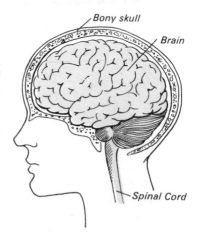

Fig. 3-1. The brain.

The spinal cord is an extension of the brain. It contains the long tracts of central nerves that lead to the peripheral nerves. The nerves of the spinal cord are carried inside tubular tissues that run two thirds the length of the spine in the spinal canal. The spinal canal, formed by the vertebrae, provides openings through which nerves branch out to organs and muscles.

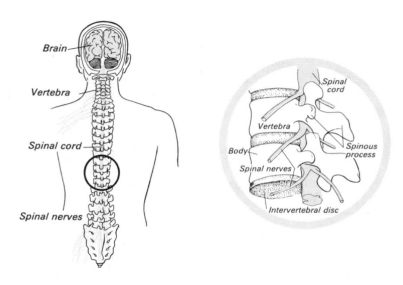

Fig. 3-2. The spinal column.   *Fig. 3-3. The spinal cord.*

PERIPHERAL NERVES

The peripheral nerves that extend from the spinal cord to all parts of the body are of two kinds; motor nerves and sensory nerves. **Motor nerves** carry the impulses from the brain that trigger movement, and **sensory nerves** transmit sensations of touch, taste, heat, cold and pain to the brain.

THE AUTONOMIC NERVOUS SYSTEM

Nerves that function automatically and continuously are called involuntary or autonomic. The autonomic nervous system controls the involuntary muscles of the body, glands and cardiac muscle. It also controls breathing and digestion, and regulates body temperature.

Notes

CHAPTER 4

THE DIGESTIVE AND URINARY SYSTEMS

The digestive and urinary systems convert food and drink into nutrients for the cells and collect and dispose of solid and fluid waste. The organs of the digestive and urinary systems are classified as hollow and solid. The hollow, tubular organs carry gastric and urinary materials while the solid organs are tissue masses with a rich blood supply.

Injury to hollow organs may allow their contents to be discharged into the abdomen causing infection. Injury to solid organs results in internal bleeding. Knowing the location and function of the organs of the digestive and urinary systems is helpful in assessing internal injuries.

DIGESTIVE SYSTEM

The mouth, oropharynx and oesophagus form the passageway through which food and drink pass to the organs of digestion in the abdomen. The principle organs of digestion are:

- the **stomach,** a pear-shaped organ located in the upper left part of the abdomen. It is partially contained within the rib cage and extends down into the abdominal area. It contains innumerable gastric glands and is richly supplied with blood and nerves. The function of the stomach is to store, warm and soften food received through the oesophagus before passing it on in small quantities to the intestine.

- the **intestine** or **bowel,** a tubular organ measuring 8.5 to 9 metres in length. This tube, comprising the small and large intestines, begins at the stomach and ends at the

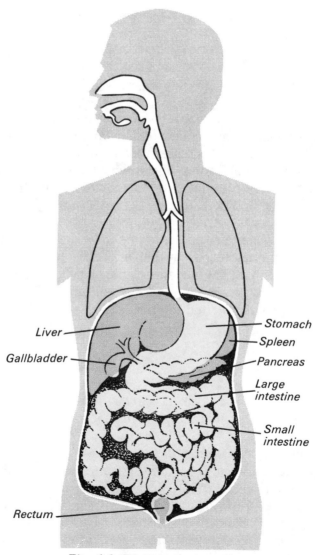

Fig. 4-1. Digestive system.

rectum. The intestine is a continuous tube that is suspended in loops in the abdominal cavity. Its main functions are to absorb nutrients through the intestine walls into the bloodstream and to collect solid waste for excretion through the rectum. Blows to the abdomen can injure the bowel. Open wounds of the abdominal wall can cause the intestines to be exposed.

- the **liver,** a large organ that takes up most of the area just beneath the diaphragm on the right side of the body. Fragile and easily injured, the liver contains many blood vessels and produces a substance called bile that aids digestion.

- the **gallbladder,** a small sac-like organ attached and connected to the underside of the liver. Its function is to store bile until it is required for digestion.

- the **pancreas,** an elongated organ directly in front of the spine and behind the stomach, aids digestion by producing insulin and pancreatic juice.

The stomach, intestine and gallbladder are hollow organs. The liver and pancreas are solid organs.

The spleen, an organ of the lymphatic system, is described in Chapter 5.

URINARY SYSTEM

The urinary system removes and collects waste products from the blood and eliminates them from the body in the form of urine. The organs of the urinary system are:

- the **kidneys,** a pair of organs situated near the spine in the upper abdomen where they are partially protected by the ribs. Blood passes into the kidneys from branches of the aorta and is carried away by the vena cava. As the blood flows through the kidneys, waste products are filtered out and a quantity of fluid (urine) is removed.

● the **ureters,** two tubes that carry urine from each kidney to the urinary bladder.

● the **urinary bladder,** a sac situated in the pelvis when empty, but which expands into the lower abdomen when it is full. Its function is to receive and hold urine until it is excreted through the urethra. The bladder, when it is full, is most susceptible to injury from direct forces or from fractures of the pelvis (see chap. 14).

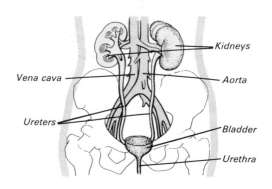

Fig. 4-2. Urinary system.

● the **urethra,** a muscular tube between the urinary bladder and the exterior of the body.

The kidneys are the solid organs in the urinary system. All other organs are classified as hollow organs.

CHAPTER 5

THE CIRCULATORY SYSTEM

The circulatory system is a complex closed circuit consisting of a muscular organ and tubular vessels, called the heart, arteries, arterioles, capillaries, venules and veins, that circulate blood throughout the body. Blood circulation is essential for the distribution of oxygen and nutrients to cells, and for the collection of waste products from cells for excretion from the body.

THE HEART

The **heart** is a muscular organ that functions as a double pump, to continuously circulate blood to the lungs and throughout the body. It is located in the thoracic cavity behind the sternum.

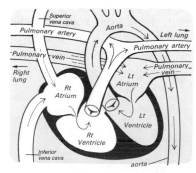

Fig. 5-1. Heart and large vessels.

The heart is divided into a right and a left side. Each side is divided into an upper collecting chamber called the **atrium** and a lower muscular pumping chamber called the **ventricle.** A valve, situated between the atrium and ventricle on each side, allows blood to flow in one direction only.

ARTERIES AND ARTERIOLES

The arteries are the strongest blood vessels, with walls strengthened by elastic and muscular tissue with a fibrous covering. They carry blood under pressure from the heart to all parts of the body. Arteries expand, according to the volume of blood being forced through them by the pumping action of the heart, and return to normal size while the heart refills for the next contraction. The largest artery is called the **aorta;** the smallest are the **arterioles.**

CAPILLARIES

Capillaries are the smallest blood vessels of the body. Roughly the diameter of a hair, they have extremely thin walls which allow the exchange of fluids and gases to and from the tissue cells. Capillaries connect the arterioles with the venules, the smallest of the veins.

VENULES AND VEINS

The **veins** take blood back to the heart. They have thinner walls than arteries and most have cuplike valves along the walls that allow blood to flow only toward the heart.

The veins of the entire body ultimately join to form two major veins, the **superior vena cava** and the **inferior vena cava.** The superior vena cava returns blood from the head, neck, shoulders and upper extremities. The inferior vena cava returns blood from the abdominal and pelvic areas and from the lower extremities. Both large veins empty into the right atrium at the right side of the heart.

THE BLOOD

Blood is the fluid that circulates through the heart, the arteries, capillaries and veins. It transports oxygen and nutrients to the cells and carries carbon dioxide and other waste products to the lungs, kidneys and other organs of excretion.

Blood is composed of plasma, red cells, white cells and platelets. **Plasma** is a yellow liquid in which the cells and platelets are suspended. Other chemicals and nutrients are dissolved in plasma and transported to the cells. **Red cells** give the blood its characteristic colour. One of the components of red cells is called **haemoglobin.** It combines with oxygen, transports it to the body tissues and exchanges it for carbon dioxide. Oxygenated blood is brighter red in colour than that which has a high carbon dioxide content.

White cells are less numerous than red and vary in size. The largest ones are attracted to foreign material and quickly pass through the thin capillary walls into surrounding tissues to engulf and destroy harmful bacteria or other foreign matter. When a large number of white cells are killed by bacteria, pus is formed indicating infection.

The **platelets** are produced from other cells in the bone marrow and aid in the clotting of blood.

THE CIRCULATION

The blood circulation system forms a closed loop beginning and ending at the heart. It includes:

- **pulmonary circulation,** which begins at the right side of the heart where blood is pumped to the lungs;

- **systemic circulation** begins at the left side of the heart, where blood is pumped throughout the body.

With each relaxation of the heart, blood pours into the right and left atrium which then contract to fill the ventricles. With each contraction of the heart, blood is forced from the ventricles through both circulatory systems.

In pulmonary circulation, venous blood that has been collected by the veins drains into the right atrium. The blood passes from this chamber through a valve into the right ventricle. The right ventricle then contracts to force the venous blood through the pulmonary arteries to the lungs. During its passage through the pulmonary capillaries, the blood gives off carbon dioxide, which is exhaled from the lungs, and receives oxygen from the inhaled air.

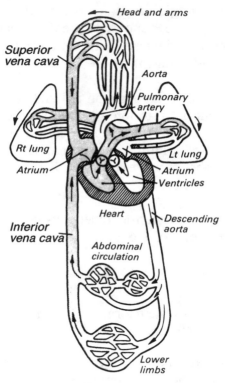

Fig. 5-2. The circulatory system.

The blood, now rich in oxygen, returns through the pulmonary veins to the left atrium, the left collecting chamber of the heart. From that chamber, it passes into the left ventricle. The left ventricle contracts and forces blood through the arteries into the systemic circulation.

The systemic circulation is the means by which the supply of oxygen and nutrients is distributed throughout the body and by which waste products are carried to the organs of excretion. The blood returns through the capillaries into the venules and veins, and into the right atrium. This cycle is repeated continuously.

BLOOD PRESSURE

Blood pressure is the force that the blood exerts against the walls of the blood vessels. The pressure wave of the blood in the arteries can be detected as a pulse, but the pressure wave in the veins is too weak to be felt.

Three factors control blood pressure:

● the blood volume (the amount of blood circulating in the body);

● the capacity and elasticity of the blood vessels (the latter provides a variable resistance to blood flow);

● the strength of the heartbeat.

To keep the blood volume under pressure at all times, the size of the arteries and veins is automatically controlled by the nervous system to provide a variable resistance to flow. When a person loses blood, the arteries and veins adjust to the new volume. The automatic adjustment to maintain adequate pressure, particularly in the arteries, maintains circulation to essential organs. However, if the loss of blood is great, the system fails and the person collapses or goes into a state of **shock** (see chap. 10).

THE PULSE

The **pulse** is the pressure wave that occurs in the arteries each time the heart pumps blood through the aorta. This wave or pulse can be felt with the fingertips along major and medium arteries where they come near the surface of the body. Common sites for checking the pulse are at the wrist – **radial pulse;** at the neck – **carotid pulse;** and at the upper arm – **brachial pulse.** The pulse is an important sign for assessing a person's physical condition. It is called a **vital sign** because it indicates the presence or absence of a heart beat.

Pulse Rate and Characteristics

The pulse rate of a healthy infant at rest varies from 80 to 140 beats per minute. The pulse rate of a healthy child at rest varies from 80 to 100 beats per minute. A healthy adult at rest can have a resting pulse rate that varies from 50 to 100 beats per minute, averaging about 72 beats per minute. It is slower in old age and in young athletes. The normal pulse is strong and has a regular rhythm. Physical activity will increase the rate and strength of a healthy person's pulse but not the rhythm. Illness and injury can cause the pulse to become abnormally fast or slow; can cause the pulsations to be bounding and full, or faint and weak; and can result in an irregular beat. Take the pulse for a full minute to determine the rate and to assess the quality of its strength and rhythm. Do not apply excessive pressure when taking a pulse. This could compress the artery and cut off circulation.

Radial Pulse

The most common site for taking a pulse on an adult is at the wrist where an artery passes close to the distal radius — hence the term **radial pulse.** To take a radial pulse, place the tip of one or two fingers on the front of the forearm, about 2.5 cm (one inch) above the creases of the wrist and about 1.25 cm (one-half inch) from the outside edge. Light pressure with

Fig. 5-3. Taking a radial pulse.

the fingertips may be necessary in order to feel the pulsations of the blood as it expands the artery. You should not use your thumb to take a pulse because it has its own pulse and may cause confusion.

Carotid Pulse

The **carotid pulse** is preferred when checking the pulse of a person whose blood pressure may be low, such as an unconscious person in respiratory or cardiac arrest (see chaps. 7 and 8). The carotid arteries are on each side of the neck, in the groove

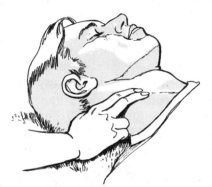

between the trachea and the large neck muscles. To check a carotid pulse, locate the Adam's apple at the front of the neck with two fingertips. Slide the fingertips backward on the side nearest you to locate the carotid artery between the neck muscle and trachea. **Do not feel for or compress both carotid arteries at the same time.**

Fig. 5-4. Carotid pulse

Brachial Pulse

In infants, the carotid pulse may be difficult to find and may be unreliable. The **brachial pulse** is preferred and should be checked by placing two fingertips on the inside of the upper arm. Press lightly between the large muscle of the arm and the bone until the pulse beat is felt.

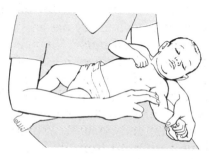

Fig. 5-5. Brachial pulse.

THE LYMPHATIC SYSTEM

As the blood flows in the systemic circulation, **lymph** (fluid similar to blood plasma) passes through capillary walls and bathes tissue cells. The lymph gives its quota of oxygen, nutrients and water to the cells and collects waste products, including carbon dioxide. It then passes back into the bloodstream through the capillaries and lymph channels.

In this system, very fine tubules called **lymph vessels** form an extensive network throughout the body. The network includes small structures called the **lymph nodes,** which act as barriers to the spread of germs that have entered the body. For example, when a person has an infected finger, the lymph glands in the armpit or at the elbow may become swollen and tender indicating the reaction of the nodes to the infection. The lymph vessels may become inflamed, a condition characterized by red streaking from the infected site up the limb to the lymph gland.

THE SPLEEN

The **spleen** is a small elongated organ located in the upper left side of the abdomen just beneath the diaphragm (see Fig. 4-1). This organ acts as a blood reservoir. It is delicate and can be damaged in accidents. Bleeding from a ruptured spleen is severe and cannot be controlled by first aid measures.

CHAPTER 6

THE RESPIRATORY SYSTEM

RESPIRATION

Respiration is the process of exchanging oxygen (O_2) and carbon dioxide (CO_2) in the body. **External respiration** is the exchange of oxygen and carbon dioxide in the lungs; **internal respiration** is the exchange of these gases between the blood and the cells of the body.

Normal air is a mixture of gases containing about 21% oxygen. Exhaled air contains about 16% oxygen, sufficient to sustain life when giving a direct method of artificial respiration.

THE AIRWAY

Air, drawn into the lungs through the nose and mouth, passes down the **pharynx** (back of the throat), through the **larynx** (voice box), to enter the **trachea** (windpipe). The entire passage is called the **airway.** The top of the larynx is protected by a flap called the **epiglottis** that remains open for breathing, but closes when food and fluid are being swallowed.

THE LUNGS

The trachea divides into two branches called the right and left **bronchi.** Each bronchus passes into a lung where it divides into a number of small **bronchioles** that, in turn, divide into millions of **alveoli** (air sacs).

Capillaries, a fine network of blood vessels, surround the alveoli. The walls of the alveoli are so thin that gases can pass through them, enabling the red blood cells to discharge carbon dioxide and pick up oxygen from the air breathed in.

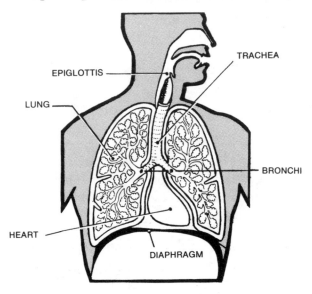

Fig. 6-1. Respiratory System.

THE PLEURA

The **pleura** is a smooth slippery tissue that forms a sac enclosing each lung. It is a continuous double-layered tissue; one layer adhering to the lung and the other to the inside of the chest wall. The functions of the pleura are to provide a lubricant for the normal movement of the lungs against the chest wall and to ensure that the lungs expand with the action of the chest wall.

THE DIAPHRAGM

The **diaphragm** is a strong muscle that separates the thoracic and abdominal cavities. It is dome-shaped in its relaxed state and flat when it is contracted. This change of shape decreases and increases the space within the thoracic cavity.

CHEST CAGE AND INTERCOSTAL MUSCLES

The **intercostal muscles** (between the ribs) are arranged in two layers. When the external muscles contract, they pull the ribs upward and outward, expanding the chest as we breathe in. When these muscles relax, the ribs drop, reducing the space in the chest cavity and expel air from the lungs. The internal muscles pull the ribs downward and inward.

RESPIRATORY CENTRE

The **respiratory centre** is located in the brain near the base of the skull. It controls respiration and is affected by various forms of chemical stimulation. From the First Aider's point of view, the most important stimuli are an increase of carbon dioxide and/or a decrease of oxygen in the blood.

MECHANISM OF BREATHING

The respiratory centre reacts to an increased level of carbon dioxide in the body, sending stimuli along nerves to the diaphragm and muscles of the chest to increase the depth and rate of respiration. As the space in the chest cavity increases, a negative pressure or vacuum is created, drawing air into the lungs.

As the alveoli give off carbon dioxide and absorb oxygen, the carbon dioxide level of the body is reduced. The respiratory centre ceases to stimulate the intercostals and the diaphragm, and those muscles relax. The ribs drop downward and inward and the diaphragm resumes its dome shape, decreasing the space in the chest cavity and expelling the used air.

The body cells consume oxygen and produce carbon dioxide at a rate related to the degree of physical activity. Therefore, when the level of carbon dioxide reaches the critical point, the respiratory centre is stimulated to increase the rate and depth of breathing movements.

Breathing — Rate, Rhythm, Depth

The rate, rhythm and depth of breathing are important indicators of a person's state of health. These signs give early warning of physical changes and of life-threatening conditions. Breathing is classified as one of the **vital signs.** Because of this, you should learn to recognize "normal breathing" so that abnormal breathing can be more accurately assessed. Normal breathing is quiet and effortless with an even, steady rhythm.

The **rate of breathing** is the number of breaths (inhalations and exhalations) in one minute. Although the normal breathing rate varies for persons of different ages and sex, the average rate for a healthy adult at complete rest falls in the range of 10 to 18 breaths per minute. The rates for children and infants are faster; 18 to 28 breaths per minute is considered a normal range for a five to seven year old and 41 to 55 breaths per minute for an infant.[1]

Breathing rhythm refers to the interval between breaths. In normal breathing, the intervals are even and breathing appears effortless. This is described as **regular breathing. Irregular breathing** can be recognized by uneven intervals between breaths. This usually indicates a respiratory disorder or distress.

Depth of breathing refers to the amount of air moved in and out of the lungs with each breath. You should learn to judge between normal breathing depth and shallow or deep breathing. Abnormal breathing depth is often associated with other breathing difficulties such as gasping breaths, laboured breathing or noisy breathing.

---

[1] Respiration and Circulation. *Philip L. Altman and Dorothy S. Dittner, Editors, for the series Biological Handbooks. The Federation of American Societies for Experimental Biology, Bethesda, Maryland, 1971, p. 42.*

Breathing Assessment

Assess breathing for a minimum of thirty seconds, using a watch, and multiply by two to establish the rate per minute. Make this assessment as a continuation of a pulse check to avoid alerting the person that his breaths are being counted. Otherwise, breathing will become a conscious act and the rate and depth may not be reliable. After checking the pulse, leave the fingers in place, but count the breaths, while noting the rhythm and depth of breathing. Observe carefully for very slow, rapid, laboured or noisy breathing. These indicate serious conditions that require medical aid urgently.

Notes

CHAPTER 7

ASPHYXIA AND ARTIFICIAL RESPIRATION

ASPHYXIA

Asphyxia is the condition in which a lack of oxygen in the circulating blood results in damage to vital tissues and eventually in death. The causes of asphyxia can be grouped under three headings; lack of oxygen in the inhaled air, loss of effective function of the lungs and heart, and airway obstruction.

Oxygen supply can be depleted through normal breathing in confined spaces such as airtight cabinets, mines and sewers. Toxic gases can displace oxygen in the air, resulting in reduced oxygen levels in the blood. Carbon monoxide fumes from combustion engines and gases formed in farm silos and manure holding tanks are examples of oxygen displacement.

Lung and heart functions are controlled through nerve impulses and require the mechanical action of muscles and ribs. Conditions affecting the respiratory and circulatory systems, such as electric shock, spinal injuries, or the use of drugs and certain poisons, may affect breathing and heart action. Injury to the ribs, sternum and muscles of the chest will decrease movement of the chest wall and result in a partial or complete loss of lung function.

Airway obstruction may be caused by foreign matter lodged in the throat, by blood and mucus from injuries to the mouth or by vomitus, but it is most often caused by the unconscious person's tongue falling to the back of the throat and blocking the airway.

The airway can also be blocked by muscular spasm caused by water or food entering the airway or by swelling of throat tissues caused by allergies, diseases or injuries.

SIGNS OF RESPIRATORY DISTRESS

Abnormal breathing and respiratory distress can be recognized by one or more of the following signs:

- rate of respirations is irregular, too fast or too slow;

- depth of breathing is shallow or abnormally deep;

- breathing is noisy, raspy or the person is gasping and struggling for breath;

- blood vessels of the head and neck are swollen with blood (congestion);

- lips, ears and fingernail beds show bluish discolouration (cyanosis) indicating a lack of oxygen;

- chest does not rise and fall and air movement cannot be heard or felt.

Unconsciousness and asphyxia will occur rapidly and death will soon follow unless artificial respiration is given.

ARTIFICIAL RESPIRATION

Vital organs of the body, such as the brain and heart, must have a continuous supply of oxygen to survive. **The brain may be permanently damaged if it is deprived of oxygen for more than four minutes.** Artificial respiration is the technique of supplying air to the lungs of a casualty who is unable to breathe. When respiratory functions fail, it is vital that artificial respiration be started immediately. Seconds count!

Giving artificial respiration to a non-breathing casualty requires five simple techniques:

- response assessment;

- breathing assessment;

- airway opening;

- lung ventilation;

- pulse assessment.

RESPONSE ASSESSMENT

A person who appears unconscious must not be handled until a state of unconsciousness has been confirmed. Gently tap or shake the shoulder while shouting, "Are you okay?", to determine the person's ability to respond. If the history of the accident suggests a possible head or neck injury, steady and support the head and neck before assessing responsiveness.

BREATHING ASSESSMENT

Assess a casualty's breathing or determine the absence of breathing by putting your ear close to the casualty's mouth and nose to listen for sounds of breathing. At the same time, feel with your cheek for air movement. Look careful-

Fig. 7-1. Assess breathing.

ly at the chest for upward and downward movement as the chest expands and contracts. This assessment should take 3 to 5 seconds. To minimize head and neck movement, assess breathing before opening the airway—not all unconscious casualties are in respiratory arrest.

AIRWAY OPENING

When a person becomes unconscious, the muscles of the mouth and throat relax. If the casualty is on his back, his tongue will fall to the back of the throat, closing off the air passage to the lungs. Breathing will stop. This results in brain damage and death unless you act quickly. Opening the airway by lifting the

tongue away from the back of the throat may be all that is needed to restore breathing. The airway may be opened in one of two ways — head tilt with chin lift or jaw thrust without head tilt.

Fig. 7-2. Airway closed.

Fig. 7-3. Airway partially open.

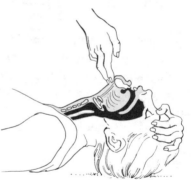

Fig. 7-4. Airway open.

Head Tilt—Chin Lift

The head tilt—chin lift manoeuvre is the most effective method of opening the airway when no neck injuries are suspected. Tilting the head back straightens the air passage and lifts the tongue away from the back of the throat. Lifting the chin forward brings the jaw and tongue up further to provide maximum airway opening.

Place one hand on the casualty's forehead and push backward. At the same time, place the fingers of the other hand under the chin on the bony part of the jaw and lift forward. Take care not to compress the soft tissue under the chin; this might obstruct the airway.

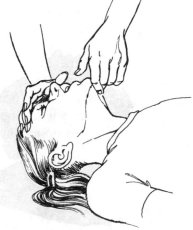

Fig. 7-5 (a). Head tilt — chin lift – adult.

To open the airway in an infant, tilt the head back gently into a neutral or sniffing position. Tilt the head slightly further for a child. Avoid overextension of the neck, especially in infants, and take care not to close the mouth or push on the soft parts under the chin. Closing the mouth completely and pressing on the soft underparts of the chin may obstruct the airway.

Fig. 7-5 (b). Head tilt — chin lift – infant.

Jaw Thrust Without Head Tilt

If neck injuries are suspected, the safest method of opening the airway is the jaw thrust without head tilt. The jaw must be lifted forward without flexing or extending the neck and with the head held in a fixed position in line with the body.

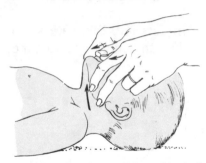

Fig. 7-6. Jaw thrust without head tilt – infant.

Place the hands on both sides of the casualty's head, immobilizing the head and neck. Grasp the angle of the mandible (lower jaw) with the fingers of each hand and lift forward. Use the thumbs to depress the lower lip to open the mouth. Seal the casualty's nose with your cheek as you breathe air into the mouth.

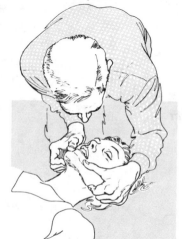

Fig. 7-7. Jaw thrust without head tilt – adult.

Fig. 7-8. Seal the nose with your cheek.

If the lungs do not inflate, tilt the head back slightly and try again. There is a risk that tilting the head may aggravate a neck injury, but it must be taken in order to get air into the lungs.

LUNG VENTILATION

Breathe for the casualty by blowing air into the lungs. There is sufficient oxygen in your exhaled air to keep a person alive if the ventilations are properly given.

Blow air into the lungs of a non-breathing casualty through the mouth, the nose, the mouth and nose, or a stoma in the case of neck breathers. Ensure that the airway is well opened and that there is a tight seal between your mouth and the casualty's airway. Seal off any other airway openings through which air might escape. In mouth-to-mouth artificial respiration, for example, the nose must be pinched shut. Take a deep breath and blow air slowly into the casualty's lungs; take 1 to 1.5 seconds for each breath. Slow breaths reduce the risk of opening the oesophagus and forcing air into the stomach.

After each breath, move your mouth away and look toward the chest, while keeping your ear and cheek near the casualty's face. Look for chest movement, listen for air sounds and feel with your cheek for air being exhaled. These signs will tell you that air is reaching the lungs.

Fig. 7-9. Mouth-to-mouth ventilation.

Fig. 7-10. Watch for chest movement.

If there are no signs of air movement, reposition the head and add more lift to the chin or jaw. Recheck the seals and try again. If the lungs still do not inflate, suspect an airway obstruction and give first aid for choking (see chap. 9)

Ventilations — Depth and Rate

Ventilations should be given slowly, taking 1 to 1.5 seconds per breath, with just enough force to expand the casualty's chest. The rate of ventilations should be as close as possible to normal breathing. This will allow for maximum air exchange in the casualty and will prevent hyperventilation in the rescuer.

Adults (8 years and older). Ventilate an adult casualty with a full breath once every five seconds or about 12 breaths per minute.

Children (Ages 1 to 8 years). A child's lungs are smaller and the normal breathing rate is faster than an adult. Ventilations should be given with light breaths, taking 1 to 1.5 seconds per breath. The rate of ventilations should be one breath every four seconds or about 15 breaths per minute.

Infants (Less than 1 year). Infants have much smaller lungs and they breathe faster than children. Reduce the depth of breaths to light puffs of air. Ventilate at a rate of one puff every three seconds or 20 per minute.

Gastric Distention

If ventilations are given with too much pressure, air will enter the stomach. If air goes into the stomach, there will be upward pressure on the diaphragm, making artificial respiration more difficult. It also increases the risk of the casualty vomiting and aspirating the stomach contents. If the stomach becomes distended during rescue breathing, recheck and reposition the airway, observe the rise and fall of the chest, and avoid excessive airway pressure. Continue rescue breathing without attempting to expel the stomach contents. Experience has shown that attempting to relieve stomach distention by manual pressure over the victim's upper abdomen is almost certain to cause regurgitation if the stomach is full. If stomach distention is so great that it hinders proper inflation of the lungs, turn the casualty onto his side with his head down before applying abdominal pressure. Stomach contents may be expelled along with the air from the stomach. In this case, wipe out the mouth quickly and resume artificial respiration.

PULSE ASSESSMENT

If the heart is not beating, blood will not circulate and oxygen will not be carried to vital tissues, such as the brain, even though you are breathing for the casualty. You must determine if the heart is beating by assessing the pulse.

After giving two breaths and verifying that the lungs are inflating, check the carotid pulse in an adult or child and the brachial pulse in an infant. Take 5 to 10 seconds to detect what may be a weak, slow pulse. If no pulse is felt, start CPR if you are trained (see chap. 8) or continue artificial respiration and send someone for medical aid.

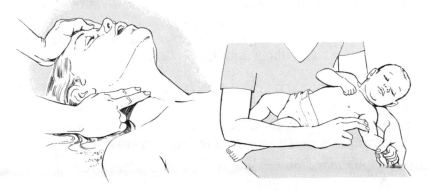

Fig. 7-11. Checking the carotid pulse.   *Fig. 7-12. Checking the brachial pulse.*

If a pulse is present, continue giving artificial respiration and recheck the pulse after one minute and every few minutes thereafter.

DIRECT METHODS OF ARTIFICIAL RESPIRATION

Artificial respiration may be given by a direct method, namely **mouth-to-mouth, mouth-to-nose, mouth-to-mouth-and-nose,** or **mouth-to-stoma.** The direct methods are considered superior because:

- they provide the greatest volume of air to the lungs.

- they can be started immediately and continued while the casualty is being moved to safety or to medical aid. This is particularly important when artificial respiration is being given to near-drowning casualties while they are being taken from the water.

- they can be applied as soon as the rescuer reaches the casualty and clears the mouth of obstructions. There may be no need to move the casualty. However, it is best to have the casualty lying on her back on a solid, flat surface.

- they provide immediate warning if the airway is obstructed.

- they are not physically demanding and can be carried out for long periods without significant fatigue.

MOUTH-TO-MOUTH METHOD

When giving mouth-to-mouth artificial respiration, ensure that the airway is correctly opened. Pinch the nostrils closed with the thumb and index finger to prevent loss of air.

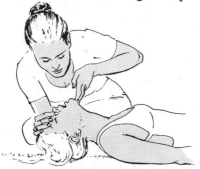

Fig. 7-13. Open the airway and pinch the nostrils.   *Fig. 7-14. Make a tight seal.*

Take a deep breath, open your mouth wide and place it over the casualty's mouth, making a tight seal, and breathe into the person's mouth.

Start by giving two breaths. After each inflation, raise your mouth away from the person's face to allow air to escape. Look, listen and feel for air flow from the mouth and nose and for movement of the chest.

Fig. 7-15. Watch for chest movement.

If air is getting into the lungs during the first two breaths and if a pulse is present, continue artificial respiration. Dentures should be left in place unless they interfere with air flow. They help to maintain a tight seal with your mouth.

MOUTH-TO-NOSE METHOD

The mouth-to-nose method may be used for casualties with mouth injuries or when it is not possible to fully cover the mouth.

Proceed in the same manner as for the mouth-to-mouth method except that you will blow air through the casualty's nose. Tilt the head back with one hand, but do not pinch the nostrils. Lift the chin with the other hand, using the thumb to close the casualty's mouth. Cover the casualty's nose with your mouth and give two breaths. Open the person's mouth between breaths to allow air to escape on exhalation. If air is getting into the lungs and a pulse is present, continue breathing rhythmically in the same manner as you would for mouth-to-mouth.

Fig. 7-16. Mouth-to-nose method.

MOUTH-TO-MOUTH-AND-NOSE METHOD

The mouth-to-mouth-and-nose method is preferred **for infants** . It is essentially the same as mouth-to-mouth artificial respiration for adults, with the following differences:

- when opening the airway, lift the chin, but do not force the head back too far. Too much backward tilt may obstruct the airway by kinking the trachea. Take care not to close the mouth or push on the soft under parts of the chin. This may obstruct the airway.

- make a tight seal with your mouth over both the mouth and nose.

- give puffs of air rather than full breaths.

Fig. 7-17. Mouth-to-mouth and nose.

Fig. 7-18. Watch for chest movement.

- locate and assess the brachial pulse. If a pulse is detected . . .

- continue giving artificial respiration and reassess the pulse frequently. If a pulse is not detected, start CPR (see chap. 8).

MOUTH-TO-STOMA METHOD

Certain persons, due to previous surgery, breathe through an opening or **stoma** in the trachea. The condition is caused usually by the removal of the larynx. People who have had this operation are called **laryngectomees** or **neck breathers.**

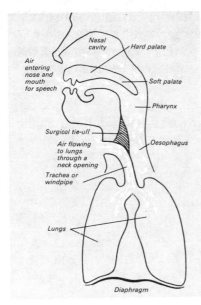

Fig. 7-19. Total laryngectomy.

Although the occasions to give artificial respiration to a laryngectomee may be rare, it must be done promptly when required, using the mouth-to-stoma method.

The basic procedure for mouth-to-stoma artificial respiration is the same as that for other direct methods, with certain modifications. Remember, no air can get to the lungs through the mouth and nose of a neck breather; air must enter the lungs through the opening in the neck called a stoma.

Quickly determine that the casualty is a neck breather and proceed as follows:

- bare the entire neck and remove all coverings over the stoma;
- put a pad under the shoulders to keep them slightly elevated, keep the head in line with the body and keep the chin raised;

Fig. 7-20. Mouth-to-stoma method.

- make a seal with your mouth and breathe directly into the stoma;
- look, listen and feel for air movement to ensure that the stoma is not obstructed;
- maintain a clean air passage using a cloth to clean the opening; never use paper tissues.

Some laryngectomees may have a tube in the tracheal opening. This may be cleared of any blockage with a clean cloth or handkerchief. Do not delay. A partially cleared airway that allows air to get to the lungs immediately is better than a clear airway when it is too late.

Partial laryngectomees have an air passage through the mouth and nose that allows air to escape. Close the mouth and pinch the nose to make an airtight seal.

SEQUENTIAL STEPS IN ARTIFICIAL RESPIRATION

Whenever there is reason to believe that a person may not be breathing, make the area safe and take the following actions quickly, but deliberately:

1. **Assess responsiveness.** Gently tap the shoulder and shout, "Are you O.K.?" If there is no response . . .

2. **Assess breathing.** Look, listen and feel for signs of breathing (3 to 5 seconds). If none of these signs are present . . .

3. **Call out for help.** Shout or use any other method to attract the attention of anyone who may call medical aid and assist with first aid.

4. **Position the casualty.** Place the casualty on her back, supporting the head and neck, and turn the body as a unit.

5. **Open the airway.** Use either the head tilt—chin lift or the jaw thrust without head tilt to open the airway. While keeping the airway open . . .

6. **Reassess breathing.** Look, listen and feel again for signs of breathing (3 to 5 seconds). Opening the airway may have restored spontaneous breathing. If no signs of breathing are detected . . .

7. **Start ventilations.** Ventilate the lungs. After two initial ventilations, maintain an open airway and . . .

8. **Assess the pulse.** Locate and assess the carotid pulse in adults and children or the brachial pulse in infants. Allow 5 to 10 seconds in the initial check to detect and assess what may be a weak, slow pulse. If a pulse is detected . . .

9. **Send for help.** Have someone call for medical aid. Ensure that they have all the needed information to pass on to the police or the emergency services dispatcher (see chap. 1). **Do not leave a non-breathing casualty, whose heart is beating, to call medical aid.**

10. **Resume artificial respiration.** Ventilate the lungs every 5 seconds for an adult, every 4 seconds for a child and every 3 seconds for an infant. Look for movement of the chest and listen and feel with your cheek for air flow from the lungs after each breath.

11. **Reassess the pulse.** Assess the carotid or brachial pulse (5 seconds should be sufficient on recheck) after the first minute of artificial respiration and every few minutes thereafter.

Air may enter the stomach during artificial respiration and this may cause vomiting during the procedure or in the recovery stages. If this occurs during artificial respiration, immediately turn the casualty over to allow drainage from the mouth. Clear the mouth of any foreign matter, wipe it clean and resume artificial respiration.

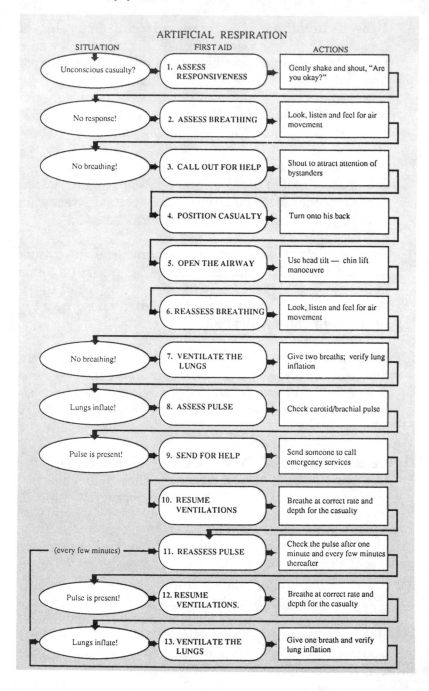

ARTIFICIAL RESPIRATION

SITUATION	FIRST AID	ACTIONS
Unconscious casualty?	1. ASSESS RESPONSIVENESS	Gently shake and shout, "Are you okay?"
No response!	2. ASSESS BREATHING	Look, listen and feel for air movement
No breathing!	3. CALL OUT FOR HELP	Shout to attract attention of bystanders
	4. POSITION CASUALTY	Turn onto his back
	5. OPEN THE AIRWAY	Use head tilt — chin lift manoeuvre
	6. REASSESS BREATHING	Look, listen and feel for air movement
No breathing!	7. VENTILATE THE LUNGS	Give two breaths; verify lung inflation
Lungs inflate!	8. ASSESS PULSE	Check carotid/brachial pulse
Pulse is present!	9. SEND FOR HELP	Send someone to call emergency services
	10. RESUME VENTILATIONS	Breathe at correct rate and depth for the casualty
(every few minutes)	11. REASSESS PULSE	Check the pulse after one minute and every few minutes thereafter
Pulse is present!	12. RESUME VENTILATIONS.	Breathe at correct rate and depth for the casualty
Lungs inflate!	13. VENTILATE THE LUNGS	Give one breath and verify lung inflation

FOLLOW-UP CARE

When the casualty starts to breathe, place her in the recovery position (see chap. 11). If neck injuries are suspected and the casualty must be left unattended, apply a cervical collar before turning the casualty (see chap. 16). The recovery position helps to maintain an open airway and it will help to prevent the aspiration of fluids or vomitus.

Casualties who have experienced a breathing emergency must be monitored carefully in case further breathing difficulties arise. They should be taken to medical aid promptly.

INDIRECT METHODS OF ARTIFICIAL RESPIRATION

Indirect or manual methods of artificial respiration provide air to the lungs by physical compression and expansion of the thoracic cage. Compression is provided by manual pressure on the back or chest, and expansion by extension of the arms. Two methods of indirect artificial respiration are the **back pressure – arm lift** or Holger Nielsen method and the **chest pressure – arm lift** or Sylvester method.

Although the indirect methods are not nearly as effective as the direct methods, there are instances when it may not be possible to use direct artificial respiration. Severe mouth and face injuries or toxic gas poisoning are conditions that may require the use of a manual method. Selection of either the Holger Nielsen method or the Sylvester method will depend on the casualty's physical condition.

When using either method of manual artificial respiration, the First Aider should follow these general rules:

● clear and maintain an open airway by extending the neck.

- place the casualty on a firm flat surface, preferably at floor level.

- assess the carotid pulse after the first minute or twelve complete cycles. If a pulse is detected, resume compressions and recheck the pulse every few minutes.

BACK PRESSURE—ARM LIFT (HOLGER NIELSEN) METHOD

The Holger Nielsen method can be used for casualties with injuries that cause drainage into the throat. The method is not advisable for obese persons, women in the advanced stages of pregnancy or casualities with injuries of the neck, back or upper extremities.

Position of the Casualty

Place the casualty face down with the hands one on top of the other under the forehead. Turn the head slightly to one side to allow drainage from the mouth. Extend the neck by placing soft padding under the head. Tilt the chin upward to help maintain an open airway. Ensure that the nose and mouth are clear of obstructions.

Position of the First Aider

Position yourself on one knee at the casualty's head. Place your knee near the casualty's head and the other foot ahead of the knee to give solid support. Place your hands on the casualty's back; the heels of the hands in line with the armpits. Spread the fingers downward and outward. The thumbs should be barely touching over the person's spine and your arms should be straight.

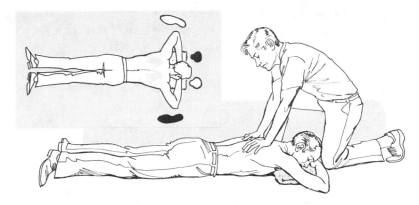

Fig. 7-21. Position of casualty and First Aider.

Respiration Cycle

For ease of learning, the respiration cycle is described in four phases. The entire cycle should be performed rhythmically to achieve a breathing rate of 12 per minute. One cycle, therefore, should take about 5 seconds. A steady, even rhythm is of greater importance than exact timing.

Compression phase (expiration). Keep your arms straight, rock gently forward until the arms are vertical. This applies body weight to the casualty's back. Use just enough pressure to force air out of the lungs. During this procedure, count: **ONE ONE-THOUSAND, TWO ONE-THOUSAND . . .**

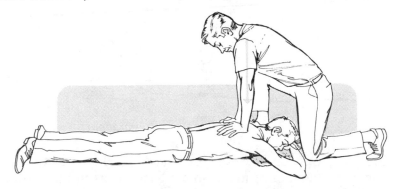

Fig. 7-22. Compression phase (expiration).

Transition phase 1. Rock back, sliding your hands past the casualty's shoulders and grip the upper arms near the elbows, while counting: **THREE ONE-THOUSAND ...**

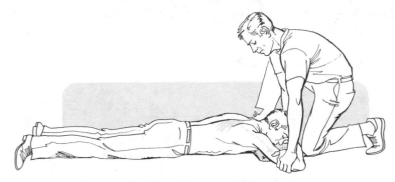

Fig. 7-23. Transition phase 1.

Expansion phase (inspiration). Rock back, raising and pulling the casualty's elbows until you feel tension. Your arms must be kept straight and the casualty's chest should not rise from the ground. During this procedure, count: **FOUR ONE-THOU-SAND, FIVE ONE-THOUSAND ...**

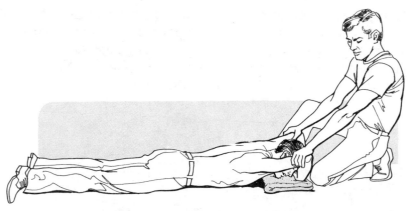

Fig. 7-24. Expansion phase (inspiration).

Transition phase 2. Slide your hands up the casualty's arms and place them once more on the back, heels in line with the armpits to start the compression phase.

Holger Nielsen for Children

For children, age five and over, the procedures are the same, except that pressure on the back should be reduced and applied with the fingertips only.

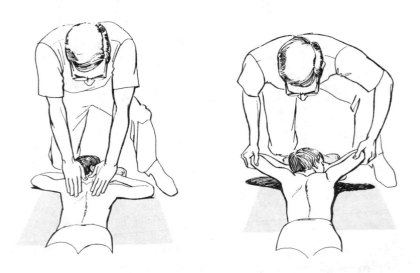

Fig. 7-25. Holger Nielsen method for children.

The procedure for children under five years of age is:

- lay the child facedown with arms at the sides; place a pad under the forehead to extend the neck and turn the head slightly to one side;

- hold the child's shoulders with your thumbs and fingers (thumbs on the scapula);

- apply thumb pressure while counting: **ONE AND TWO AND . . .,** to cause expiration;

- lift the shoulders to expand the chest, while counting: **THREE AND FOUR AND . . .,** to cause inspiration.

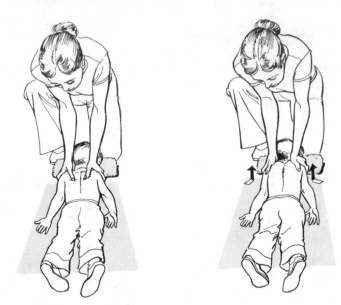

Fig. 7-26. Holger Nielsen method for children under five.

Repeat the expiration and inspiration phases to maintain a rhythm of about 15 breaths per minute or one cycle every 4 seconds.

CHEST PRESSURE – ARM LIFT (SYLVESTER) METHOD

The Sylvester method may be used for obese persons, for women in advanced stages of pregnancy and for other casualties who cannot be placed facedown. The method is not recommended for casualties with injuries causing drainage into the throat or casualties with injuries of the neck, back or upper extremities.

Position of the Casualty

Place the casualty on his back on a firm surface. Extend the neck by placing a rolled blanket or a jacket folded into a narrow pad under the shoulders. That allows the head to tilt back and helps maintain an open airway. Remove any obvious obstruction in the mouth and throat. Place the casualty's hands and lower arms across the chest, parallel to each other.

Position of the First Aider

Kneel at the casualty's head, knees to either side and in line with the person's head. Keeping your arms straight, grasp the person's wrists and cross them over the lower sternum in position for the first phase of the cycle — compression.

Respiration Cycle

The respiration cycle is described in three phases. The complete cycle should be performed rhythmically to achieve a breathing rate of about 12 breaths per minute for adults and 15 to 20 breaths per minute for children. Be constantly aware of the danger of rib fractures when compressing the ribs and sternum. Pressure must be reduced for slender casualties and for children.

Compression phase (expiration). With a firm grasp on each wrist, rock forward to put your body weight on the casualty's chest to expel air from the lungs, while counting: **ONE ONE-THOUSAND, TWO ONE-THOUSAND ...**

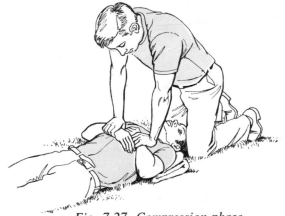

Fig. 7-27. Compression phase.

Expansion phase (inspiration). Rock back on the heels, extending the casualty's arms outward and upward to full extension. That will expand the chest and cause an inflow of air. During the procedure, count: **THREE ONE-THOUSAND, FOUR ONE-THOUSAND ...**

Fig. 7-28. Expansion phase.

Transition. Return the person's wrists to the start position across the chest, while counting: **FIVE ONE-THOUSAND ...** Repeat the cycle at the appropriate rate for the age of the casualty.

CHAPTER 8

CARDIOPULMONARY RESUSCITATION

Cardiopulmonary resuscitation (CPR) is a combination of two basic life support procedures — artificial circulation (cardioresuscitation) and artificial respiration (pulmonary resuscitation). These combined procedures are applied to sustain life in a person who has stopped breathing and whose heart has stopped beating. Artificial circulation, created by external chest compressions, causes blood to flow from the heart to the lungs where it picks up oxygen to be carried to vital organs. Artificial respiration, sometimes called rescue breathing, provides oxygen to the lungs. These procedures, properly applied by one or two rescuers, can sustain life until normal cardiopulmonary functions are restored.

INDICATIONS FOR CPR

CPR should be started when breathing assessment and a pulse assessment indicate that the casualty is not breathing and the heart has stopped beating. This person is said to be in respiratory and cardiac arrest. Cardiac arrest can occur suddenly or it can follow a period of unattended respiratory arrest when oxygen remaining in the body is depleted. The immediate application of artificial respiration to a person who has stopped breathing can prevent the more serious condition of cardiac arrest.

Cardiac arrest in a child or infant rarely occurs from a heart attack. It is most commonly caused by low oxygen levels that result from breathing difficulties. Starting artificial respiration before the heart stops may prevent cardiac arrest. For this reason, you must learn to recognize the early signs of breathing emergencies in children and infants and act quickly. Remember that artificial respiration is the single most important first aid procedure for a non-breathing child or infant.

Learn to recognize the signs and symptoms of an impending heart attack (see chap. 25) so that emergency medical services can be obtained before a cardiac arrest occurs.

CPR MANOEUVRES

The application of CPR requires the use of six manoeuvres. Response assessment, breathing assessment, airway opening, lung ventilation and pulse assessment are described in the procedures for artificial respiration (see chap. 7) and their application in CPR is highlighted here. Chest compressions are described in detail with variations in their application for adults, children and infants.

ADULT – CHILD – INFANT

Adult CPR manoeuvres are modified for use on children and infants. Although these age groups are not rigidly defined, for the purposes of CPR they are considered to be:

● adult – 8 years or older,

● child – 1 to 8 years,

● infant – less than 1 year.

The most important factor in determining the correct application of CPR is the size of the casualty. For this reason, ranges of pressures are recommended and good judgement dictates that forces used for chest compressions and breaths be moderated for smaller children and frail adults.

RESPONSE ASSESSMENT

Gently tap or shake the shoulder and shout, "Are you OK?" to determine if the person is unconscious. This should be done with care if a head or neck injury is suspected.

BREATHING ASSESSMENT

A 3 to 5-second check should determine if there are any signs of air movement that indicate the presence of breathing.

AIRWAY OPENING

Opening the airway, using either the head tilt—chin lift or the jaw thrust without head tilt method, often results in a return of spontaneous breathing. Always reassess breathing after opening the airway.

Whenever possible, maintain the airway open during CPR. A second person can hold an adult's head tilted back while you give chest compressions; a child's head can be held back with one hand while compressions are given with the other; and the infant can be positioned so that the head tilts back during compressions.

LUNG VENTILATION

Lung ventilations are performed slowly, taking 1 to 1.5 seconds for each breath, with a pause to allow the casualty to exhale. Use full breaths to ventilate an adult, lighter breaths for a child and puffs of air for an infant.

Give two breaths when the assessment confirms absence of breathing. In CPR, subsequent breaths are coordinated with chest compressions in a ratio dependent on the age of the casualty and the number of rescuers:

- **adult – one rescuer** — after each sequence of 15 compressions, give 2 breaths for a **ratio of 15:2;**

- **adult – two rescuers** — after each sequence of 5 compressions, give 1 breath for a **ratio of 5:1;**

- **child – one or two rescuers** — after each sequence of 5 compressions, give 1 breath for a **ratio of 5:1;**

- **infant – one rescuer** — after each sequence of 5 compressions, give 1 puff of air for a **ratio of 5:1.**

PULSE ASSESSMENT

To take the pulse, press the appropriate pulse area gently with two fingers, avoiding compression of the artery. Take time to detect what might be a weak, irregular pulse to ensure that you do not give chest compressions if the heart is beating. This could result in serious medical complications. You may need 5 to 10 seconds for the initial pulse check. Subsequent checks should not take more than 5 seconds.

Pulse assessments are made:

- after the initial 2 ventilations;

- after the first minute of CPR;

- every few minutes during CPR;

- by a second rescuer before taking over CPR;

- by a two-rescuer team before taking over CPR and when switching positions;

- continually to assess the effectiveness of compressions during two-rescuer CPR.

Discontinue chest compressions when a spontaneous pulse is felt. Continue artificial respiration if breathing is absent, but continue to check the pulse every few minutes.

CHEST COMPRESSIONS

Chest compressions increase the pressure within the chest and may exert direct pressure on the heart, causing blood to flow to the lungs, heart and brain. The oxygen picked up by the blood as it passes through the lungs will be carried to the heart and brain to prevent tissue damage until normal circulation and breathing can be restored.

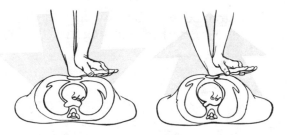

Fig. 8-1. Increasing pressure within the chest.

To give effective chest compressions, place the casualty on a hard, flat surface. For an infant, this can be the palm of one hand. Any elevation of the head will further reduce blood flow to the brain, but elevating the lower extremities may help increase blood flow.

Apply pressure to the lower half of the sternum along its length, exerting enough force to depress the chest to a depth of:

- 3.8 to 5.0 cm (1½ to 2 inches) for an adult;

- 2.5 to 3.8 cm (1 to 1½ inches) for a child;

- 1.3 to 2.5 cm (½ to 1 inch) for an infant.

Do not apply pressure to the ribs on either side of the sternum nor to the xiphoid process (the tip of the sternum). This could cause rib fractures and internal injuries.

Chest compression to an adult

Rescuer's Position. Kneel close to the casualty's side by the shoulder. The hand nearest the casualty's feet is used for landmarking.

Landmarking. To place the hands correctly on the lower half of the sternum and above the xiphoid:

- locate the bottom edge of the casualty's rib cage nearest to you with the index and middle finger of the landmarking hand;

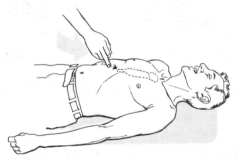

*Fig. 8-2 (a). Landmarking —
follow the ribs.*

- run these fingers up the edge of the rib cage to the notch where the ribs meet the sternum;

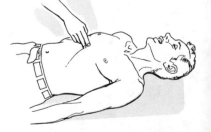

*Fig. 8-2 (b). Landmarking —
middle finger in the notch.*

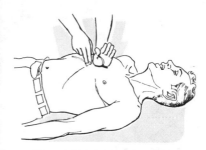

*Fig. 8-2 (c). Landmarking —
position the hand.*

- leave the middle finger in the notch and place the index finger above it on the lower end of the sternum;

- place the other hand next to this index finger so that the heel of the hand runs along the length of the sternum with the fingers raised and pointing directly across the chest;

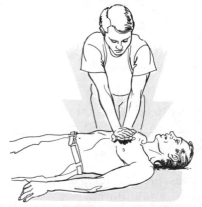

*Fig. 8-2 (d). Landmarked for
compression.*

- bring the landmarking hand up and place it on top of the first with the fingers parallel and raised or interlocked to prevent any pressure being applied to the ribs.

Chest Compressions. Apply pressure vertically on the sternum. If pressure is not straight down, the body may roll and the effect will be lost. Apply pressure only through the heels of the hands. With the hands correctly located on the sternum, you will achieve proper compression by:

- locking the elbows so that the arms are straight;

- positioning the shoulders directly over the hands;

- letting your body weight apply enough pressure through the arms to the heels of the hands to depress the chest to a depth of 3.8 to 5 cm (1½ to 2 inches);

Fig. 8-3. Chest compressions.

● releasing the pressure completely to allow blood to flow into the heart, but keeping the hands in their original position and in light contact with the chest;

● repeating the two phases — pressure and release — rhythmically so that each phase is of equal duration.

Use any suitable mnemonic, such as ONE AND, TWO AND, THREE AND, FOUR AND, FIVE. Count at a constant speed to help maintain a smooth rhythm at a rate of 80 to 100 compressions per minute.

Pause at the appropriate times (after each 5th or 15th compression) to ventilate the lungs or to allow a second rescuer to give ventilations. Landmark again to reposition the hands if they have been moved to give ventilations.

Chest Compressions to a Child

The techniques for giving chest compressions to a child are similar to those for an adult with the following differences.

Landmarking. Use the hand nearest the feet of the child to landmark and to apply compressions. Maintain head tilt with the other hand to keep the airway open. To position the hand correctly for chest compressions:

- locate the bottom edge of the rib cage nearest you with the index and middle finger of the landmarking hand;

- run these fingers up the edge of the rib cage to the notch where the ribs meet the sternum;

- leave the middle finger in the notch and place the index finger above it on the lower end of the sternum;

- rotate the landmarking hand to bring the heel of the hand to rest on the chest just above the spot marked by the index finger;

- align the heel of the hand along the length of the sternum and raise the fingers well off the chest.

Fig. 8-4. Chest compressions to a child.

Chest Compressions. Lock the elbow of the arm used to give compressions so that the arm is straight. Let your body weight apply pressure vertically through the arm to the heel of the hand to depress the chest to a depth of 2.5 to 3.8 cm (1 to 1½ inches).

Pause to give one ventilation after each 5th compression and landmark visually if the hand is moved. Visual landmarking will enable you to start chest compressions quickly and to maintain the appropriate rate of 80 to 100 compressions per minute.

Chest Compressions to an Infant

Position of Rescuer and Casualty. Place an infant on a horizontal, hard flat surface. The palm of the hand under the shoulders is ideal because it allows the head to drop back slightly to help keep the airway open.

Landmarking. Use two fingers to compress an infant's chest. Place the fingertips along the sternum at a point one finger's width below a line between the nipples. Position the fingers for chest compressions as follows:

- locate the centre of the sternum along an imaginary line between the nipples;

- place the tip of the index finger on the sternum just under this line and let the next two fingers fall in place next to the index finger;

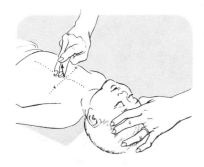

- raise the index finger, leaving the other two fingers in place ready to compress the chest.

Fig. 8-5. Landmarking and chest compressions — infant.

Chest Compressions. Depress the sternum vertically to a depth of 1.3 to 2.5 cm (½ to 1 inch). Release the pressure at the end of each compression to allow the chest to return to its normal shape, but do not move the fingers from the sternum. Make the pressure and release phases of equal duration and administer them smoothly without jerky movements. Count ONE AND, TWO AND, THREE AND, FOUR AND, FIVE to help maintain the correct rhythm and rate of at least 100 compressions per minute.

Give a puff of air after each 5th compression and landmark to return the fingers to their original position to resume chest compressions.

CPR MANOEUVRES — VARIATIONS BY AGE

CPR MANOEUVRES		ADULT (over 8 yrs)		CHILD (1 to 8 yrs)	INFANT (under 1 yr)
		1 RES-CUER	2 RES-CUERS	1 OR 2 RESCUERS	1 RES-CUER ONLY
VENTILATIONS	Method of Application	Mouth-to-Mouth		Mouth-to-Mouth	Mouth-to-Mouth-and-Nose
	Volume of Breaths	Full Breaths		Light Breaths	Puffs of Air
	PULSE ASSESSMENT	Carotid Pulse		Carotid Pulse	Brachial Pulse
CHEST COMPRESSIONS	Method of Application	Heels of Two Hands		Heel of One Hand	Tips of Two Fingers
	Depth	3.8 to 5 cm (1½ to 2 ins)		2.5 to 3.8 cm (1 to 1½ ins)	1.3 to 2.5 cm (½ to 1 in)
	Rate	80-100 per min		80-100 per min	At least 100 per min
RATIO – COMPRESSIONS: VENTILATIONS		15:2	5:1	5:1	5:1

CPR PERFORMANCE

CPR can be performed by one rescuer on adults, children and infants. It may be performed by two rescuers on adults and children. Training in the one-rescuer method is preferred for most people. Training in two-rescuer procedures is recommended for those whose work requires them to provide a first response to emergencies. Two-rescuer CPR requires more training time to achieve a well-coordinated effort.

CPR, once initiated, should be continued until there is either a return of spontaneous pulse and breathing or a hand-over to more qualified rescuers.

ONE-RESCUER CPR – ADULT

The sequential steps in the performance of one-rescuer CPR for an adult are as follows:

1. **Assess Responsiveness.** Tap or gently shake the shoulders of an apparently unconscious person and shout, "Are you OK?" to determine the degree of responsiveness. If there is no response . . .

2. **Assess Breathing.** Place your ear near the casualty's mouth and look for chest expansion. Look, listen and feel for signs of air movement. If breathing is absent . . .

3. **Call Out For Help.** Shout or use any means to attract the attention of bystanders.

4. **Position the Casualty.** Place the casualty on his back on a firm, flat surface, supporting the head and neck during the move.

5. **Open the Airway.** Use the head tilt—chin lift manoeuvre to open the airway.

6. **Reassess Breathing.** Look, listen and feel for any signs of air movement. If breathing is absent . . .

7. **Ventilate the Lungs.** Pinch the casualty's nostrils shut, take a full breath, make a good seal over the casualty's mouth. Breathe into the mouth, taking 1 to 1.5 seconds. Pause to let the casualty exhale and repeat, giving one more breath. Maintain the head tilt and . . .

8. **Assess the Pulse.** Locate the carotid artery on the side of the neck nearest to you and feel for a pulse. Check carefully to detect what may be a weak, irregular pulse. If there is no pulse . . .

9. **Send for Help.** If someone responded to your call for help, send him to call emergency services, giving sufficient information to ensure a prompt response to your call (see chap. 1). Direct that person to return to you when the call has been completed.

10. **Begin Chest Compressions.**

   ● Landmark for correct hand position, lock the elbows, and bring your shoulders directly over the sternum.

   ● Press down on the hands to compress the chest to a depth of 3.8 to 5.0 cm (1½ to 2 inches) and relax to allow the chest to return to its normal shape. Pressure and relaxation should be of equal time and take less than 1 second.

   ● Repeat compressions at a rate of 80 to 100 per minute for a total of 15 compressions. This should not take more than 9 to 11 seconds. Counting at a constant speed — ONE AND, TWO AND, THREE AND, FOUR AND, **FIVE** AND, ONE AND, TWO AND, THREE AND, FOUR AND, **TEN** AND, ONE AND, TWO

AND, THREE AND, FOUR AND, **FIFTEEN** — will help maintain rhythm, rate and count.

- Ventilate the lungs twice.

- Perform four full cycles of 15 compressions and 2 ventilations, which should take about 1 minute.

11. **Reassess Pulse.** Check the carotid pulse for a return of spontaneous pulse. If there is no pulse . . .

12. **Ventilate the lungs.** Give 2 breaths.

13. **Continue CPR.** Resume compressions and ventilations in the ratio of 15:2 and recheck the pulse every few minutes.

If no one responded to your earlier call for help, you should call emergency medical services after one minute of CPR. Do not leave the casualty for more than four minutes — remember, the brain may be damaged if it is deprived of oxygen for longer than this.

Relief Rescuer

A relief rescuer, possibly the person you sent to call medical aid, can assume your role as the CPR rescuer if you become tired. He should identify himself by saying, "I know CPR. Can I help?" If you indicate that you wish to be relieved, the handover should be made in the following manner at the time when you would normally interrupt CPR to reassess the pulse. When you have completed a cycle ending with two breaths:

- relief rescuer locates and assesses the carotid pulse (step 11). If a 5-second check indicates no pulse . . .

- relief rescuer opens the airway and ventilates twice.

- relief rescuer landmarks and resumes compressions and ventilations in the ratio of 15:2.

- while the relief rescuer is giving CPR, you maintain the airway open and monitor the carotid pulse to assess the effectiveness of chest compressions. Check every few minutes for return of spontaneous pulse.

Stand by ready to take over the role of CPR rescuer when the relief rescuer becomes fatigued.

ONE-RESCUER CPR – CHILD

One-rescuer CPR for a child follows the same sequence of steps as adult CPR. However, CPR manoeuvres are modified so that ventilating breaths are of less volume, chest compressions are given with the heel of one hand only and to a lesser depth, and the ratio of compressions to ventilations is five to one (5:1). The steps are performed as follows:

1. **Assess Responsiveness.** Tap or gently shake the shoulders of an apparently unconscious child and shout, "Are you OK?" to determine the degree of responsiveness. If there is no response . . .

2. **Assess Breathing.** Place your ear near the child's mouth. Look for chest expansion while you listen and feel for signs of air movement. If breathing is absent . . .

3. **Call Out For Help.** Shout or use any means to attract the attention of bystanders.

4. **Position the Casualty.** Place the child on his back on a firm, flat surface, supporting the head and neck during the move.

5. **Open the Airway.** Use the head tilt—chin lift manoeuvre to open the airway.

6. **Reassess Breathing.** Look, listen and feel for any signs of air movement. If breathing is absent . . .

7. **Ventilate the Lungs.** Pinch the child's nostrils shut and cover the mouth or cover both the mouth and nose of a small child with your mouth to make a tight seal. Breathe a volume of air appropriate to the size of the child into the mouth or into the mouth and nose. Give two breaths, taking 1 to 1.5 seconds for each breath. Pause between the two breaths to let the child exhale. Maintain the head tilt and . . .

8. **Assess the Pulse.** Locate the carotid artery on the side of the neck nearest to you and feel for the pulse. Check carefully to detect what may be a weak, irregular pulse. If there is no pulse . . .

9. **Send for Help.** If someone responds to your call for help send him to call emergency services, giving sufficient information to ensure a prompt response to your call (see chap. 1). Direct that person to return to you when the call has been completed.

10. **Begin Chest Compressions.**

    ● Landmark to position the heel of one hand along the lower half of the sternum. Bring your shoulders directly over the sternum. Maintain the head tilt with the other hand.

    ● Press the heel of the hand down to compress the chest to a depth of 2.5 to 3.8 cm (1 to 1½ inches) and release the pressure to allow the chest to return to its normal shape. Pressure and release should be of equal time and take less than 1 second. Give a total of five compressions, at a rate of 80 to 100 per minute. This should take 3 to 4 seconds. Counting at a constant speed — ONE AND,

TWO AND, THREE AND, FOUR AND, FIVE — will help maintain rhythm and rate.

- Ventilate the lungs. Open the airway and give one light breath.

- Perform 10 full cycles of 5 compressions and 1 ventilation taking about 1 minute.

11. **Reassess Pulse.** Check for a return of spontaneous pulse. If there is no pulse . . .

12. **Ventilate the lungs.** Give one light breath.

13. **Continue CPR.** Continue to give compression-ventilation cycles and reassess the pulse every few minutes.

If no one responded to your earlier call for help, go yourself to call emergency medical services, but do not leave the child for more than 4 minutes.

Relief Rescuer

A relief rescuer, possibly the person you sent to call emergency medical services, can take over your role as the CPR rescuer. The method of hand-over is described in one-rescuer CPR for adults.

TWO-RESCUER CPR

CPR rescuers, who are trained to coordinate their efforts, can use a team approach to perform two-rescuer CPR. Two-rescuer CPR is less fatiguing and, because the positions of compressor and ventilator can be switched, it can be carried on for longer periods than one-rescuer CPR.

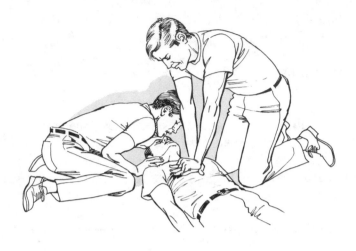

Fig. 8-6. Two-rescuer CPR.

TWO RESCUERS — UNATTENDED CARDIAC ARREST

Two rescuers, arriving on a scene where a casualty is in cardiac arrest and CPR has not been started, should inititate one-rescuer CPR while one goes to call emergency medical services. If there is a bystander who can be directed to call emergency medical services, two-rescuer CPR can be started immediately.

TWO-RESCUER CPR — ADULT OR CHILD

In two-rescuer CPR, one rescuer assumes the role of VENTILATOR and the other as COMPRESSOR. The first aid steps are carried out as follows:

1. VENTILATOR **Assess Responsiveness.** Tap or gently shake the shoulder of an apparently unconscious person and shout, "Are you okay?" to determine the degree of responsiveness. If there is no response . . .

2. VENTILATOR **Assess Breathing.** Place your ear near the casualty's mouth and nose and look toward the chest. Look,

listen and feel for signs of air movement. If breathing is absent, say, "No breathing!"

3. VENTILATOR **Position the Casualty.** Place the casualty on his back, supporting the head and neck during the move.

4. VENTILATOR **Open the Airway.** Use the head tilt-chin lift manoeuvre to open the airway.

5. VENTILATOR **Reassess Breathing.** Look, listen and feel for any signs of air movement. If breathing is absent, say "No breathing."

6. VENTILATOR **Ventilate the Lungs.** Pinch the nostrils shut, make a good seal over the casualty's mouth and give one breath. Pause to let the casualty exhale and give one more breath. Maintain head tilt and ...

7. VENTILATOR **Assess the Pulse.** Locate the carotid artery on the nearest side and feel for a pulse. Check carefully to detect what may be a weak, irregular pulse. If there is no pulse, say, "No pulse!" Send for medical aid.

8. COMPRESSOR **Start Chest Compressions.** From the position and landmarking assumed during the pulse check, give 5 chest compressions, using the heels of two hands for an adult and the heel of one hand for a child. Count aloud "ONE AND, TWO AND, THREE AND, FOUR AND, FIVE". Pause to allow one breath to be given, but keep the hand(s) in place.

9. VENTILATOR **Ventilate the Lungs.** Give one breath then maintain an open airway and monitor the pulse for effectiveness of chest compressions.

10. COMPRESSOR **Continue CPR.** Compress the chest at a
    AND   rate of 80 to 100 per minute, pausing after
    VENTILATOR   each 5th compression to allow the ven-
                       tilator to give one breath.

11. VENTILATOR **Reassess the Pulse and Ventilate.** After 10 cycles (about one minute) of compressions—ventilations say, "Stop CPR", give one breath and check for a return of spontaneous pulse. If there is no pulse say, "No pulse!" and give one breath.

12. COMPRESSOR **Resume CPR.** Compressions—ventila-
    AND   tions resumed. Ventilator calls for a re-
    VENTILATOR   check of the pulse every few minutes.

Switch-over

The compressor signals that he is tired and wants to switch positions. Instead of using the mnemonic ONE AND, TWO AND, THREE AND, FOUR AND, FIVE, he maintains the same rate and says "NEXT, TIME, CHANGE, AFTER, FIVE" (any other mnemonic may be used). On completion of the respiration of the next cycle, the ventilator assumes the position of the compressor and landmarks in readiness to give CPR. The compressor moves to the position of the ventilator to assess the carotid pulse.

13. VENTILATOR **Reassess the Pulse.** Check the carotid pulse. If no pulse is detected, say "No pulse!"

14. VENTILATOR **Ventilate the Lungs.** Give one breath, maintain the head tilt and keep the fingers on the carotid pulse to assess the effectiveness of the chest compressions.

15. COMPRESSOR **Resume CPR.** Compress the chest at the same rhythm and rate at a ratio of five compressions to one breath.

TWO-RESCUER CPR — ATTENDED CARDIAC ARREST

Two rescuers trained in two-rescuer CPR who arrive at a scene where one-rescuer CPR is in progress should first tell the single rescuer they are a two-rescuer team and initiate the hand-over procedure by taking charge of the situation. Second, they should determine whether emergency medical services have been called. Immediately after the single rescuer has completed a cycle of 15 compressions and two breaths, the ventilator, who is now in charge, moves to the head, opens the airway and checks for a pulse while the compressor landmarks for hand position — this should take 5 seconds. At this point, the single rescuer should be sent to call emergency medical services, if necessary. Once the ventilator has confirmed the absence of a pulse and given one breath, compressions are resumed.

ONE-RESCUER CPR – INFANT

Infant CPR follows the same sequence as for adult CPR, but manoeuvres are modified to accommodate the smaller size of the infant. Variations in manoeuvres are recommended for opening the airway; ventilating the lungs; checking the pulse; landmarking for chest compressions; the application, depth and rate of compressions; and the ratio of compressions to ventilations. Perform the steps as follows:

1. **Assess Responsiveness.** Tap or gently shake the apparently unconscious infant to determine the degree of responsiveness. If there is no response . . .

2. **Assess Breathing.** Place your ear near the infant's mouth. Look for chest expansion while you listen and feel for signs of air movement. If breathing is absent . . .

3. **Call Out For Help.** Shout or use any means to attract the attention of bystanders who will be able to call emergency services.

4. **Position the Infant.** Turn the infant on his back on a firm, flat surface, supporting the head and neck during the move.

5. **Open the Airway.** Use the head tilt—chin lift manoeuvre to open the airway, but avoid overextension of the neck. Do not close the mouth completely or push on the soft underparts of the chin.

6. **Reassess Breathing.** Look, listen and feel for any signs of air movement. If breathing is absent . . .

7. **Ventilate the Lungs.** Cover the infant's mouth and nose with your mouth, making a tight seal, and breathe into the infant. Give two puffs of air, taking 1 to 1.5 seconds for each puff and pausing between the two to let the infant exhale. Maintain the airway open and . . .

8. **Assess the Pulse.** Locate the brachial artery with two fingertips and feel for signs of a pulse. Check carefully to detect what may be a weak, irregular pulse. If there is no pulse . . .

9. **Send for Help.** If someone responded to your call for help, send him to call emergency services, giving sufficient information to ensure a prompt response to your call (see chap. 1). Direct that person to return to you when the call has been completed.

10. **Begin Chest Compressions.**

   • Landmark to position two fingertips along the length of the sternum, one finger's width below the line between the infant's nipples.

   • Compress the chest vertically to a depth of 1.3 to 2.5 cm (½ to 1 inch). Release the pressure to allow the chest to return to its normal shape, but keep the fingers in place. Pressure and release should be of equal time and take less than 1 second. Give five compressions at a rate of at least 100 per minute. This should take 3 seconds. Counting at a constant speed — ONE AND, TWO AND, THREE AND, FOUR AND, FIVE — will help maintain rhythm and the correct rate.

   • Ventilate the lungs. Open the airway and give one puff of air.

Complete 10 compression-ventilation cycles in the ratio of 5:1, taking about 45 seconds.

11. **Reassess the Pulse.** Maintain the airway open and reassess the brachial pulse (about 5 seconds). If there is no pulse . . .

12. **Ventilate the lungs.** Give one puff of air.

13. **Continue CPR.** Give compression-ventilation cycles and reassess the pulse every few minutes.

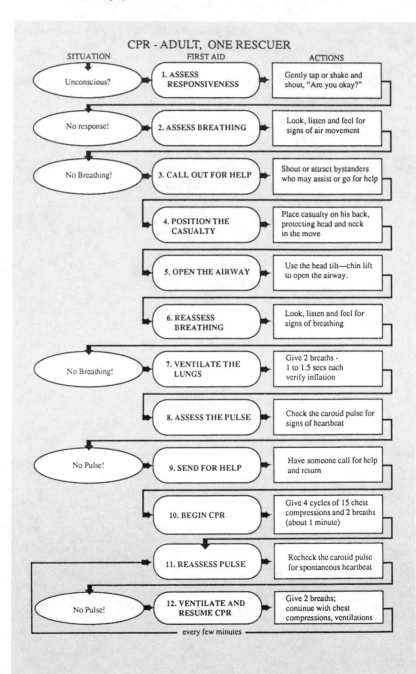

CPR - ADULT, ONE RESCUER

SITUATION	FIRST AID	ACTIONS
Unconscious?	1. ASSESS RESPONSIVENESS	Gently tap or shake and shout, "Are you okay?"
No response!	2. ASSESS BREATHING	Look, listen and feel for signs of air movement
No Breathing!	3. CALL OUT FOR HELP	Shout or attract bystanders who may assist or go for help
	4. POSITION THE CASUALTY	Place casualty on his back, protecting head and neck in the move
	5. OPEN THE AIRWAY	Use the head tilt—chin lift to open the airway.
	6. REASSESS BREATHING	Look, listen and feel for signs of breathing
No Breathing!	7. VENTILATE THE LUNGS	Give 2 breaths - 1 to 1.5 secs each verify inflation
	8. ASSESS THE PULSE	Check the carotid pulse for signs of heartbeat
No Pulse!	9. SEND FOR HELP	Have someone call for help and return
	10. BEGIN CPR	Give 4 cycles of 15 chest compressions and 2 breaths (about 1 minute)
	11. REASSESS PULSE	Recheck the carotid pulse for spontaneous heartbeat
No Pulse!	12. VENTILATE AND RESUME CPR	Give 2 breaths; continue with chest compressions, ventilations

every few minutes

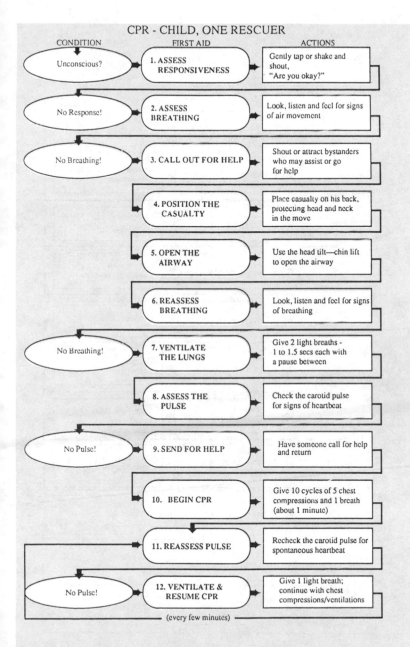

CPR - CHILD, ONE RESCUER

CONDITION	FIRST AID	ACTIONS
Unconscious?	1. ASSESS RESPONSIVENESS	Gently tap or shake and shout, "Are you okay?"
No Response!	2. ASSESS BREATHING	Look, listen and feel for signs of air movement
No Breathing!	3. CALL OUT FOR HELP	Shout or attract bystanders who may assist or go for help
	4. POSITION THE CASUALTY	Place casualty on his back, protecting head and neck in the move
	5. OPEN THE AIRWAY	Use the head tilt—chin lift to open the airway
	6. REASSESS BREATHING	Look, listen and feel for signs of breathing
No Breathing!	7. VENTILATE THE LUNGS	Give 2 light breaths - 1 to 1.5 secs each with a pause between
	8. ASSESS THE PULSE	Check the carotid pulse for signs of heartbeat
No Pulse!	9. SEND FOR HELP	Have someone call for help and return
	10. BEGIN CPR	Give 10 cycles of 5 chest compressions and 1 breath (about 1 minute)
	11. REASSESS PULSE	Recheck the carotid pulse for spontaneous heartbeat
No Pulse!	12. VENTILATE & RESUME CPR	Give 1 light breath; continue with chest compressions/ventilations

(every few minutes)

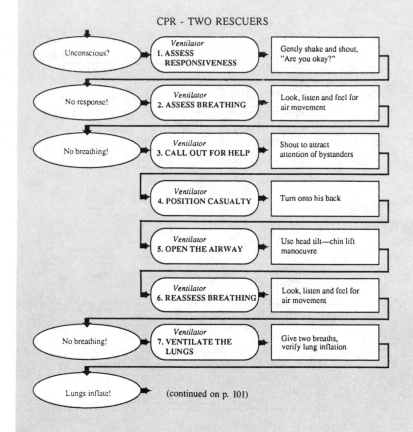

CPR - TWO RESCUERS

Unconscious?	*Ventilator* **1. ASSESS RESPONSIVENESS**	Gently shake and shout, "Are you okay?"
No response!	*Ventilator* **2. ASSESS BREATHING**	Look, listen and feel for air movement
No breathing!	*Ventilator* **3. CALL OUT FOR HELP**	Shout to attract attention of bystanders
	Ventilator **4. POSITION CASUALTY**	Turn onto his back
	Ventilator **5. OPEN THE AIRWAY**	Use head tilt—chin lift manoeuvre
	Ventilator **6. REASSESS BREATHING**	Look, listen and feel for air movement
No breathing!	*Ventilator* **7. VENTILATE THE LUNGS**	Give two breaths, verify lung inflation
Lungs inflate!	(continued on p. 101)	

(continued from p. 100)

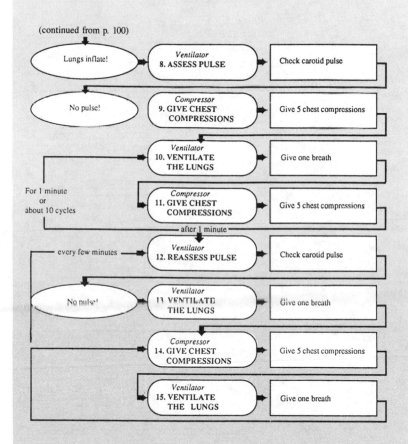

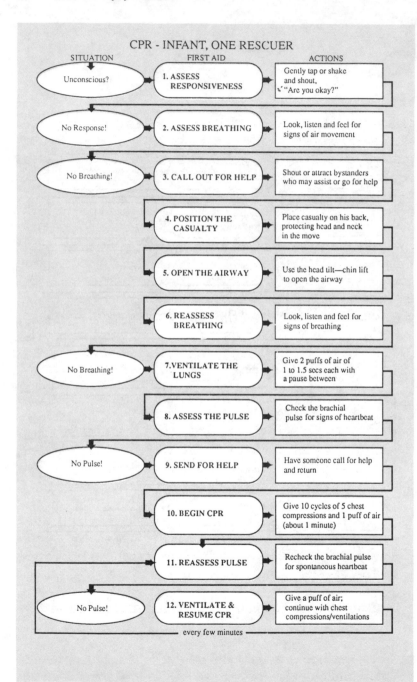

CPR - INFANT, ONE RESCUER

SITUATION	FIRST AID	ACTIONS
Unconscious?	**1. ASSESS RESPONSIVENESS**	Gently tap or shake and shout, "Are you okay?"
No Response!	**2. ASSESS BREATHING**	Look, listen and feel for signs of air movement
No Breathing!	**3. CALL OUT FOR HELP**	Shout or attract bystanders who may assist or go for help
	4. POSITION THE CASUALTY	Place casualty on his back, protecting head and neck in the move
	5. OPEN THE AIRWAY	Use the head tilt—chin lift to open the airway
	6. REASSESS BREATHING	Look, listen and feel for signs of breathing
No Breathing!	**7. VENTILATE THE LUNGS**	Give 2 puffs of air of 1 to 1.5 secs each with a pause between
	8. ASSESS THE PULSE	Check the brachial pulse for signs of heartbeat
No Pulse!	**9. SEND FOR HELP**	Have someone call for help and return
	10. BEGIN CPR	Give 10 cycles of 5 chest compressions and 1 puff of air (about 1 minute)
	11. REASSESS PULSE	Recheck the brachial pulse for spontaneous heartbeat
No Pulse!	**12. VENTILATE & RESUME CPR**	Give a puff of air; continue with chest compressions/ventilations

every few minutes

CHAPTER 9

AIRWAY OBSTRUCTION

Obstruction of the upper airway is the condition in which the air passage to the lungs is partially or completely blocked, preventing air from entering the lungs. Upper airway obstruction in the conscious person is most often caused by foreign objects, such as food or small toys, lodged in the throat. In the unconscious person, the tongue may fall to the back of the throat and close off the air passage. These causes can be treated by first aid. Other causes of airway obstruction, such as injury or swelling of the tissues of the throat from allergic reaction or disease, require medical aid urgently. If air is prevented from entering the lungs, the person will become unconscious. Unless immediate first aid is given, this could lead to cardiopulmonary arrest and death.

PREVENTION OF AIRWAY OBSTRUCTION

Choking on food and other objects can be avoided by taking these precautions:

- cut food, especially meat, into small pieces and chew thoroughly before swallowing. Cut hotdogs lengthwise before serving them to children.

- avoid talking, laughing or drinking while chewing food.

- avoid excessive drinking of alcoholic beverages before and during meals.

- caution children not to run with food or other objects in their mouths.

- keep small objects and balloons out of the reach of infants and children.

- supervise infants and children when they are eating and drinking.

- be aware that certain foods tend to cause choking in infants and small children — avoid peanuts, popcorn and thickly-spread peanut butter.

- choose toys that have been safety approved.

RECOGNITION OF AIRWAY OBSTRUCTION

Early recognition of upper airway obstruction is most important to a successful rescue, especially in infants and younger children. Consider choking as a possible cause in any casualty who suddenly stops breathing, shows signs of cyanosis (blueness about the lips) and falls unconscious. Be alert for the possibility of choking in anyone who suddenly leaves during a meal. This may be an attempt to avoid embarrassment, but it also isolates the person from help. Go with this person to ensure that help is available. Choking as the result of a foreign body can cause either a partial or a complete airway obstruction.

PARTIAL AIRWAY OBSTRUCTION

A partial airway obstruction allows some air to enter the lungs, which is evident from attempts to cough. The quality of the air exchange must be assessed quickly to determine what first aid action is needed.

Good Air Exchange. Forceful coughing, even though there may be wheezing between coughs, indicates good air exchange. Stand by, encourage coughing, but do not interfere with this person's efforts to clear his airway.

Poor Air Exchange. A weak and ineffective cough, a high-pitched noise while inhaling, increased respiratory difficulty and cyanosis are signs of poor air exchange. Consider this casualty to have a complete airway obstruction and give first aid for choking.

COMPLETE AIRWAY OBSTRUCTION

Fig. 9-1. Sign of choking.

If the airway obstruction is complete, the person will be unable to breathe, cough or speak. The casualty will show signs of distress and clutch the throat. Initial congestion (redness of the face) will change to cyanosis, and unconsciousness will soon follow. First aid for choking must be started immediately.

FIRST AID MANOEUVRES FOR CHOKING

First aid for choking requires the use of one or more of the following manoeuvres, depending on the age and physical condition of the casualty:

- abdominal thrusts;

- chest thrusts;

- back blows;

- finger sweeps or foreign body checks of the mouth;

- ventilations.

Each manoeuvre is described in detail. However, its application, either alone or in combination with other manoeuvres, must be performed in rapid sequence to be effective. These manoeuvres are potentially dangerous and they must never be practised with full force, except on manikins.

ABDOMINAL THRUSTS

The abdominal thrust (Heimlich manoeuvre) is more accurately described as a subdiaphragmatic thrust. The intent of the abdominal thrust is to apply pressure under the diaphragm to force air out of the lungs, creating an artificial cough. If the casualty is standing or sitting, pressure is applied with the fist on the upper abdomen. If the casualty is lying on his back, the heels of the hands are used. There is a risk of causing internal injuries, but correct application of the manoeuvre should keep this risk to a minimum. Abdominal thrusts must not be used on infants and they are not recommended for a markedly obese person or a woman in advanced stages of pregnancy.

Abdominal Thrust – Casualty Standing or Sitting

To give abdominal thrusts to a person who is standing or sitting, stand behind the casualty and wrap your arms around the waist.

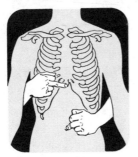

Fig. 9-2 (a). Abdominal thrusts — landmarking.

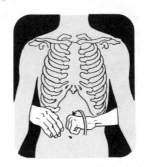

Fig. 9-2 (b). Abdominal thrusts — fist position.

Locate the tip of the xiphoid with the middle finger of one hand and the umbilicus (navel) with the middle finger of the other. Without shifting position, make a fist with the lower hand and roll it upward so that the thumb is against the abdomen, in the midline, just above the navel and well below the tip of the xiphoid. Grasp the fist with the other hand and press upward quickly and forcefully. Make each a distinct thrust with the intent of dislodging the obstruction.

Fig. 9-2 (c). Abdominal thrusts — grasp the fist.

Fig. 9-2 (d). Abdominal thrusts.

Abdominal thrusts are given to a conscious choking person until the obstruction is relieved or until the person becomes unconscious.

Abdominal Thrust – Casualty Lying Down

To give abdominal thrusts to an unconscious person, place him on his back. Kneel astride the casualty at the thighs or lower, so that the heels of your hands reach the upper abdominal area comfortably. Locate the tip of the xiphoid with the middle finger of one hand and the navel with the middle finger of the other. Without shifting position, let the hand at the xiphoid drop down so that the heel of the hand falls just above the navel. Place the other hand on top, ensuring that the fingers are parallel to the midline of the body. Keep the fingers raised or interlocked to ensure that pressure will be delivered only through the heels of the hands. Thrust upward quickly, giving a series of six to ten distinct thrusts, each with the intent of dislodging the obstructing material.

Each series of six to ten thrusts is followed by attempts to ventilate the lungs and they are discontinued when the obstruction is relieved.

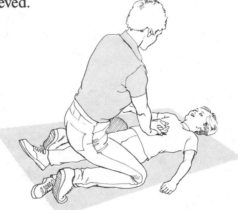

Fig. 9-3. Abdominal thrusts — lying down.

Abdominal Thrusts – Self-Administered

A conscious choking person can administer abdominal thrusts to himself to assist in his efforts to cough up a foreign body. Self-administered abdominal thrusts are given by making a fist and placing it, thumb side in, in the midline, just above the navel and well below the xiphoid process. Grasp the fist with the other hand and press forcefully and quickly upward into the diaphragm. Repeat these thrusts until successful.

The back of a padded chair or the edge of a counter or table can also be used for self-administered abdominal thrusts. Position the upper abdomen along the edge of a counter, table or chair back. Press forcefully into the counter edge to apply pressure to the diaphragm. Repeat until successful.

CHEST THRUSTS

Chest thrusts may have to be used instead of abdominal thrusts for the choking adult who is in an advanced stage of pregnancy or who is markedly obese. Abdominal thrusts, in these cases, cannot be applied effectively. Chest thrusts, in combination with back blows, are to be used for the choking infant. Chest thrusts can be administered to a conscious adult casualty who is in a sitting or standing position or to an unconscious adult casualty lying on his back. Chest thrusts to infants are always administered in the lying position.

Chest Thrusts – Conscious Adult Standing or Sitting

To give chest thrusts to a pregnant or obese person who is standing or sitting, stand behind the casualty, slide your arms

under the armpits and position your fist, thumb side in, on the middle of the sternum. Take care to avoid the xiphoid process and the ribs on either side of the sternum. Grasp the fist with the other hand and pull forcefully backward. These backward thrusts will compress the chest and force air out of the lungs, creating an artificial cough. Give each thrust with the intent of dislodging the obstructing material.

Fig. 9-4. Chest thrusts — standing.

Chest thrusts are repeated until the obstruction is relieved or the casualty becomes unconscious.

Chest Thrusts – Unconscious Adult Lying Down

To deliver chest thrusts to the pregnant or obese person who is unconscious, place the casualty face up on a firm, flat surface with the arms at the sides. Kneel close to the casualty's chest and landmark to find the lower half of the sternum in the same manner as in CPR (see chap. 8). Deliver a series of six to ten thrusts slowly and distinctly, depressing the sternum 3.8 to 5 cm (1½ to 2 inches), with the intent of dislodging the obstruction. Each series of six to ten chest thrusts is followed by finger sweeps and attempts to ventilate the lungs. They are discontinued when the obstruction is relieved.

Chest Thrusts – Infants

Chests thrusts, preceded by back blows, are used to relieve airway obstruction in infants (younger than 1 year), because abdominal thrusts pose greater dangers of internal injury to this age group.

Chest thrusts to an infant who is choking are delivered with two fingers placed on the sternum, one finger's width below the nipple line as in CPR (see chap. 8). Hold the infant on your thigh

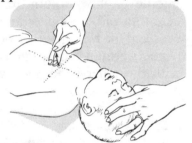

and support the head and neck, with the head lower than the trunk. Deliver four thrusts, at a slower rate than for CPR, depressing the chest 1.3 to 2.5 cm (½ to 1 inch). Release the pressure between each thrust to allow the chest wall to return to its normal position.

Fig. 9-5. Chest thrusts — infant.

BACK BLOWS

To administer back blows, straddle the infant over your arm, support the head by firmly holding the jaw, and position the head lower than the trunk. Rest your forearm on your thigh. With your fingers in line with the body, deliver four distinct blows with the heel of the hand to the area between the shoulder blades. Follow the series of four back blows by chest thrusts.

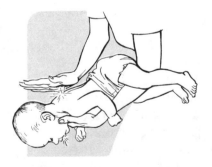

Fig. 9-6. Back blows — infant.

FINGER SWEEP – FOREIGN BODY CHECK

Finger sweep of the mouth or foreign body check is a two-part manoeuvre that is used to dislodge and remove a foreign body

Fig. 9-7. Tongue-jaw lift and finger sweep.

that may be obstructing the airway of an unconscious casualty. Place your thumb inside the casualty's mouth to hold the tongue, while grasping the chin with the fingers. With the tongue and jaw held firmly between the thumb and fingers, lift the jaw (tongue-jaw lift). This may loosen the foreign body, allowing it to be "hooked" out of the mouth as you sweep deeply into the mouth with the index finger.

When making a foreign body check in the mouth of an infant or small child, do not make a blind sweep. Your finger may accidentally push the obstructing matter deeper into the throat. Attempt to remove only foreign matter that you can see.

Although finger sweeps may not result in the removal of a foreign body, lifting the tongue away from the back of the throat may partially relieve the obstruction and allow air to pass into the lungs as you attempt to ventilate.

VENTILATIONS

After each finger sweep/foreign body check manoeuvre, open the airway and attempt to ventilate the lungs. If the chest rises, continue with artificial respiration. If the lungs do not inflate, continue with first aid for choking to relieve the airway obstruction.

PERFORMING FIRST AID FOR CHOKING

When it is determined that a person has an airway obstruction, quickly apply the appropriate manoeuvres in proper sequence, depending on the casualty's state of consciouness, size and general physical condition.

CHOKING ADULT OR CHILD – CONSCIOUS

1. **Assess Obstruction.** As long as there is good air exchange, encourage coughing to relieve the obstruction and stand by ready to help. Ask, "Are you choking?" When air exchange is poor or absent, the obstruction is complete.

2. **Give Abdominal Thrusts.** Stand behind the casualty and wrap your arms around the waist. Locate the tip of the xiphoid with one hand and the navel with the other. Position a fist just above the navel, but well below the xiphoid process. Grasp the fist with the other hand and give repeated quick upward thrusts until successful in dislodging the obstructing material or until the casualty becomes unconscious.

CHOKING ADULT OR CHILD – BECOMES UNCONSCIOUS

3. **Position the Casualty.** Ease the person to the floor or other firm flat surface on his back with his arms to the sides.

4. **Call Out/Send For Help.** Shout to attract bystanders and, if someone responds, send him to call emergency services. Provide all the information needed to ensure a prompt response to your call (see chap. 1).

5. **Finger Sweep/Foreign Body Check.** Open the mouth with the tongue-jaw lift and attempt to dislodge or remove the foreign body with a hooked finger. DO NOT MAKE

BLIND SWEEPS OF A CHILD'S MOUTH, and remove only foreign matter that can be seen.

6. **Ventilate the Lungs.** Open the airway and attempt to ventilate the lungs. Watch the chest for any signs of expansion. This will indicate that air is getting past the obstruction and that artificial respiration should be continued. If the lungs do not inflate . . .

7. **Give Abdominal Thrusts.** Kneel astride the casualty so that you can reach the upper abdomen comfortably with your hands. Locate the tip of the xiphoid with one hand and the navel with the other. Place the heel of one hand just above the navel and the other hand on top. With the fingers raised or interlocked and in line with the centre line of the body give 6 to 10 quick upward thrusts, each a separate and distinct movement.

8. **Repeat Finger Sweeps/Foreign Body Checks, Ventilations and Abdominal Thrusts.** Begin again at Step 5 and repeat finger sweeps/foreign body checks, ventilations and abdominal thrusts until you are successful or until medical aid arrives on the scene.

CHOKING ADULT OR CHILD – FOUND UNCONSCIOUS

1. **Assess Responsiveness.** Tap or gently shake the person and shout, "Are you okay?" to verify that the person is unconscious. If there is no response . . .

2. **Assess Breathing.** Place your ear and cheek near the casualty's mouth and nose. Observe the chest for movement. If there are no signs of breathing . . .

3. **Call Out For Help.** Shout to attract bystanders to assist with a call to emergency services.

4. **Position the Casualty.** Turn the casualty over onto his back, taking care to protect the head and neck as you turn the body over as one unit without twisting.

5. **Open the Airway.** Use the head tilt—chin lift manoeuvre to open the airway.

6. **Reassess Breathing.** Look, listen and feel with your cheek for any signs of air movement. If there are no signs of breathing . . .

7. **Ventilate the Lungs.** Take a breath, pinch the casualty's nostrils closed, make a tight seal with your mouth over the casualty's mouth and breathe into his mouth. Look for chest expansion to check if the lungs are being inflated. If the lungs do not inflate . . .

8. **Reopen the Airway, Recheck Seals, Ventilate.** Increase head tilt and chin lift. Ensure that the nostrils are pinched closed and that you are making good seals with your mouth as you try again to ventilate the lungs. If the lungs do not inflate . . .

9. **Send For Help.** Send someone to call emergency services. Provide all the information needed to ensure a prompt response to your call. If you are alone, do not leave the casualty; continue giving first aid.

10. **Give Abdominal Thrusts.** Position yourself astride the casualty so that you can comfortably reach the upper abdomen with your hands. Locate the tip of the xiphoid with one hand and the navel with the other. Position the heels of the hands just above the navel with the fingers parallel to the centre line of the body and raised or interlocked. Give 6 to 10 quick upward thrusts. If the obstruction persists . . .

11. **Finger Sweep/Foreign Body Check.** Open the mouth with the tongue-jaw lift and attempt to hook the foreign body to

dislodge it or to remove it completely. DO NOT MAKE BLIND FINGER SWEEPS OF A CHILD'S MOUTH; remove a foreign body only if it can be seen.

12. **Ventilate the Lungs.** Open the airway and attempt to ventilate the lungs. Look for signs of chest expansion. If the lungs do not inflate, return to Step 10 and continue to give abdominal thrusts, finger sweeps/foreign body checks and attempts to ventilate until you are successful or until medical aid arrives on the scene.

FIRST AID FOR CHOKING – INFANTS

Foreign body airway obstruction should be suspected in an infant who develops sudden respiratory distress associated with coughing, gagging or high-pitched noisy breathing. If the breathing difficulty is due to an upper respiratory infection or to an allergic reaction, do not waste time trying to relieve the obstruction. Get this infant to a medical facility immediately.

Give first aid for choking to an infant when foreign body aspiration has been witnessed or is strongly suspected. Use the choking manoeuvres on an unconscious, non-breathing infant when attempts to ventilate the lungs are unsuccessful and the airway remains obstructed after airway opening manoeuvres have been attempted.

CHOKING INFANT – CONSCIOUS

1. **Assess Obstruction.** Encourage the infant's efforts if coughing is forceful and breathing is spontaneous. When coughing becomes ineffective with high-pitched breathing sounds or breathing sounds are absent . . .

2. **Give Four Back Blows.** Straddle the infant over your forearm, supporting the head in your hand at a level lower than the trunk and supported on your thigh. Give four

distinct blows with the heel of the hand between the infant's shoulder blades.

3. **Give Four Chest Thrusts.** Continue to support the head and neck as you turn the infant over onto his back, supported on your thigh with the head lower than the trunk. Place two fingers on the mid-sternum as in CPR and give four chest thrusts to compress the chest 1.3. to 2.5 cm (½ to 1 inch).

4. **Repeat Back Blows and Chest Thrusts.** Continue giving a series of four back blows and four chest thrusts until successful in dislodging the obstructing material or until the infant becomes unconscious.

CHOKING INFANT – BECOMES UNCONSCIOUS

5. **Call Out/Send For Help.** Shout to attract bystanders and, if someone responds, send him to call emergency services. Provide all the information needed to ensure a prompt response to your call.

6. **Foreign Body Check.** Open the mouth with the tongue-jaw lift and attempt to remove any foreign matter that can be seen. DO NOT MAKE BLIND FINGER SWEEPS.

7. **Ventilate the Lungs.** Open the airway and attempt to ventilate the lungs. Cover the infant's mouth and nose with your mouth and give a light puff of air. Observe the chest for signs of expansion. If the chest expands, continue with artificial respiration. If the lungs do not inflate . . .

8. **Give Four Back Blows.** Straddle the infant over your forearm, supporting the head in your hand at a level lower than the trunk. Rest your forearm on your thigh and give four distinct blows with the heel of the other hand between the infant's shoulder blades.

9. **Give Four Chest Thrusts.** Continue to support the head and neck as you turn the infant over onto his back, supported on your thigh with the head lower than the trunk. Place two fingers on the midline of the sternum, as in CPR, and give four chest thrusts to compress the chest 1.3 to 2.5 cm (½ to 1 inch).

10. **Foreign Body Check.** Open the mouth with the tongue-jaw lift and attempt to remove any foreign matter that can be seen. DO NOT MAKE BLIND FINGER SWEEPS.

11. **Ventilate the Lungs.** Use the head tilt—chin lift to open the airway, make a good seal over the infant's mouth and nose and give a puff of air.

If the lungs do not inflate, repeat the sequence, starting with Step 8 and give back blows, chest thrusts, foreign body checks, and attempts to ventilate. Repeat these manoeuvres until successful or until medical aid arrives.

CHOKING INFANT – FOUND UNCONSCIOUS

1. **Assess Responsiveness.** Tap or gently shake the infant's shoulder to verify unconsciousness. If there is no response . . .

2. **Assess Breathing.** Place your ear and cheek near the infant's mouth and nose to listen and feel for air movement. Observe the chest for movement. If there are no signs of breathing . . .

3. **Call Out For Help.** Shout to attract bystanders to assist with a call to emergency services.

4. **Position the Infant.** Turn onto his back while supporting the head and neck.

5. **Open the Airway.** Use the head tilt—chin lift manoeuvre to open the airway.

6. **Reassess Breathing.** Look, listen and feel with your cheek for any signs of air movement. If there are no signs of breathing . . .

7. **Ventilate the Lungs.** Cover the infant's mouth and nose with your mouth and give a puff of air. If the lungs do not inflate . . .

8. **Reopen the Airway, Recheck Seal, Ventilate.** Reposition the head and chin, ensure a tight seal about the infant's mouth and nose and attempt again to ventilate the lungs. If the lungs do not inflate . . .

9. **Send For Help.** Send someone to call emergency services. Provide all the information needed to ensure a prompt response to your call (see chap. 1).

10. **Give Four Back Blows.** Straddle the infant over your forearm, supporting the head in your hand at a level lower than the trunk. Rest your forearm on your thigh and give four distinct blows with the heel of the hand between the infant's shoulder blades.

11. **Give Four Chest Thrusts.** Continue to support the head and neck as you turn the infant over onto his back, supported on your thigh. Place two fingers on the midline of the sternum, as in CPR, and give four chest thrusts to compress the chest 1.3. to 2.5 cm (½ to 1 inch).

12. **Foreign Body Check.** Open the mouth with the tongue-jaw lift and attempt to remove any foreign matter that can be seen. DO NOT MAKE BLIND FINGER SWEEPS.

13. **Ventilate the Lungs.** Open the airway, make a good seal

over the infant's mouth and nose and attempt to ventilate the lungs.

If the lungs do not inflate, begin again at Step 10 and repeat back blows, chest thrusts, foreign body checks and attempts to ventilate until successful or medical aid arrives.

FOLLOW-UP CARE

Discontinue choking manoeuvres at any time that the obstruction is sufficiently relieved to allow spontaneous breathing or to allow artificial respiration to be given.

When spontaneous breathing resumes, stay with the casualty to ensure that no further breathing difficulties develop. Take this person to emergency medical services or encourage him to see his own physician. Choking manoeuvres can cause internal injuries, and this casualty needs medical care.

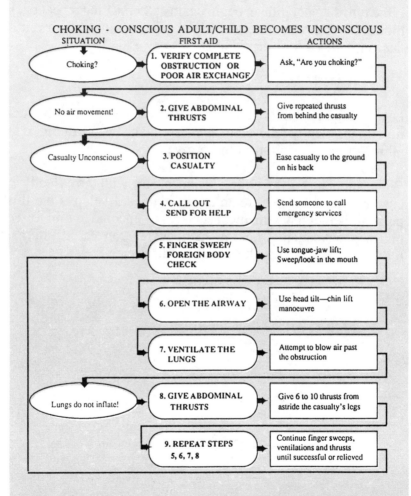

CHOKING - CONSCIOUS ADULT/CHILD BECOMES UNCONSCIOUS

SITUATION	FIRST AID	ACTIONS
Choking?	1. VERIFY COMPLETE OBSTRUCTION OR POOR AIR EXCHANGE	Ask, "Are you choking?"
No air movement!	2. GIVE ABDOMINAL THRUSTS	Give repeated thrusts from behind the casualty
Casualty Unconscious!	3. POSITION CASUALTY	Ease casualty to the ground on his back
	4. CALL OUT SEND FOR HELP	Send someone to call emergency services
	5. FINGER SWEEP/ FOREIGN BODY CHECK	Use tongue-jaw lift; Sweep/look in the mouth
	6. OPEN THE AIRWAY	Use head tilt—chin lift manoeuvre
	7. VENTILATE THE LUNGS	Attempt to blow air past the obstruction
Lungs do not inflate!	8. GIVE ABDOMINAL THRUSTS	Give 6 to 10 thrusts from astride the casualty's legs
	9. REPEAT STEPS 5, 6, 7, 8	Continue finger sweeps, ventilations and thrusts until successful or relieved

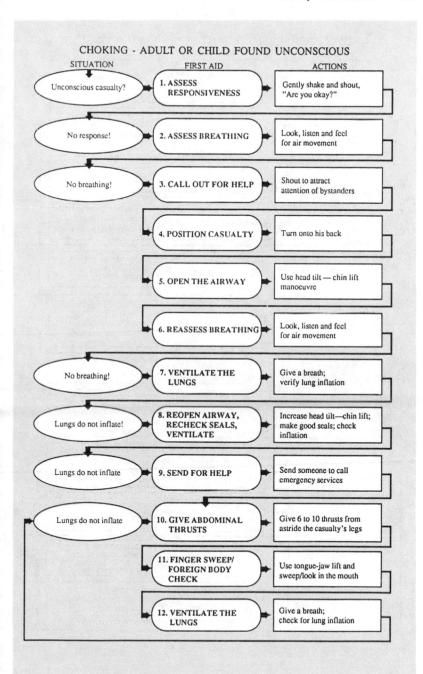

CHOKING - ADULT OR CHILD FOUND UNCONSCIOUS

SITUATION	FIRST AID	ACTIONS
Unconscious casualty?	1. ASSESS RESPONSIVENESS	Gently shake and shout, "Are you okay?"
No response!	2. ASSESS BREATHING	Look, listen and feel for air movement
No breathing!	3. CALL OUT FOR HELP	Shout to attract attention of bystanders
	4. POSITION CASUALTY	Turn onto his back
	5. OPEN THE AIRWAY	Use head tilt — chin lift manoeuvre
	6. REASSESS BREATHING	Look, listen and feel for air movement
No breathing!	7. VENTILATE THE LUNGS	Give a breath; verify lung inflation
Lungs do not inflate!	8. REOPEN AIRWAY, RECHECK SEALS, VENTILATE	Increase head tilt—chin lift; make good seals; check inflation
Lungs do not inflate	9. SEND FOR HELP	Send someone to call emergency services
Lungs do not inflate	10. GIVE ABDOMINAL THRUSTS	Give 6 to 10 thrusts from astride the casualty's legs
	11. FINGER SWEEP/ FOREIGN BODY CHECK	Use tongue-jaw lift and sweep/look in the mouth
	12. VENTILATE THE LUNGS	Give a breath; check for lung inflation

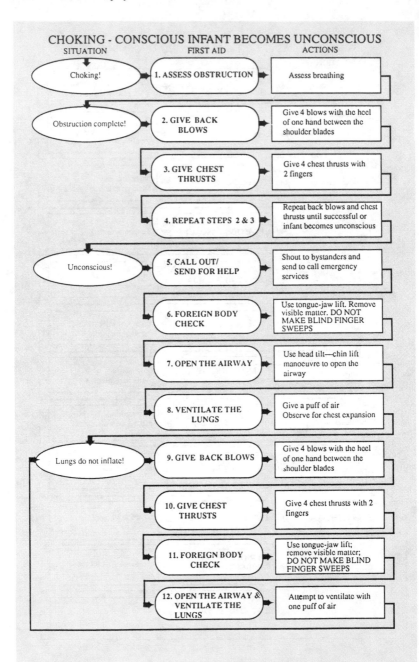

CHOKING - CONSCIOUS INFANT BECOMES UNCONSCIOUS

SITUATION	FIRST AID	ACTIONS
Choking!	1. ASSESS OBSTRUCTION	Assess breathing
Obstruction complete!	2. GIVE BACK BLOWS	Give 4 blows with the heel of one hand between the shoulder blades
	3. GIVE CHEST THRUSTS	Give 4 chest thrusts with 2 fingers
	4. REPEAT STEPS 2 & 3	Repeat back blows and chest thrusts until successful or infant becomes unconscious
Unconscious!	5. CALL OUT/ SEND FOR HELP	Shout to bystanders and send to call emergency services
	6. FOREIGN BODY CHECK	Use tongue-jaw lift. Remove visible matter. DO NOT MAKE BLIND FINGER SWEEPS
	7. OPEN THE AIRWAY	Use head tilt—chin lift manoeuvre to open the airway
	8. VENTILATE THE LUNGS	Give a puff of air Observe for chest expansion
Lungs do not inflate!	9. GIVE BACK BLOWS	Give 4 blows with the heel of one hand between the shoulder blades
	10. GIVE CHEST THRUSTS	Give 4 chest thrusts with 2 fingers
	11. FOREIGN BODY CHECK	Use tongue-jaw lift; remove visible matter; DO NOT MAKE BLIND FINGER SWEEPS
	12. OPEN THE AIRWAY & VENTILATE THE LUNGS	Attempt to ventilate with one puff of air

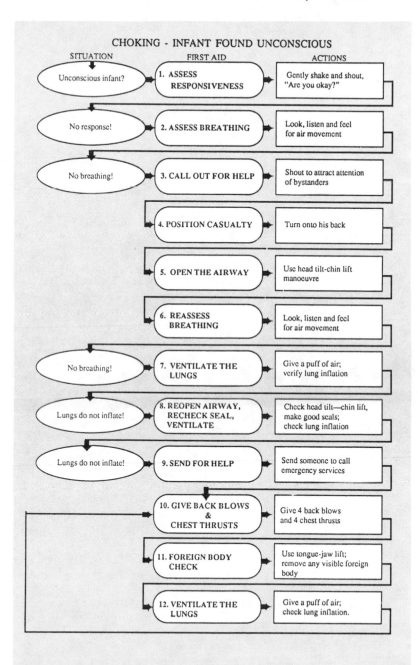

CHOKING - INFANT FOUND UNCONSCIOUS

SITUATION	FIRST AID	ACTIONS
Unconscious infant?	1. ASSESS RESPONSIVENESS	Gently shake and shout, "Are you okay?"
No response!	2. ASSESS BREATHING	Look, listen and feel for air movement
No breathing!	3. CALL OUT FOR HELP	Shout to attract attention of bystanders
	4. POSITION CASUALTY	Turn onto his back
	5. OPEN THE AIRWAY	Use head tilt-chin lift manoeuvre
	6. REASSESS BREATHING	Look, listen and feel for air movement
No breathing!	7. VENTILATE THE LUNGS	Give a puff of air; verify lung inflation
Lungs do not inflate!	8. REOPEN AIRWAY, RECHECK SEAL, VENTILATE	Check head tilt—chin lift, make good seals; check lung inflation
Lungs do not inflate!	9. SEND FOR HELP	Send someone to call emergency services
	10. GIVE BACK BLOWS & CHEST THRUSTS	Give 4 back blows and 4 chest thrusts
	11. FOREIGN BODY CHECK	Use tongue-jaw lift; remove any visible foreign body
	12. VENTILATE THE LUNGS	Give a puff of air; check lung inflation.

Notes

CHAPTER 10

SHOCK

Shock is a condition of inadequate circulation to the body tissues. It can deprive the brain and other vital organs of oxygen and can lead to unconsciousness and death. Shock may be due to the loss of blood or other body fluids as in severe bleeding and burns. It may also be the result of fright, pain, nerve injury, heart attack, or allergic reaction. Some degree of shock is present with any injury or illness. It is a serious condition which can be fatal if it is not prevented from worsening.

The following conditions, if untreated, may result in severe shock:

- **severe external bleeding** and **internal bleeding** into the body cavities;

- **burns,** with a loss of blood plasma into the surrounding injured area;

- **crush injuries,** which may result in the loss of blood and plasma into the surrounding injured tissues;

- **cardiac emergencies,** when the heart can no longer pump sufficient blood through the circulatory system;

- **respiratory emergencies,** such as an obstructed airway, a sucking chest wound, a flail chest or paralysis of the intercostal muscles, which prevent the casualty from breathing enough air to supply oxygenated blood to the vital organs;

- **spinal cord or nerve injuries** affecting control of the size of blood vessels;

- **severe allergic reactions** from an insect sting, an animal bite, specific foods or drugs.

- **infection** associated with abdominal emergencies. This type of shock is usually seen after a period of illness and is rarely the concern of the First Aider.

Pain, loss of body heat, anxiety and fear are aggravating factors that will speed the onset and increase the degree of shock.

SIGNS AND SYMPTOMS

The condition of a casualty who is in shock may vary from faintness to a deeper level of unconsciousness. Any or all of the following signs and symptoms may be present and may increase in intensity as shock progresses:

- restlessness and anxiety may precede all other signs;

- pallor or blue-grey colour of the skin, especially the lips, fingernail beds and earlobes, indicating lack of oxygen;

- cold and clammy skin with profuse sweating;

- weak and rapid pulse;

- shallow and rapid breathing and, in later stages, gasping for air;

- thirst;

- nausea and vomiting;

- changes in the level of consciousness.

FIRST AID

Learn to recognize the conditions that cause shock and give appropriate first aid to slow down its progress.

There must be no delay in getting medical aid for casualties in shock. Until medical aid is obtained, give first aid promptly:

- treat the obvious causes of shock such as severe bleeding, fractures and burns.

- reassure the casualty.

- handle the casualty gently to avoid causing pain.

- loosen clothing around the neck, chest and waist.

- prevent loss of body heat when treating for shock. Body heat can be retained by putting blankets over and under the casualty. Do not overheat a person in shock and do not use hot water bottles or heating pads unless directed to do so by a physician.

- give nothing by mouth if shock is severe. Moisten the lips if the casualty complains of thirst.

- place an unconscious person in the recovery position (see chap. 11) and obtain medical aid as quickly as possible.

POSITIONING A CASUALTY IN SHOCK

A casualty in shock should be positioned to slow down the progress of shock and to provide maximum comfort. The ideal position for a casualty in shock is on his back with his head low and the lower extremities raised 15 cm to 30 cm (6 to 12 inches) to increase the blood flow to the brain.

The casualty's injuries or physical condition may not permit you to place him in the ideal shock position. Raising the legs and feet of a casualty with pelvic fractures can cause increased pain and may aggravate the injury. This person is best kept flat on his back, preferably on a stretcher. However, the foot of the stretcher can be elevated if the casualty is well immobilized. Those who have suffered chest injuries, who have a lung disease or who have just had a heart attack usually find it easier to breathe if they are semisitting. Unconscious casualties or those who show signs of vomiting should be placed in the recovery position.

CHAPTER 11

UNCONSCIOUSNESS

LEVELS OF CONSCIOUSNESS

Many illnesses and injuries are complicated by the loss of consciousness. Head injurics, asphyxia, poisoning, shock and heart attack are some of the conditions that may affect a person's level of consciousness.

Consciousness is the state in which a person is fully awake, speaks coherently, controls muscular activity, responds to speech or pain and is fully aware of his surroundings. Any change in this state, other than for normal sleep, is an important sign of injury or illness. Progressive loss of consciousness indicates a deterioration of a person's condition. Therefore, it is essential that you assess a casualty's state of consciousness, periodically monitor the level of consciousness and note any change.

ASSESSING LEVELS OF CONSCIOUSNESS

The **Glasgow Coma Scale** was devised to assess and describe levels of consciousness. The assessment is based on the ability of the casualty **to open his eyes, to speak** coherently and **to use his muscles**. The scale ranges from a full use of these faculties (conscious), through degrees of functional impairment (semi-conscious), to a complete lack of response (unconscious).

This scale has been modified for first aid purposes, but the principle of its application remains the same. The best response from a casualty is rated on the following scale:

- **Eye opening response**
  – open spontaneously;
  – open to speech or pain;
  – do not open.

- **Best verbal response**
  – oriented and alert;
  – confused/incom-prehensible;
  – no response.

- **Best motor response**
  – obeys commands;
  – responds to pain – flexes and extends;
  – no response.

Using this scale, an altered state of consciousness can be described as follows: "eyes open to pain, speech is confused and at times incomprehensible and muscles flex slightly when the inside of the forearm is pinched." The condition may deteriorate so that there would be "no eye opening response, no verbal response and no motor response."

Pain Stimulus

During the examination, it is possible that pain will be caused unintentionally and that the casualty will react. The degree of reaction should be noted to assess the state of consciousness. If it is necessary to use pain as a stimulus in the initial or in subsequent assessments, it can be done in a number of ways without causing harm. Pinching the tip of the earlobe or the skin on the inside of the forearm generally will produce enough pain to cause a reaction. Pressure to the proximal edge of the finger-nail bed with the edge of a pencil will also cause enough pain to get a response.

Impediments To Appropriate Response

Be alert to those conditions that might affect the casualty's ability to make a response appropriate to his actual level of consciousness. Eye injuries and swelling of surrounding tissue may restrict the person's ability to open his eyes although he may be fully conscious. Similarly, throat injuries, a speech impediment or linguistic differences may restrict verbal response, and nerve injuries may limit motor response. If paralysis is suspected, ask the casualty to blink his eye or stick out his tongue so that you can assess motor response.

Information about changes in levels of consciousness, including whether the onset was sudden or slow and when the changes were noticed, is important to the physician who will eventually treat the casualty.

CARE OF AN UNCONSCIOUS CASUALTY

When there are several casualties, look for unconscious persons first. The cause of unconsciousness may not be readily apparent, but that should not delay initial first aid.

The unconscious casualty's muscles relax and, if the person is lying on his back, the tongue may fall to the back of the throat and obstruct the airway. Unconscious persons may also lose the natural swallowing and coughing reflexes. This will allow mucus, vomitus and blood to enter and obstruct the airway. The immediate objectives in the care of an unconscious casualty are to ensure an open airway and adequate breathing. To do so:

- maintain an open airway;

- begin artificial respiration immediately if the casualty is not breathing (see chap. 7);

- if there are obvious injuries about the face and jaw, check the mouth for knocked-out teeth; remove these to prevent them from being inhaled or swallowed and care for them as amputated tissue (see chap. 5);

- loosen constrictive clothing at the person's neck, chest and waist;

- identify and give first aid for the cause of unconsciousness;

- place the casualty in the recovery position if his injuries permit and monitor breathing;

- give nothing by mouth to an unconscious person.

Note the person's level of consciousness and make a mental note or written notes of changes observed. Note the times that changes were observed.

A person who has regained consciousness and is not transferred immediately to medical aid should be handed over to the care of responsible people and advised to see a physician as soon as possible.

RECOVERY POSITION

To move a person who is lying on his back to the recovery position:

- kneel at the person's side and bring his far leg toward you to cross at the ankles.

- tuck the arm and hand nearest you along the person's side. Bring the other arm across the chest.

- position your knees close to the person, place one hand under the head to support it, and grip his clothing or belt at the waist on the side away from you.

Fig. 11-1 (a). The recovery position.

- roll the person toward you in one smooth but firm motion, protecting his head and neck during the roll and bringing his chest and abdomen to rest on your thighs.

Fig. 11-1 (b). The recovery position.

- move back and bend the person's upper knee toward you to prevent his body from rolling forward. Position his head so the neck is in an extended position to maintain an open airway.

Fig. 11-1 (c). The recovery position.

● bend the arm nearest you at the elbow to support his upper body. Position the person's other arm comfortably along his side to prevent him from rolling over onto his back.

Fig. 11-1 (d). The recovery position.

MEDICAL ALERT INFORMATION

Persons with medical problems that require specific treatment often wear or carry medical information in the form of a brace-

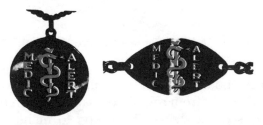

Fig. 11-2. Medic-Alert pendant and bracelet.

let, necklace or pocket card that specifies their condition and the treatment required. When examining an unconscious casualty, search for such medical information. It may assist in assessment and first aid, or warn of allergies or health problems that may be aggravated by the use of certain first aid or medical procedures.

FAINTING

Fainting results from a temporary shortage of oxygenated blood to the brain. A person who faints will be unconscious, even if only for a few moments. The aim of first aid for fainting is to increase the supply of oxygen to the brain.

Common causes of fainting are:

- fatigue, long periods of standing or sitting in one position, hunger and lack of fresh air;

- emotional strain such as fear, anxiety or the sight of blood;

- illness, injury or severe pain.

There may be some warning of an impending faint. You may feel unsteady, become pale and start to perspirc. If you feel faint, take the following preventive measures:

- sit with your head lowered, or lie down with legs raised 15 cm to 30 cm (6 to 12 inches);

- ensure that you have a supply of fresh air (open windows or doors), but that you are protected from extremes of temperature;

- loosen tight clothing at your neck, chest and waist.

When a person has fainted, you should:

● ensure that his airway is open and that he is breathing;

● loosen tight clothing at the neck, chest and waist;

● place him in the recovery position;

● ensure a good supply of fresh air and protect him from extremes of temperature;

● make the person comfortable as consciousness returns and keep him lying down for 10 to 15 minutes.

A temporary loss of consciousness is one of the signs of a transient ischemic attack or little stroke (see chap. 25). Do not ignore the possibility of such an attack if fainting occurs in older adults and the cause of fainting is not readily apparent. If recovery from a faint is not rapid and complete, obtain medical aid.

CHAPTER 12

DRESSINGS AND BANDAGES

Dressings and bandages are the basic tools of first aid. They are essential for wound care and for the care of injuries to muscles, bones and joints. The First Aiders must not only be skilled in the use of commercially prepared dressings and bandages, but must be able to use readily available materials as improvised dressings and bandages. To improvise, you will need to know the characteristics and qualities of materials best suited for these purposes.

DRESSINGS

A dressing is a protective covering applied to a wound to help control bleeding, to absorb blood discharged from the wound, and to prevent further contamination and infection.

A dressing should be:

- **sterile** or as clean as possible;

- **highly absorbent and porous** to keep the wound dry;

- **compressible, thick and soft,** especially for severe bleeding, so that pressure can be transmitted evenly over the affected area;

- **nonadherent and lint-free** to reduce the possibility of the dressing sticking to the wound. Gauze, cotton or linen make good dressings. Wool or other fluffy materials are not suitable.

Dressings are available in a variety of sizes and designs. The dressings most frequently used in first aid are:

● **adhesive dressings;** prepared sterile gauze dressing with their own adhesive strips. They are sealed in a paper or plastic covering. They are available in various sizes and shapes, according to their intended use. They are used primarily in the care of minor wounds with minimal bleeding.

● **gauze dressings;** in varying sizes, folded and packaged individually or in large numbers. Packaged gauze is usually sterile.

● **pressure dressings;** prepared sterile dressings of gauze and other absorbent material, usually with an attached roller bandage. They are used to apply pressure on a wound with severe bleeding.

● **improvised dressings;** prepared from lint-free sterile or clean material, preferably white. They may be made from a towel, a sheet, a pillow slip, pads of facial tissue or paper towel, or any other clean absorbent material such as a sanitary pad. Plastic wrap or aluminum foil may be used to make an airtight seal for penetrating wounds of the chest.

To use a dressing effectively, you should observe the following rules:

● **cleanliness** is essential to mimimize contamination and infection. Wash your hands before dressing a wound. Use the cleanest material available as a dressing. When placing a dressing on a wound, be careful not to touch or breathe on any part of it that will be in direct contact with the wound.

● **completely cover the wound** and extend the dressing beyond the edges of the wound.

- **reinforce gauze dressings** with absorbent cotton or other material before bandaging.

- **do not remove a dressing** from a wound. If blood soaks through, leave the dressing in place and cover with additional dressings and secure more firmly with bandages.

- **secure a dressing in place** with tape or bandages.

BANDAGES

A bandage is any material that is used to hold a dressing in place, maintain pressure over a wound, support a limb or joint, immobilize parts of the body and secure a splint. Bandages may be improvised or commercially prepared.

Observe the following rules when using bandages:

- **apply firmly** to ensure that bleeding is controlled or that immobilization is achieved;

- **check distal circulation frequently** to ensure that the bandage is not too tight;

- **do not use bandages as padding or dressing** for wounds when other materials are available. They may be needed for other injuries.

TRIANGULAR BANDAGE

One of the most versatile prepared or improvised bandages is the triangular bandage. It is made by cutting a one-metre square of linen or cotton on the diagonal, producing two triangles. The parts of the triangular bandage, identified for ease of instruction, are:

- the **BASE,** the longest side of the bandage;

- the **ENDS,** each end of the BASE;

- the **POINT,** furthest away from the BASE;

- the **SIDES,** the two edges between the ENDS and the POINT.

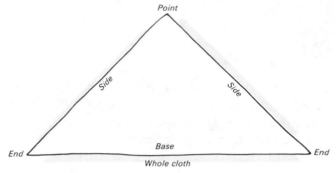

Fig. 12-1. The triangular bandage.

A triangular bandage may be used in the following forms:

- as a **whole cloth.** When it is opened to its fullest extent, it may be used as a sling or to hold a large dressing in place.

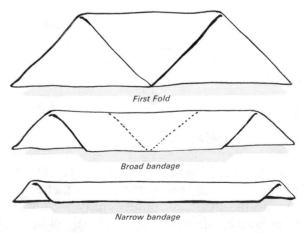

Fig. 12-2. The broad and narrow bandage.

- as a **broad bandage.** Fold the POINT to centre BASE and fold in half again from the top to the BASE. In this form it is used to hold splints in place or to apply pressure evenly over a large area.

- as a **narrow bandage.** Fold a broad bandage in half again from the top to the BASE, to secure dressings and splints or to immobilize ankles and feet in a figure-8.

- as a **ring pad.** Make a narrow bandage. Form a loop around one hand by passing one END of the bandage twice around the four fingers. Pass the other END through the loop and wrap it around and around until the entire bandage is used and a firm ring is made. Tie two narrow bandages together to make a ring pad with a larger loop if required. Use the ring pad to control bleeding when pressure cannot be applied directly to the wound, as in the case of an embedded object or a protruding bone. Prepare a ring pad and keep it in your first aid kit ready for use.

Fig. 12-3. Preparing a ring pad.

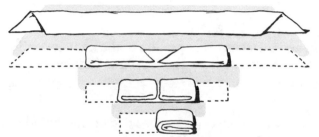

Fig. 12-4. Folding a triangular bandage.

When not in use, fold the triangular bandage as a narrow bandage and then fold ends-to-centre until it is small enough for storage.

THE REEF KNOT

The reef knot is recommended for tying bandages and slings because it is flat and more comfortable than other knots, it will not slip and it can be loosened easily when necessary.

To tie a reef knot, take one end of a bandage in each hand. Lay the end from the right hand over the one from the left hand and pass it under to form a half-knot. This will transfer the ends from one hand to the other. The end now in the left hand should be laid over the one from the right and passed under to form another half-knot. This will give the effect of two intertwined loops that can be tightened by pulling one loop against the other or by pulling on the ends only.

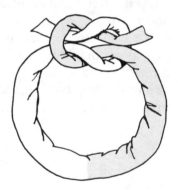

Fig. 12-5. The reef knot.

Remember the sequence for tying a reef knot, by memorizing the following mnemonic:

RIGHT OVER LEFT AND UNDER, LEFT OVER RIGHT AND UNDER.

If the end and the shank on one side of the knot are pulled away from each other, the knot will be loosened and the other end can be slipped off.

Place knots so that they do not cause discomfort by pressing on skin or bone, particularly at the site of a fracture or at the neck when tying a sling. If the knot is uncomfortable, place soft material underneath it as padding. Tuck knot ends away neatly so they do not get caught or pulled when the casualty is moved.

FIGURE-8

A figure-8 is a method of applying a bandage to immobilize the ankles and feet, to apply a splint to the sole of the foot, or to support an injured ankle.

To apply a figure-8:

- position the centre of a narrow or broad triangular bandage under the ankle or ankles. The bandage may be positioned over a dressing or splint.

- bring the ENDS around the ankles, cross over on top of the legs and bring the ENDS around the feet.

- tie off, or repeat the figure-8 in the opposite direction, tying off at the starting point.

Fig. 12-6. The figure-8.

SLINGS

Slings provide support and protection for the upper limbs. They may be used to elevate or immobilize a limb or transfer its weight from one side of the body to the other.

The Arm Sling

The arm sling supports the forearm and hand when there are injuries to the upper limb. To apply the arm sling:

- support the forearm of the injured limb across the body, with the wrist and hand slightly higher than the elbow;

- place a triangular bandage as a whole cloth between the forearm and the chest with its POINT toward the elbow and extending well beyond it;

- bring the upper END over the person's shoulder on the uninjured side, around the back of the neck to the front of the affected side;

- still supporting the forearm, bring the lower END of the bandage over the hand and forearm and tie off with the other END at the natural hollow above the collarbone;

- bring the POINT around to the front of the elbow and secure to the bandage with a safety pin, or twist the POINT into a "pigtail" and tuck it inside the sling;

Fig. 12-7. The arm sling.

- position the BASE of the bandage at the knuckle joint of the little finger so that all fingernails are exposed for observation.

St. John Tubular Sling

The St. John tubular sling is used to support the hand and forearm in a well-raised position. It may be used to elevate the hand, or to transfer the weight of the upper limb from one side to the other when there are injuries to the shoulder or collarbone. To apply a St. John tubular sling:

- support the forearm on the injured side diagonally across the chest, with the fingers pointing toward the opposite shoulder;

- place a triangular bandage as a whole cloth over the forearm and hand, its POINT extending well beyond the elbow, its upper END over the shoulder on the uninjured side; and its BASE in line with the body on the uninjured side;

Fig. 12-8. St. John tubular sling.

- while supporting the forearm, ease the BASE of the bandage under the hand, forearm and elbow, and bring the lower END diagonally across the back and over the shoulder on the uninjured side;

- gently adjust the height of the arm as you tie off the ENDS of the bandage at the natural hollow above the collarbone;

- tuck the POINT in between the forearm and the bandage, and secure with a safety pin. If a safety pin is not available, the point may be twisted into a "pigtail" and tucked in.

Collar and Cuff Sling

As the name implies, the collar and cuff sling is formed of two
parts; a cuff around the wrist and a collar around the casualty's
neck. It may be made of one or two triangular bandages. This
sling allows an arm to be immobilized in any position of flexion,
depending on the degree of movement permitted by the injuries.
It is especially useful in the care of joint injuries of the shoulder
and elbow when movement of the shoulder joint or bending the
elbow may cause more pain.

To apply a collar and cuff sling:

● place the centre of a narrow triangular bandage on
the forearm, letting the
ENDS fall on either side,
one near the wrist and one
near the elbow to form a
long diagonal;

● bring one END around the
forearm and pass it under
the center to form a loop
around the arm;

● bring the other END
around the forearm in the
opposite direction and
pass it under the center to
form another loop;

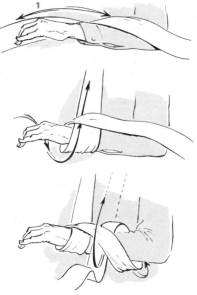

*Fig. 12-9 (a). Collar and cuff
sling — application.*

● bring both ENDS up to form a cuff around the wrist, keeping
it wrinkle free and fairly loose so that it supports the wrist
comfortably;

● bring the ENDS around the casualty's neck and tie off in the
hollow above the collar bone on the injured side;

Fig. 12-9 (b). Collar and cuff sling.

- if additional length is needed, tie the END of another narrow triangular bandage to one END of the first and bring it around the casualty's neck;

- tie off the other two ENDs so that the arm is positioned at the desired level.

Improvised Slings

Improvised slings can be devised by:

- placing the hand inside a buttoned jacket;

- supporting the limb with a scarf, belt, necktie or other item around the casualty's neck;

Fig. 12-10. Improvised slings.

- pinning the sleeve of a shirt or jacket to the clothing;

- turning up the lower edge of the casualty's jacket over the injured limb and pinning it to itself.

BANDAGING

Triangular bandages are used to hold dressings to various parts of the body such as the head, the elbow and knee, and the hand and foot.

To bandage the **head:**

- stand behind the casualty;

- use a triangular bandage as a whole cloth with a narrow hem folded along its BASE;

- place the centre BASE on the midpoint of the forehead close to the eyebrows and bring the POINT over the top of the head, covering the dressing, and down the back of the head;

- bring the ENDS around the back of the head, crossing over the POINT and continuing around the head to tie off low on the forehead;

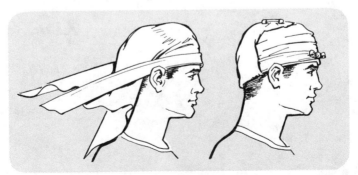

Fig. 12-11. Bandage for holding dressing on the scalp.

- steady the head with one hand while drawing the POINT of the bandage down with the other to put the desired pressure on the dressing. Fold the POINT up toward the top of the head and secure carefully with a safety pin.

The method of bandaging the hinge joints of **elbow** and **knee,** is similar:

- use a triangular bandage as a whole cloth with a narrow hem folded along its BASE.

- place the centre BASE on the forearm to bandage an elbow, and on the shin below the kneecap to bandage a knee. Position the POINT upward and over the dressing. Bring the ENDS around the limb, crossing over in front of the elbow or at the back of the knee.

- tie off on the upper part of the limb.

- draw the POINT up to put the desired pressure on the dressing and then fold it downward and secure it with a safety pin.

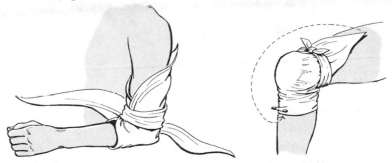

Fig. 12-12. Bandaging the elbow.   *Fig. 12-13. Bandaging the knee.*

To bandage the **hand** or **foot:**

- use a triangular bandage as a whole cloth, placing it on a flat surface with the POINT away from the casualty;

- place the hand or foot on the triangular bandage with the fingers or toes toward the POINT, leaving sufficient bandage at the wrist and ankle to enclose the part;

- bring the POINT up and over the hand or foot to rest on the wrist or lower leg;

- bring the ENDS up and around the wrist or ankle, crossing over the POINT and repeating turns around the part to use up any extra bandage before tying it off;

- draw the POINT through the tie to apply the desired pressure, then fold it downward and secure with a pin.

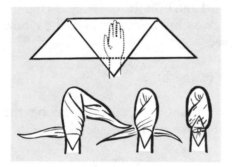   

Fig. 12-14. Bandaging the hand.   *Fig. 12-15. Bandaging the foot.*

ROLLER BANDAGE

The roller bandage, either the clinging or open-weave type, may also be used for holding dressings in place over a wound. It should be applied so that it is comfortable and firm, but not so tight that swelling of the injured part will restrict circulation.

To apply a roller bandage in a simple spiral, start at the narrow part of the limb and wrap diagonally toward the wider part. Overlap each turn by one quarter to one third of its width to cover the dressings and to make the bandage more secure. The bandage must be anchored at its first turn as follows:

- place the end of the bandage on a bias at the starting point;

- encircle the injured part, allowing the corner of the bandage end to protrude;

- turn down the protruding tip of the bandage and encircle the injured part again.

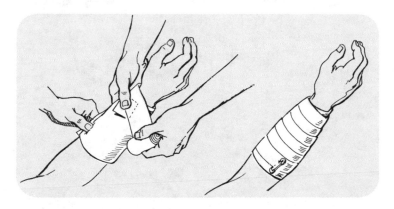

Fig. 12-16. The simple spiral bandage.

Make full width overlaps with the final two or three turns and secure with a pin or adhesive tape.

TUBULAR GAUZE AND ELASTICISED NET BANDAGES

When bleeding has been controlled and direct pressure is not required, quick and efficient bandaging can be accomplished with **tubular gauze** or **elasticized net.** Both types of bandages come in various sizes to fit different parts of the body. The required length is cut from the roll and is either applied with a specially designed applicator or is stretched by hand to fit over the dressing.

Tubular gauze and elasticized net are especially useful for holding dressings to the head, shoulder, thigh or finger where roller bandaging is difficult and time-consuming. Instructions for application are usually included with the bandage.

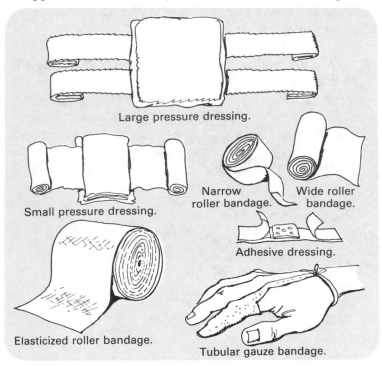

Large pressure dressing.

Small pressure dressing.

Narrow roller bandage.

Wide roller bandage.

Adhesive dressing.

Elasticized roller bandage.

Tubular gauze bandage.

Fig. 12-17. Commercially prepared dressings and bandages.

MONITORING CIRCULATION

Certain injuries and first aid procedures may result in the impairment of circulation to the extremities. A joint injury or fracture may pinch an artery and restrict the flow of blood to the limb. A bandage tied around a limb to immobilize a fracture, to hold a dressing or to control bleeding may have been put on too tight or the limb may have become swollen after its application. In either case, the limb will be constricted and blood flow to the extremity will be impaired. If oxygenated blood does not reach the tissues, the damage that results could lead to the loss of the limb. This serious condition must be corrected. Loosen any bandages. If this does not help, seek medical aid immediately.

Monitor circulation in any extremity that has sustained a fracture, a joint injury or that has been bandaged. Check for pulse at any point distal to (further from the body than) the injury or bandages. If a pulse site is not accessible, compare the temperature of the fingers or toes of the injured limb to the unaffected limb. Any drop in temperature in the injured limb indicates a restriction of blood flow to that limb. Perform the nail bed test to determine the degree of circulatory impairment. Press on a fingernail or toenail until the nail bed turns white. Release the pressure and note how long it takes for its normal colour to return. If it returns quickly, blood flow is unrestricted. If it remains white or regains colour slowly, circulation is severely impaired and must be corrected immediately.

Loosen bandages and, in the case of joint injuries, reposition the limb to relieve blood-flow restriction. Resecure the limb and check again to ensure that circulation is unimpeded. Continue to monitor circulation until handed over to medical aid. If circulation cannot be restored, medical aid is needed urgently.

Notes

CHAPTER 13

WOUNDS AND BLEEDING

A **wound** is any break in the continuity of the tissues of the body. It usually results in bleeding and may permit the entrance of germs that cause infection. **Bleeding** is the escape of blood from the vessels into surrounding tissues, body cavities or externally from the body. The soft tissues of the body are the most susceptible to injury, resulting in wounds and bleeding.

PREVENTION

Wounds are often the result of poor safety practices while using machinery, tools and equipment. The majority of accidental injuries occur in the home and during recreation. Prevent soft tissue injuries by eliminating the hazards from the environment. A "WHAT IF" approach [1] will help to prevent many such injuries. Be safety conscious — think of the consequences:

- WHAT IF knives are stored in a drawer, sharp side up?

- WHAT IF someone uses their fingers to reach into food processors and grinders?

- WHAT IF chain saws, lawnmowers, hedge trimmers, etc. are used without safety guards or personal safety equipment?

- WHAT IF children are allowed to use chain saws and snow-blowers?

[1] *Industrial Accident Prevention Association, Hazards Recognition and Control Seminar – HRC 004, November 1986*

- WHAT IF helmets, masks, gloves etc. are not worn when playing a hazardous sport?

- WHAT IF guns and ammunition are stored in the same unlocked area? WHAT IF guns are left loaded?

Farm tools and machines are extremely hazardous because they are frequently operated in poor weather conditions, on rough terrain, in poor light and by overtired, untrained or inexperienced operators. Adjusting and clearing power takeoffs (PTOs) on tractors with the engine running has caused many serious injuries. The operator must ensure that the guard remains in place until the power is off and the equipment stops.

Awareness of potential dangers in the home, in industry and on the farm, and a personal commitment to safe practices can eliminate many causes of injury.

CLASSIFICATION OF WOUNDS

When someone is injured, recognizing the type of wound sustained helps in giving appropriate first aid. Soft tissue wounds are classified as follows:

- **contusions** or bruises are usually caused by a fall or a blow from a blunt instrument with no break in the skin. The chance of contamination is slight.

- **abrasions** or scrapes are surface breaks in the skin that may not bleed much, but dirt embedded in the skin may lead to infection.

- **incisions** or clean-cuts in soft tissue are caused by sharp instruments such as knives or broken glass. These wounds may not be as dirty as abrasions, but they may contain fragments of glass or other material.

- **lacerations** or tears of the skin and underlying tissue are caused by such things as machinery, barbed wire or the claws of an animal. The edges of the wound are jagged and irregular. Dirt is likely to be present, increasing the risk of infection.

- **puncture or stab wounds** are caused by sharp pointed instruments, such as knives, nails or an animal's teeth. These wounds may have small openings, but often penetrate deeply into the tissue. There may be contamination deep in the wound and internal organs may be damaged.

- **gunshot wounds** are a special type of puncture wound. They usually have a small entry wound and a large exit wound. Some gunshot injuries have no exit wound, but there is usually extensive internal injury and severe bleeding.

CARE OF WOUNDS

The aims in the care of wounds are to **stop the bleeding** and **prevent infection.** Although some bleeding may help to wash contamination from the wound, excessive blood flow must be stopped quickly to minimize shock.

BLEEDING

Bleeding can be either internal or external and either venous or arterial. The major difference between venous and arterial bleeding is that in venous bleeding, blood flows steadily and will stop readily with direct pressure, elevation and rest, while with arterial bleeding the blood spurts with each pulse beat and is harder to control.

SIGNS AND SYMPTOMS OF BLEEDING

Signs and symptoms of bleeding vary widely, depending on the amount of blood loss and the rate of bleeding. Severe loss of blood will result in the following signs and symptoms that also indicate the progress of shock:

- pale, cold and clammy skin;

- rapid pulse, gradually becoming weaker;

- faintness and dizziness;

- thirst and nausea;

- restlessness and apprehension;

- shallow breathing, causing the casualty to yawn, sigh and gasp for air; a condition known as air hunger.

The care for shock is detailed in chapter 10.

CONTROL OF BLEEDING

The body has natural defences against loss of blood that help to close a wound and reduce bleeding. When a blood vessel is severed, the damaged ends constrict to reduce blood flow. As bleeding continues, blood pressure is reduced, decreasing the flow of blood to the wound. Blood will clot to form a natural barrier at the wound site. You can help these natural processes by:

- **direct pressure.** Pressure applied over a dressing on the wound will stop blood flow and allow clots to form. When bleeding is controlled, pressure should be continued with dressings and bandages.

- **elevation.** Raising an injured limb above the level of the heart uses gravity to help reduce blood flow to the wound area. The injured limb should be elevated as much as the injury and comfort will permit.

● **rest.** Place the casualty at rest to reduce the pulse rate. The preferred position is lying down with the head low, unless the bleeding is from a head wound.

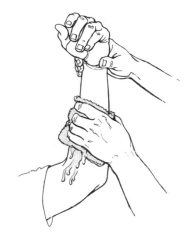

These actions, applied simultaneously, will control all but the severest bleeding. The mnemonic RED may help to remember these three actions to control bleeding — **R**est, **E**levation and **D**irect pressure.

Fig. 13-1. Pressure and elevation.

The Tourniquet

Direct pressure, elevation and rest should control bleeding, but if bleeding from a limb does not stop or if you must go to other casualties with life-threatening conditions, a tourniquet may have to be used. **A tourniquet should be applied only as a last measure** and in the following manner:

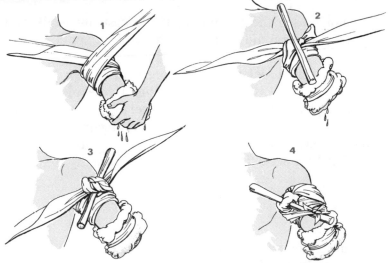

Fig. 13-2. Applying the tourniquet.

- fold a triangular bandage to a narrow width (7 to 10 cm) or improvise with any bandage of similar width. Do not use rope or wire that could cut into the skin.

- wrap the bandage tightly twice around the limb above the wound and as close to it as possible.

- tie a half-knot, place a stick or other rod on the half-knot, and then tie a full knot.

- twist the stick to tighten the tourniquet just enough to stop bleeding.

- secure the stick in place with the remaining ends of the bandage.

- tag or mark the casualty in a clearly visible place with the letters "TK". Mark it on the casualty's forehead if a tag is not available. Make a note of the time the tourniquet was applied.

- ensure that the tourniquet is always visible.

- do not loosen the tourniquet if the casualty is likely to receive medical aid within one hour of its application.

- if medical aid is delayed beyond one hour, loosen the tourniquet hourly to assess the bleeding. If the bleeding has stopped, leave the loosened tourniquet in place so that it can be tightened quickly if bleeding starts again. However, if blood flows from the wound, re-tighten the tourniquet immediately. Check the condition of the casualty frequently.

All casualties on whom a tourniquet has been applied must be taken to medical aid.

PREVENTION OF FURTHER CONTAMINATION

All wounds are contaminated to some degree. You can prevent further contamination by taking the following precautions:

- wash your hands with soap and water before starting first aid;

- do not cough or breathe directly over a wound;

- wash away any visible dirt from the wound and clean the surrounding skin with soap and water, taking care to swab away from the edges of the wound;

- do not allow your fingers to touch the wound or the side of the dressing that will come in contact with the wound;

- cover the wound promptly with a sterile dressing or at least one that is clean.

- wash your hands and any other skin area that may have been in contact with the casualty's blood to prevent cross-infection (see chap. 1).

Contaminated wounds may become infected in time. Infected wounds can be recognized by reddening of the skin area around the wound or red streaking away from the wound. The wound area may be hard, swollen and warm to the touch. As infection becomes older, it will show a yellow-green discolouration or discharge as a result of the accumulation of pus. These infected wounds need medical care.

Tetanus Infection

Any wound may be contaminated by spores that cause tetanus, a potentially fatal disease that is characterized by muscle spasms commonly referred to as lock-jaw. Deep wounds, especially those caused by animal bites or those that may have been contaminated by soil, dust and animal feces, are at high risk of such infection. A casualty with such a wound must be advised to go to medical aid for immuniation to prevent the onset of tetanus.

FIRST AID FOR WOUNDS

Contusions or bruises will cause blood to escape into the surrounding tissue. First aid consists of reducing the blood flow to the adjacent areas and relieving pain and swelling. This is best accomplished by the application of cold compresses or an ice bag (15 minutes on, 15 minutes off), elevating the injured limb and keeping the person at rest.

Cold Application

Prepare a cold compress by soaking a towel in cold water, wringing out the excess water and wrapping the towel around the affected part. Cold water can be added to the compress from time to time or it can be replaced with a fresh one. An **ice bag** can be prepared by filling a rubber or plastic bag two-thirds full of crushed ice, expelling excess air from the bag, and sealing the opening to make it watertight. Wrap the bag in a towel and apply it carefully to the injured part—15 minutes on, 15 minutes off. Replace the ice as necessary. **Do not apply an ice bag directly to the skin because the cold can cause injury.** Commercial **cold packs** may be used instead of ice. Follow the manufacturer's directions to activate the chemicals and to apply these packs.

Minor wounds with bleeding, such as abrasions, small incisions and minor lacerations, may be washed under running water if they are dirty. They should be dried with sterile or clean gauze and covered with prepared or improvised dressings and bandages.

Major wounds with severe bleeding require continuous direct pressure. If the wound is large and gaping, it may be necessary to bring the edges together before applying pressure. There may only be time to wipe away loose debris from the wound. Embedded objects should not be disturbed. If the wound is free of embedded objects, give first aid as follows:

- apply a sterile pressure dressing and bandage firmly with a triangular bandage or roller bandage;

- if the wound is to a limb, elevate the limb to help control bleeding;

- if blood soaks through, do not remove the dressing but apply additional dressings and secure with fresh bandages, adding more pressure and increased elevation;

- immobilize and support a limb to maintain elevation and to avoid disturbing clots.

Wounds with an embedded object require special care, because the object may be sealing severed blood vessels deep in the wound.

Do not disturb or remove objects that are deeply embedded or firmly lodged. Dress the wound, pad around the embedded object to prevent its movement, bandage to apply pressure away from the embedded object and immobilize the limb to prevent further injury. Care for fractures with protruding bone is much the same as for wounds with embedded objects (see chap. 14).

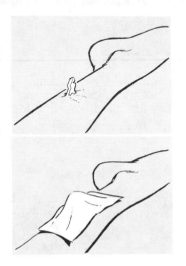

If the embedded object is short and does not protrude too far out of the wound, give first aid as follows:

- gently cover the wound and object with dressings, taking care not to put pressure on the object;

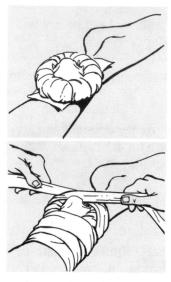

- make a ring pad large enough to go around the entire wound;

- place the ring pad over the dressings and around the wound, "tenting" the dressings to avoid pressure on the object;

- bandage the ring pad in place with a narrow bandage.

Fig. 13-3. First aid for wound with an embedded object.

If the embedded object is long and protrudes too far to allow dressings over the object and wound:

- place dressings around the base of the object to cover the wound;

- build up around the object with bulky dressings to keep it from moving;

- bandage the dressings in place with a narrow bandage, taking care that pressure is not exerted on the object.

Fig. 13-4. Stabilizing a long embedded object.

Puncture wounds may not show much external bleeding, but you should suspect internal bleeding, especially if the wound is in the chest or abdomen. Some puncture wounds, such as those from a gunshot, may have both an entry and an exit wound. These wounds are serious because there is internal tissue damage, severe bleeding and contamination deep in the wound. Control bleeding and give first aid for the wounds.

Crush injuries are extensive bruises of limbs or of the whole body, caused by the weight of sand, masonry, machinery or other heavy objects. Tissue damage is generalized and internal organs may be ruptured. Crush injuries may be complicated by fractures. Crush injuries of a limited nature, such as a hand, are serious, but are not usually life threatening (see chap. 14).

Major crush injuries may cause the **crush syndrome** in which muscle products and acids from damaged muscles combined with shock, lead to a low output of urine, general body swelling and kidney failure. The crush syndrome is also known as post-traumatic acute renal (kidney) failure.

Shock, resulting from a drop in blood pressure, is therefore a serious complication of crush injuries. Even though the casualty may show little or no signs and symptoms of shock when extricated from the site of the accident, first aid for shock should be started immediately to keep it from getting worse (see chap. 10). First aid for wounds and fractures will help to stop bleeding and relieve pain. The following first aid should be given for crush injuries as soon as other conditions have been stabilized and while waiting for transportation to medical aid:

- do whatever is possible to minimize pain and move the person as little as possible;

- apply ice bags to the injured part; do not apply direct heat;

- treat for shock.

Wounds of the palm of the hand usually cause severe bleeding because many blood vessels may be damaged. Give first aid for a transverse wound (across the palm) as follows:

● cover the wound with a pad of dressings;

● bend the fingers over the pad to make a fist and to put pressure on the wound;

● bandage the clenched hand by placing the centre of a narrow triangular bandage on the inside of the wrist and bring the ENDS around the back of the hand diagonally to cross over the fingers and to tie off at the wrist;

● elevate and support the limb in a St. John tubular sling.

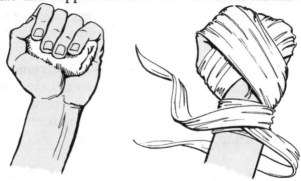

Fig. 13-5. First aid for a transverse wound of the hand.

If the wound is longitudinal (along the length of the palm) place dressings over the wound and bandage the hand with the fingers

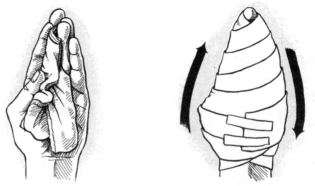

Fig. 13-6. First aid for a longitudinal wound of the hand.

extended. A roller bandage applied around the hand will help to keep the wound closed and will reduce bleeding. Elevate and support the hand in a St. John tubular sling.

Bleeding from the gums, which occurs after tooth extraction or from fractures of the jaw (see chap. 16), should receive first aid as follows:

- place a gauze pad firmly on the tooth socket or injury site, using a pad thick enough to keep the teeth apart when biting;

- instruct the person to bite on the pad, supporting the chin with the hands, until the bleeding stops (normally in 10 to 20 minutes);

- seek medical or dental advice if the bleeding cannot be controlled.

Do not wash out the mouth after bleeding has stopped as it may dislodge clots and cause bleeding to resume.

Bleeding from the tongue or cheek. Use a sterile dressing or clean cloth and compress the bleeding part between the finger and thumb until bleeding stops.

Bleeding from the scalp is often severe and may be complicated by a fracture of the skull or an embedded object. When giving first aid for these wounds, avoid direct pressure, probing and contaminating the wound. Care must be taken to:

- clean away loose dirt;

- apply a thick, sterile dressing that is large enough to extend well beyond the edges of the wound and bandage it firmly in place;

- if there is an embedded object, apply a large ring pad over the dressing to maintain pressure around but away from the wound;

- if there is a suspected underlying skull fracture, use a thick, compressible, soft dressing instead of a ring pad and hold it in place with a head bandage.

- transport the casualty to medical aid.

Nosebleeds may occur spontaneously or they may be caused by blowing the nose, by direct injury or, in more serious cases, by indirect injury such as a fractured skull (see chap. 16). Do not restrict blood flow in nosebleeds that result from head injuries. Give first aid for other nosebleeds as follows.

- place the casualty in a sitting position with the head slightly forward;

- instruct the casualty to pinch the nostrils firmly with the thumb and index finger for about 10 minutes;

- loosen clothing around the person's neck and chest if it is uncomfortably tight;

- keep the casualty quiet to avoid increasing blood pressure and increased bleeding.

Instruct the casualty to breathe through his mouth and not to blow his nose for some hours after bleeding has stopped so that blood clots will not be disturbed. If bleeding does not stop with this first aid or if bleeding recurs, get medical aid.

Varicose veins is a condition in which the venous valves fail to function properly. This allows blood to pool in the veins, creating pressure that may cause the veins to rupture. Internal bleeding appears as swelling and discolouration. External bleeding, normally caused by a blow or a laceration, may be alarming but usually is not serious. This condition most commonly occurs in the lower legs.

To give first aid for a ruptured varicose vein:

- elevate the limb as much as possible, consistent with comfort;

- apply direct pressure over a dressing;

- remove or loosen any articles of clothing that may restrict blood flow from the limb;

- secure the dressing with a bandage while keeping the limb elevated and supported;

- transport to medical aid.

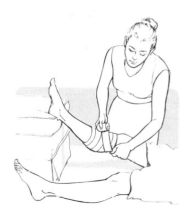

Fig. 13-7. First aid for bleeding from a varicose vein.

Wounds of the abdomen may be closed or open. Closed wounds are those in which internal abdominal tissues are damaged but the skin remains intact. Open abdominal wounds are those in which the skin has been broken. Open abdominal wounds may gape and must be prevented from opening wider by positioning the patient with head and shoulders slightly raised and supported, and with the knees raised. The method of dressing a wound of the abdominal wall depends on whether or not internal organs are protruding:

- if organs do not protrude, apply a dressing to the wound and bandage firmly.

- if organs protrude, do not attempt to reinsert them. Cover the wound and the protruding organs with a large moist gauze dressing or a soft clean moist towel and secure it without pressure.

Do not give anything by mouth. If the casualty coughs or vomits, support the abdomen with broad bandages. This casualty will be in shock and contamination of the wound will result in serious infection. Transport him to medical aid promptly.

CARE OF AMPUTATED TISSUE

Completely or partially amputated parts must be preserved, regardless of their condition, and taken to the medical facility with the casualty. There is a good chance these parts can be re-attached if they are given proper care and brought to medical aid promptly.

To care for a **partially amputated part:**

● keep it as near as possible to its normal position (position of function).

● cover it with sterile gauze dressings, bandaged and supported.

● keep it dry and cool. Place an ice bag or other watertight cold compress on the wound but outside the bandages covering the wound.

To care for a **completely amputated part:**

● wrap it in clean, moist dressing and place it in a clean watertight plastic bag. Seal the bag and attach a record of the date and time this was done. If unable to moisten the dressing, use a clean dry dressing.

● place it in another plastic bag or container partially filled with crushed ice.

● transport it with the casualty to the medical facility.

Fig. 13-8. Care of the amputated part.

To care for a **knocked-out tooth:**

● do not handle the tooth by the root;

● gently replace the tooth in the socket if possible, otherwise, place it in moistened gauze or a cup of water;

● seek medical or dental aid quickly for best chance of reimplantation.

Do not attempt to clean amputated parts and do not use any antiseptic solutions.

INTERNAL BLEEDING

Internal bleeding may result from an injury such as a closed fracture, a crush injury or a puncture wound. It may also result from certain medical conditions with no history of injury. Internal bleeding may remain concealed or it may be recognized by external signs. If bleeding is severe, the signs and symptoms of shock may be apparent.

Concealed internal bleeding should be suspected in the following conditions:

● fractures of the vault of the skull.

● closed fractures of long bones showing signs of severe swelling.

● severe blows to the abdomen, especially in the area of the liver or spleen. Bleeding from those organs is very serious, and signs and symptoms of shock will develop progressively.

Internal bleeding may become evident in the following ways:

● blood may be discharged from the ear canal or the nose, or it may appear as a bloodshot eye or black eye in head injuries.

- red frothy blood may be coughed up in chest injuries.

- blood may be seen in vomitus. It will be bright red if bleeding into the stomach has been recent; brown and granular like coffee grounds if it has been in the stomach for some time.

- bleeding into the upper bowel will cause stools to be black and tarry. Blood in the lower bowel retains its normal colour and will be red in the stools.

- bleeding from the kidneys or bladder will be seen in the urine, making it reddish or smoky brown in appearance.

- remove to medical aid as quickly as possible.

FIRST AID FOR INTERNAL BLEEDING

The aims of first aid for internal bleeding are to minimize shock and to obtain medical aid promptly. First aid for suspected internal bleeding is as follows:

- place the conscious casualty at complete rest, with the feet and legs elevated 15 to 30 cm (6 to 12 in) if the injuries permit. Warn the casualty not to move.

- place the unconscious casualty in the recovery position.

- do not give anything by mouth.

- loosen all tight clothing about the neck, chest and waist.

- reassure the casualty, explaining the need to relax mentally as well as physically.

- keep the casualty warm and protected from extremes of temperature.

- remove to medical aid as quickly as possible.

Keep a record of the following conditions for the attending physician:

● the rate and quality of breathing and pulse, noting whether breathing is normal or irregular, and whether the pulse is full and bounding or weak and almost imperceptible;

● skin temperature;

● occurrences such as vomiting, uncontrolled urination or bowel movement;

● the time of major changes in the casualty's appearance or condition.

Bleeding from the ears may be accompanied by a discharge of straw-coloured fluid. This indicates a fracture of the skull, which is very serious (see chap. 16). Make no attempt to stop the flow of blood or other fluids. Do not pack the ear with gauze. Arrange for prompt medical aid and then give first aid as follows:

● apply a cervical collar;

● secure a sterile dressing loosely over the ear;

● lay the casualty down on the injured side, carefully supporting the head and neck, with his upper body slightly raised;

● if the casualty vomits or if you must leave him, place him in the recovery position on the injured side;

● check breathing and circulation frequently.

● care for shock (see chap. 10).

Notes

CHAPTER 14

FRACTURES

A fracture is any break or crack in a bone. It is caused by **direct force,** such as a blow or kick; or by **indirect force,** when a bone breaks some distance from the spot where the force is applied. Fracture of the collarbone caused by a fall on the outstretched arm is an example of indirect force. Fractures may also occur as the result of **muscular action.** For example, a fracture of the patella (kneecap) can occur from violent contraction of the muscles attached to it. Certain bone **diseases** may cause fractures to occur from very slight pressure.

PREVENTION

Most fractures can be prevented by adopting good safety habits. Motor vehicle accidents are the cause of many bone injuries. Defensive driving reduces the number of accidents, and the use of seat belts decreases the incidence and severity of injuries. Adopt a WHAT IF attitude [1] to every hazardous condition in the workplace and at home. Potential falls exist on every working and walking surface. Prevent the fall — avoid the injury. Ask yourself:

- WHAT IF work areas are cluttered and untidy? What if tools, hoses, extension cords are left lying about?

- WHAT IF floors are wet, greasy and slippery? What if floor coverings — carpets, rugs at the tops and bottoms of stairs, tiles and floorboards are loose?

[1] *Industrial Accident Prevention Association. Hazards Recognition and Control Seminar HRC 004, November 1986.*

- WHAT IF stairs are poorly lighted, cluttered with shoes and bottles, have no handrails, are covered with ice and snow? What if chairs are used to reach high places, step-ladders are in poor repair, ladders are not secured?

- WHAT IF life-lines and safety belts are not used when working in high places? What if children are left on balconies unattended?

The appropriate safety action in each of the above situations will take only a moment, but could save someone many hours and days of pain and suffering from an accidental fall.

TYPES OF FRACTURES

The most important factor in assessing a fracture is the condition of the surrounding tissue. Fractures, therefore, are generally classified as **closed** or **open:**

- **closed fractures** are those over which the surrounding skin is unbroken;

- **open fractures** are those over which the skin is broken; bone ends may protrude.

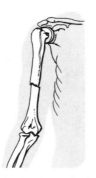

Fig. 14-1. Closed fracture.   *Fig. 14-2. Open fracture.*

A **complicated fracture** is one in which broken bones have caused damage to internal organs, such as blood vessels, liver, lungs or spleen.

Other terms are used to describe particular types of fractures but the characteristics of these fractures cannot always be determined by a First Aider. When a bone is broken into more than two pieces, it is said to be **comminuted;** bone ends driven into one another are described as **impacted;** an incomplete break is called a **greenstick fracture; epiphyseal fractures** are injuries to the growth plate at the ends of long bones; breaks caused by repeated stress on a bone are called **stress fatigue fractures;** and breaks resulting from bone disease are **pathological fractures.**

SIGNS AND SYMPTOMS

You should suspect a fracture if the injury was caused by some external force. A snap or crack may have been heard. Avoid all movement that may cause further damage during the physical examination. Clothing may have to be cut away to allow examination of the injury. Compare the injured limb with the other uninjured limb to help determine the degree of deformity. One or more of the following signs and symptoms will be present in any fracture:

- **pain and tenderness** near the injury will be made worse by the movement or touching of the injured part.

- **loss of function** or inability to move the injured part is usually caused by pain and swelling.

- **swelling,** resulting from fluid accumulating in the tissues surrounding the fracture, may make the recognition of other signs more difficult. Discolouration may also develop.

- **deformity** is any unnatural shape or angulation of a limb or joint, as compared to the other uninjured limb.

- **unnatural movement** may be observed at the site of the fracture;

- **shock** increases with the severity of the injury.

- **crepitus or grating** is a sensation or sound that can often be felt or heard when the broken ends of bone rub together. This should never be tested for intentionally.

This mnemonic, which will help you to remember the signs and symptoms of fractures, reads as follows: **P**oor **L**ittle **S**uzy **D**ied **T**uesday in **U**nusual and **S**trange **C**ircumstances —

P – pain	**T** – tenderness
L – loss of function	**U** – unnatural movement
S – swelling	**S** – shock
D – deformity	**C** – crepitus

FIRST AID FOR FRACTURES — GENERAL RULES

First aid for fractures is meant to prevent further injury and minimize pain and swelling. The following general rules of first aid for fractures should be applied:

- **give first aid at the accident site** unless you or the casualty is in danger. If so, move the casualty to the nearest safe location while temporarily supporting and stabilizing the injuries.

- **steady and support the injured part** until the fracture has been immobilized.

- **dress wounds** to stop bleeding and prevent further contamination. Protect any protruding bones with a dressing and ring pad, but do not force bones back into the wound.

- **immobilize the fracture** to prevent the movement of broken bones. Secure splints on long bones at points above and below the fracture and to immobilize the joint above and the joint below the fracture.

- **raise and support** an injured limb gently after immobilization to reduce bleeding and swelling.

- **monitor circulation** in the limb to ensure that bandages are not too tight (see chap. 12).

First aid for fractures should relieve pain. Any increase in pain indicates aggravation of the injury. Recheck the position of the limb, the location of bandages, and knots, and the circulation to the extremity.

Traction

When a bone breaks, the muscles attached to it contract. If the break is complete, the sudden contraction causes the broken ends to slip past one another and lodge in surrounding tissue. Rough handling may cause further pain and damage to muscles, nerves and blood vessels.

It may be necessary to realign an injured limb to prevent the bone ends from causing further damage. When traction is needed it is best applied by two people; one supporting the limb firmly above the fracture and the other gently but firmly pulling below the fracture to bring the limb into alignment.

The following precautions must be taken when applying traction:

- **apply only enough traction** to align the limb and to relieve the pressure of the broken bone ends on nerves and muscles. More traction may be needed to realign a limb with an angulated fracture, but do not use force. If there is resistance or increased pain, discontinue traction and immobilize in the position of deformity.

- **maintain traction** until the limb is completely immobilized.

- **do not attempt to straighten injured joints** at the shoulders, elbows, wrists or knees. That may damage major nerves and large blood vessels that pass close to those joints.

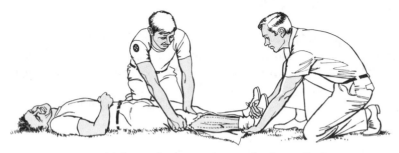

Fig. 14-3. Applying traction to the lower limb.

Note the fact that traction has been applied and inform medical aid verbally or pin a note to the casualty's clothing.

Use of Padding and Bandages in Immobilization

Bandages used to immobilize fractures should be passed underneath the casualty, using the natural hollows of the body at the neck, small of the back, knees and ankles. The bandages should be:

- **wide enough** to provide firm support without discomfort;

- **tight enough** to prevent movement;

- **knotted on the uninjured side or over the splint** to minimize discomfort and to ensure that the widest part of the bandage is on the injured side. If both legs are injured, tie the knots in the midline.

Ensure that bandages do not interfere with circulation or cause pain. Check immobilized parts at 15-minute intervals to ensure that the bandages have not become too tight due to the swelling of the surrounding tissue. This is especially important in joint injuries because of the blood vessels and nerves at a joint. Coolness or loss of colour of the extremities are indications of impaired circulation and the need to adjust bandages and padding (see chap. 12).

Parts of the body that are to be bandaged together should be separated with soft padding to prevent friction and discomfort.

Splints

A properly applied splint should prevent movement of the bone ends, reducing damage to tissue and lessening pain. A good splint should be:

● **rigid;**

● **long enough** to immobilize the joint above the fracture and the joint below it;

● **wide enough and well padded** to fit comfortably against the limb.

Improvised splints. An uninjured part of the body makes a natural splint. A splint may also be improvised from a walking stick, an umbrella, a broom handle, a piece of wood or cardboard or a firmly folded newspaper or magazine.

Commercial splints. You should not only be capable of improvising splints from materials readily at hand, you should also be familiar with and proficient in the use of commercial splints. The types of commercial splints are:

● **wire splints.** They are flexible and can be moulded to parts of the body, such as elbows.

- **preformed cardboard or plastic splints,** which are especially useful for immobilizing the extremities, because they provide maximum rigidity with minimum weight. Some can be used to apply traction to a lower limb. They do not have to be removed to take X-rays.

- **inflatable splints.** These are double-walled plastic or vinyl tubes usually closed with a zipper. They are inflated after being applied to fractured limbs. Air splints must only be inflated by mouth; inflation by pump can cause excessive pressure and restrict circulation. Avoid creasing the inflatable splint; this weakens the plastic and causes discomfort when applied.

- **traction splints** keep a fracture immobile while allowing a steady longitudinal pull on the extremity. Traction splints, such as the preformed plastic femoral splint, can only be applied to the lower limbs and their application requires two or more First Aiders.

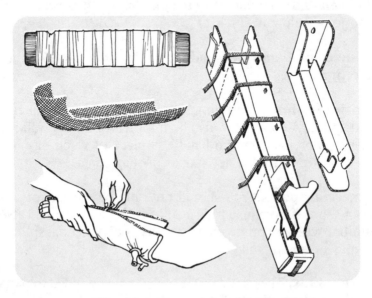

Fig. 14-4. Types of commercial splints.

● **long spine boards.** These are smooth and varnished or highly waxed so that they slide easily under a casualty. They are usually part of ambulance equipment. The long spine board can be constructed of plywood as shown. Handholds and strap holes should be located along the sides of the board. Runners, tapered at each end and fastened to the bottom of the board, make it easier to slide the board along rough surfaces and, by raising the board off the ground, make it easier to grasp the handholds.

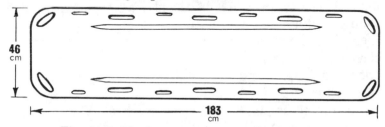

Fig. 14-5. The long spine board (bottom view).

● **short spine boards.** These are used for immobilizing back and neck injuries that occur while a person is in a sitting position, such as in a motor vehicle accident. The headpiece is notched so that straps or bandages used to hold the casualty's head in place will not slip during transportation. Strap holes along the sides of the board must not be used for carrying because that could cause the board to slip and result in further injury. Recommended dimensions of a short spine board are illustrated below. The use of the short spine board is detailed in chapter 28.

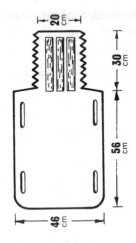

Fig. 14-6. The short spine board (back view).

FIRST AID PROCEDURES FOR FRACTURES

In addition to the signs and symptoms and the general rules of first aid for fractures, certain bone injuries have particular signs and symptoms and require specific first aid measures.

Fractures of the Clavicle

The clavicle (collarbone) may be fractured by direct or indirect force. A fall on the outstretched hand or a blow to the point of the shoulder, for example, will exert indirect force to the clavicle, causing it to break. There will be pain and tenderness at the site of the injury, and there will be loss of function of the arm. Swelling and deformity will be seen or felt over the clavicle. To relieve pain, the injured person usually supports the arm at the elbow and inclines his head toward the injured side. First aid for a fractured clavicle aims to support and immobilize the shoulder as follows:

Fig. 14-7. First aid for a fractured clavicle.

- support the arm on the injured side in a St. John tubular sling to transfer its weight to the uninjured side;

- secure the supported arm to the body with a narrow triangular bandage over the sling, starting with the midpoint at the elbow and tying off on the opposite side of the body.

Fractures of the Scapula

Fractures of the scapula (shoulder blade) are not common. They usually are caused by a direct blow. Pain may be aggravated by movement. These fractures are difficult to assess and may be mistaken for a pulled muscle. To give first aid for a fractured scapula:

● support the arm on the injured side in a St. John tubular sling to transfer its weight to the uninjured side;

● give further support by securing the upper limb to the chest with a broad bandage placed over the sling.

Fractures of the Humerus

Fractures of the humerus may involve the shoulder joint, the elbow joint or the length of the bone. Special precautions must be taken when the injury is near either joint because of possible damage to nerves and blood vessels (see chap. 17). If the joints are not involved, first aid for a fracture of the humerus is to:

● position the forearm across the lower ribs and upper abdomen;

● support the forearm in an arm sling;

● place soft padding be-tween the chest and upper arm;

Fig. 14-8. Immobilizing a fracture of the humerus

● secure the upper arm to the chest by bandages above and below the fracture;

● check to ensure that circulation is not impaired (see chap. 12).

Fractures About the Elbow

Elbow fractures require extra care because nerves and blood vessels to the hand can be further damaged by careless handling. No attempt should be made to bend or straighten the arm if this causes more pain. First aid for a fracture involving the elbow is:

- support the joint in a comfortable position, using a collar and cuff sling;

- place padding between the arm and the body;

- secure the limb to the body with broad bandages — one above and one below the elbow — tied off on the opposite side.

- check the radial pulse frequently and, if it is weak or absent, adjust the bandages and reposition the arm. If the pulse does not return, get medical aid immediately.

Fractures of the Radius and/or Ulna

Fractures of the forearm may involve either the radius or ulna, or both, and may involve the joints at the elbow or wrist. A fracture of the distal end of the radius (commonly called a Colles' fracture) makes the wrist look like an overturned dinner fork.

First aid for fractures along the length of the radius and ulna is to:

- steady and support the forearm and wrist with gentle traction and place it in the most comfortable position;

- immobilize the forearm and wrist on a padded splint placed along the palm side of the arm and extending from the elbow to the base of the fingers;

- Secure the splint to the arm with narrow bandages — one above and one below the fracture.

- place the splinted forearm across the chest, slightly elevated;

- support the forearm in an arm sling;

- monitor circulation.

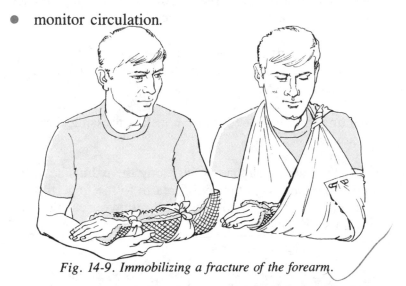

Fig. 14-9. Immobilizing a fracture of the forearm.

Fractures at the Wrist

Fractures involving the wrist should be immobilized, without traction, on a padded splint that can be moulded to the shape of the wrist and hand. Wire splints are most suitable for this purpose, but if these are not available, use sufficient padding on a rigid splint to keep the deformed wrist in a position of comfort.

Secure the ends of the splint at the elbow and hand and apply a narrow bandage above the fracture. Omit any bandage that may put pressure on the fracture site.

Fig. 14-10. Immobilizing a fractured wrist.

Support the splinted arm in an arm sling with the fingers slightly elevated. Monitor circulation carefully at the fingers (see chap. 12).

Fractures of the Hands

Many fractures of the hand will require only manual support if medical aid is readily available. However, if the injuries are more serious or if medical aid is remote, give first aid as follows:

- place the hand in the position of function, padded with a roll of loose gauze or other soft material in the palm and under the fingers;

- if the fingers are crushed, place nonstick dressings between the fingers;

- immobilize with a padded splint along the palm side of the hand, extending from the mid-forearm to the fingertips (or the hand can be enclosed in a small pillow or cushion and secured with bandages);

Fig. 14-11. Immobilizing a fractured hand.

- support the arm in an arm sling.

Fractures of the Pelvis

A fracture of the pelvis usually is caused by a direct crush or a fall and may involve injury to the organs of the pelvic area, especially the bladder and urethra. Persons with such injuries may be unable to urinate or may pass bloody urine. They should be told to try not to urinate. A casualty with a fractured pelvis may feel pain in the hips and the small of the back. Movement may cause increased pain and may prevent the person from standing or walking.

The extent of first aid for a fractured pelvis depends on the availability of medical aid, the distance to a medical facility and the smoothness of the trip. When medical aid is readily available:

- lay the casualty in the most comfortable position, usually on his back with the knees straight. If the casualty wishes to bend the knees, support them on a folded blanket or pillow.

- pad the ankles and secure the feet together with a bandage in a figure-8.

- support both sides of the pelvis with padded weights.

When medical aid may be delayed, or if transportation may be long or rough:

- place soft padding between the knees and ankles.

- apply a bandage around the ankles and feet in a figure-8.

- apply two broad bandages around the pelvis, overlapping by half. The broad parts of the bandages should be on the injured side in line with the hip joint. Tie off gently or fasten with a safety pin on the uninjured side and support both sides of the pelvic area with sandbags or other heavy weights. **If the casualty complains of discomfort, loosen or remove the bandages immediately**.

Fig. 14-12. Immobilizing fracture of the pelvis.

● apply a broad bandage around the knees.

● place the casualty on a long, padded spine board, using the logroll manoeuvre and transport to medical aid.

Fractures of the Femur

The femur (thigh bone) may be broken anywhere along its length. Fractures of the upper end or neck of the femur, referred to as hip fractures, most frequently occur in elderly persons. The cause may appear to be minor and the injury may be mistaken for a bruised hip. Suspect a fracture of the neck of the femur if an elderly person complains of pain in the hip area after a fall or minor injury, particularly if there is some loss of function or unnatural movement.

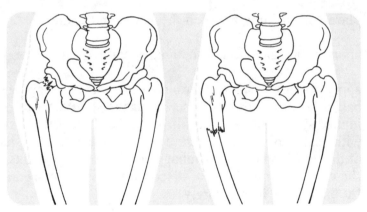

Fig. 14-13. Fractures of the neck and the shaft of the femur.

Fractures along the length of the femur are easier to assess because of marked deformity and pain. Such fractures usually are caused by a powerful force. Fractures of the distal end of the femur are often associated with injuries of the knee and of the ligaments surrounding the knee. Fractures of the femur are considered serious because the casualty may go into severe shock.

Fractures of the femur may be recognized by an outward roll of the entire leg, including an outward turn of the foot. This indicates a fracture of the neck of the femur. Marked angulation and shortening of the thigh indicates a fracture along the length of the bone.

The extent of first aid for a fractured femur is determined by the availability of medical aid, the distance to a medical facility and the smoothness of the journey. If medical aid is readily available, steady and support the limb with gentle but firm traction until help arrives.

If the casualty must be moved and the journey to a medical facility is short and smooth, use of the person's uninjured leg as a splint may be sufficient. Immobilize as follows:

- steady and support, and apply gentle traction by pulling steadily and firmly on the foot, keeping the toes and kneecap pointing upwards, and maintaining the traction until immobilization is complete;

- case five bandages under the thighs and legs, using the natural hollows of the body, and ease them into position above and below the fracture site, at the knees, lower legs and ankles.

Fig. 14-14. Immobilizing a fracture of the femur.

- place padding between the legs (a rolled blanket is ideal) and move the good leg next to the injured one;

- secure the legs together with bandages, first at the ankles with a figure-8, then above and below the fracture, next at the knees using a broad bandage, and finally at the lower legs using a broad bandage.

If the casualty must be moved and the journey to medical aid will be long and rough, a long padded splint should be applied along the length of the body on the injured side.

While maintaining traction and support on the injured limb, position seven broad bandages under the body and under both legs. Use narrow bandages above and below the fracture (for a large casualty use broad bandages) and at the feet. Use broad bandages for the other positions. Ease the bandages under the body at the small of the back, the knees and ankles and place them into position by sliding them up or down as required. Put padding between the legs, knees and ankles. Place the padded splint along side the body so that it extends from the armpit to below the foot. Secure the splint to the upper body and to the legs in the following sequence:

- at the chest below the armpits;

- at the pelvis in line with the hip joints;

- at the ankles and feet with a figure-8 to include the splint;

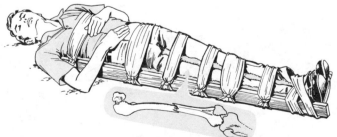

*Fig. 14-15. Immobilizing a fractured femur
for a long or rough journey.*

- at the thigh above and below the fracture;

- at the knees.

- at the lower leg.

In some instances, one bandage may have to be omitted to avoid putting pressure on the fracture.

Because a casualty with a fractured femur will be in shock from loss of blood and severe pain, first aid for shock must be started as soon as possible (see chap. 10). Place the casualty on a stretcher and elevate the foot of the stretcher.

Traction splints, such as a preformed femoral traction splint, and the Thomas splint are recommended for fractures of the femur. However, their use requires special training.

Fractures About the Knee

Fractures of the bones about the knee may occur in the distal end of the femur, in the proximal end of the tibia, or at the patella. Such fractures usually are caused by direct force, although violent muscular contraction can fracture the patella.

There may be marked deformity and severe pain. Compression of the major artery of the lower leg may impair circulation to the foot. You cannot always be sure that there has been a fracture, but treat the injury as a fracture.

First aid for fractures about the knee is to:

- support the injured limb, gently realigning it only as much as will not produce additional pain. Do not use traction.

- immobilize on a splint long enough to reach from the buttock to beyond the heel with padding under the natural hollows at the knee and ankle.

- secure the splint with bandages, using a figure-8 around the ankle, foot, and end of the splint; a broad bandage around the thigh and upper end of the splint; and a broad bandage around the lower leg and splint.

- support the splinted limb in a slightly elevated position.

- check circulation to the foot.

Pillows or blankets can be used to immobilize a knee that cannot be straightened.

Fig. 14-16. Immobilizing a fractured patella.

Fractures of the Tibia and/or Fibula

Fractures of the lower leg, involving one or both bones, are common sport injuries. Fractures at the distal end of these bones may be mistaken for a sprained ankle. In addition to the usual signs and symptoms, fractures of the lower leg may be complicated by severe deformity, including extreme angulation or rotation.

Fractures of the tibia and fibula may be immobilized in a number of ways, depending on the distance to medical aid, the method of transportation, and the availability of first aid supplies. If medical aid is near or transportation will be smooth, immobilizing by using the good leg as a splint may be adequate. If the distance is long or transportation is over rough roads, a splint placed between the legs may be necessary, and an additional splint may be needed on the outside of the leg.

Immobilization – Two Splints

If the location of the accident requires transportation on foot or in the back seat of a car, it may be necessary to retain the person's ability to use the good leg. In that case, immobilization must be effected with splints on either side of the injured leg.

- steady and support the limb, applying and maintaining traction until immobilization is completed;

- place five bandages under the leg, using the natural hollows at the knee and ankle. Ease broad bandages into position at the thigh, knee and ankle and narrow bandages — one above and one below the fracture site.

- Place padding along the leg to fill the natural hollows at the sides of the knee and ankle.

- secure the splints to either side of the leg with the bandages, at the thigh and ankle, next at the knee and finally above and below the fracture.

Immobilization – Natural Splint

If the uninjured limb is used as a splint, position bandages under the injured limb first, then place padding along the limb. Bring the uninjured limb next to the injured one, and secure the two legs together in the following sequence:

- a broad bandage at the ankles in a figure-8;

- a broad bandage at the thighs;

- a broad bandage at the knees;

- narrow bandages above the fracture and below the fracture.

Additional bandages may be used for added support, or a bandage may be omitted if it will put pressure on the fracture.

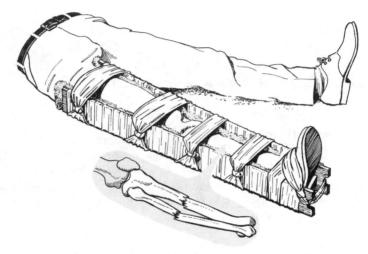

Fig. 14-17. Immobilizing a fractured leg.

Fractures of the Ankle

Fractures of the ankle are caused by a violent blow or severe twisting and may involve the tibia or the fibula or both. Pain, swelling and deformity are usually present. A fractured ankle is often assessed as a sprain. If in doubt, treat the injury as a fracture.

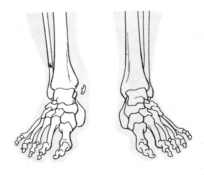

Fig. 14-18. Fracture of the ankle.

To give first aid for an ankle injury, simply immobilize the ankle with a pillow or small blanket securely fastened. A cold compress (a cold pack or an ice bag) may be used to help reduce swelling (see chap. 13).

Footwear may help to immobilize the ankle, but laces of footwear should be loosened to prevent constriction of the blood
vessels as a result of the swelling that occurs with ankle injuries.
However, when wounds of the ankle require dressing, footwear
must be removed.

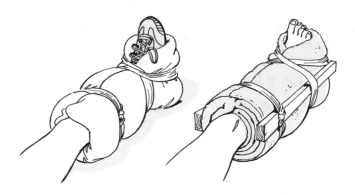

*Fig. 14-19. Immobilizing a fractured ankle
using a pillow or blanket or small splints.*

Fractures of the Foot

Fractures of the foot are usually caused by a heavy weight
dropped or rolled over the foot. Fractures may also be caused by
severe twisting or falls from a height when the person lands on
his feet. In the latter case, injuries to the spine by transferred
force should be suspected.

If wounds are present, footwear must be removed or cut away to
allow dressings and bandages to be applied. If there are no
wounds, footwear may be left on to help in immobilization, but
laces must be loosened to avoid constriction caused by swelling.
First aid for fractures of the foot is:

● immobilize the foot using a padded splint, a small pillow or
blanket fastened around the foot, or footwear secured with
bandages;

- secure the splint or footwear with a figure-8 as follows: place the centre of a broad bandage on the sole of the foot; cross over the instep and carry the ends to the back of the ankle; cross the ends at the back of the ankle, then cross them over the instep and back under the sole of the foot; tie off the ends over the splint or sole of the shoe;

- raise the foot and support it in a comfortable position, usually 15 to 30 cm (6 to 12 in);

- transport to medical aid by stretcher.

CHAPTER 15

CHEST INJURIES

Injuries of the chest, including wounds of the soft tissue of the chest, fractures of the ribs and sternum, and injuries to the organs of the chest, are potentially fatal because they may interfere with breathing and cause severe bleeding.

PREVENTION

Chest injuries are caused by a direct force such as stabbing, a blow to the chest, compression, or by a violent change in air pressure as in a blast. Wearing seat belts helps to prevent chest injuries that might be caused when the driver is forcefully thrown against the steering wheel of a car.

CLASSIFICATION

Chest wounds are classified as either open or closed. **Open chest wounds** are those in which the chest wall has been penetrated by an external object or has been perforated from within by fractured ribs. **Closed chest wounds** may show no external signs of injury, but the ribs, sternum, lungs, heart and the nervous system may have been seriously damaged.

SIGNS AND SYMPTOMS

One or more of the following signs and symptoms will be present in all chest injuries:

- **pain** at the injury site which is aggravated by breathing, usually the result of injury to the ribs, lungs or pleura;

- **difficulty in breathing** and shortness of breath, possibly caused by rib injuries, muscular paralysis, fluid in the lungs, collapse of the lung;

- **apprehension, fear and restlessness,** resulting from breathing distress;

- **inability to expand one or both sides of the chest** on inhalation, indicating a loss of muscle function because of injury to the chest wall, to the ribs or to the nerves that control chest movement (see chap. 16);

- **coughing up blood,** indicating injury to the lung tissue and bleeding into the lung and bronchi;

- **rapid and weak pulse,** a sign of shock caused by loss of blood and lack of oxygen;

- **cyanosis** (blueness of the lips, fingers, and fingernail beds), indicating a lack of oxygen in the blood, because the injured lung cannot interchange carbon dioxide and oxygen in the bloodstream.

FIRST AID FOR CHEST INJURIES

The first priority in caring for chest injuries is to ensure adequate breathing. Maintain an open airway and be prepared to give artifical respiration if breathing stops (see chap. 7). The casualty should be placed in a semisitting position to relieve pressure on the lungs from the abdominal organs and inclined toward the injured side to prevent fluid drainage into the good lung.

Chest injuries require urgent medical attention. The casualty must be transported to medical aid as quickly as possible. **Only first aid that is essential for safe transportation should be given.**

PENETRATING CHEST WOUNDS

A wound that penetrates the chest wall may allow air to flow directly into the chest cavity, causing the lung to collapse. As the casualty inhales, air may be sucked through the wound into the chest cavity. Upon exhalation, air is blown back through the wound causing bloodstained bubbles to form at the wound site. This type of wound is called a "sucking chest wound." The movement of air through the wound seriously impairs breathing and must be stopped.

Stop the flow of air into the chest cavity by applying an air-tight covering of plastic or foil. Tape this dressing on three sides to create a flutter-type valve. When the casualty inhales, the dressing will seal the wound preventing air from entering the chest cavity. When the casualty exhales, the flutter valve will open allowing air to escape. If there is an embedded object, do not remove it. Place dressings around the object and try to create a flutter-type valve. Support the arm on the injured side with a St. John tubular sling and place the casualty in the position of most comfort, often this is semisitting and inclined to the injured side.

Fig. 15-1. First aid for a penetrating wound of the chest.

If the lung has been lacerated, air may leak from the lung into the chest cavity. If there is no wound for this air to exit from, or if the wound has been sealed, a build-up of air will occur which will seriously impair both breathing and heart function. This condition, called a "tension pneumothorax," results in obvious and increasing difficulty in breathing, a rapid, weak pulse, cyanosis and extreme anxiety. Tension pneumothorax is life-threatening and immediate medical aid is required.

If you suspect a tension pneumothorax is developing from a sucking chest wound that has been bandaged, check the dressing to make sure that it is open on one side and that air is able to escape as the casualty exhales. Give first aid for shock and transport to medical aid urgently.

BLAST INJURIES

The violent shock wave of an explosion can affect the lungs and internal organs. Although there may be no signs of external injury, the casualty may complain of pain in the chest and may cough up frothy blood. The type and extent of the explosion, and the casualty's location relative to it, along with the above signs will help to confirm blast injuries to the chest.

Make the casualty as comfortable as possible in a semisitting position (head and shoulders raised and supported). Monitor and maintain respiration. Give first aid to slow the progress of shock and transport the casualty to medical aid quickly.

FRACTURED RIBS

Simple rib fractures can be supported with a broad bandage around the chest, its widest part over the fracture site. However, the bandage must be removed if it causes discomfort. Support the arm on the injured side in a St. John tubular sling to transfer its weight and to limit movement. Transport the person in a sitting position.

In cases of open rib fractures, dress the wound first to provide an airtight seal. Support the arm in a St. John tubular sling and transport the person on a stretcher in a semisitting position, inclined toward the injured side (see Fig. 15-1).

FLAIL CHEST

When several ribs are broken in more than one place, the injured section of the chest wall, called a flail segment, does not move normally during breathing. On inspiration the injured segment is sucked in, and on expiration it is blown outward. This causes painful, distressed and relatively ineffective breathing. It may cause the casualty to panic. The aim of first aid, therefore, is to stabilize the loose segment to ease breathing.

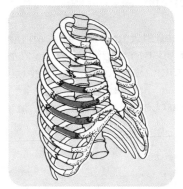

Stabilize the loose segment by placing the casualty's arm across the injury, and securing the arm to the chest with broad bandages. A firm pad or cushion, secured to the injured area with tape or bandages, may also be used as a splint.

Fig. 15-2. A flail chest.

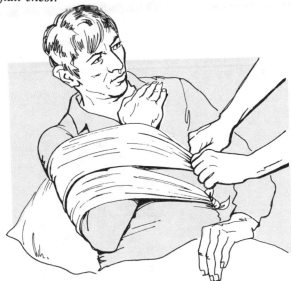

Fig. 15-3. First aid for a flail chest.

Place the casualty in a semisitting position, inclined toward the injured side. Obtain medical aid or transport to medical aid on a stretcher.

FRACTURE OF THE STERNUM

Crush injuries of the chest can cause a fracture of the sternum (breastbone). The fracture is frequently complicated by damage to underlying organs and blood vessels.

The aims of first aid for fractures of the sternum are to keep the casualty as quiet as possible in a position in which he can breathe most easily, usually semisitting. Loosen tight clothing about the neck, chest and waist. Give first aid for shock and obtain medical aid. If the casualty must be moved, transport on a stretcher.

CHAPTER 16

HEAD AND SPINAL INJURIES

First Aiders should be quick to recognize injuries to the head and spine because of their potential life-threatening complications and because immediate and proper care can reduce or eliminate those threats. Casualties with head and spinal injuries do not necessarily have spinal cord damage, but when the spine is fractured or dislocated, it may no longer be able to protect the spinal cord. Movement, therefore, may compress and damage the spinal cord and nerve roots. Proper initial handling of such injuries can prevent spinal cord damage and save the casualty from permanent paralysis or death.

INJURIES TO THE HEAD

Injuries to the head include **skull fractures, brain concussion** and **compression.** Head injuries are frequently complicated by unconsciousness (see chap 11). Fractures at the base of the skull often involve injury to the cervical spine.

FRACTURE SITES

Fractures of the skull may be the result of direct force or force transmitted through intervening bone. Fractures may occur in the cranium, at the base of the skull or in the face. Facial fractures include the nose and the orbital cavity, the maxilla (upper jaw) and the mandible (lower jaw). Fractures of the jaw are often complicated by wounds inside the mouth.

Fig. 16-1. Common fracture sites of the skull, face and jaw.

Signs

Fractures of the skull can be recognized by certain physical signs:

- a fracture of the **cranium** should be suspected if the scalp is swollen, bruised or lacerated, or if there is a depression in the bone.

- a fracture at the **base of the skull** should be suspected if blood or straw-coloured fluid comes from the ears or nose. Discolouration of the soft tissue below the eyes (black eyes) and behind the ears also indicates possible injury at the base of the skull.

- fractures of the **face** and **jaw** may be indicated by pain when moving the jaw or when swallowing. There may be displacement of teeth, swelling and bruising of the lower jaw, excessive bloody saliva and difficulty in speaking and breathing.

FIRST AID FOR HEAD INJURIES

First aid for fractures of the skull depends on the fracture site and on the signs. However, an unconscious casualty with skull injuries tends to vomit, and care must be taken to prevent aspiration of the vomitus and asphyxiation. In all cases of a head injury a spinal injury should be suspected and the casualty should be treated as if there were a fractured neck. The head and neck should be immobilized accordingly.

Give first aid for fractures of the cranium or the base of the skull as follows:

- steady and support the head and neck to prevent movement by placing hands on either side of the head.

- assess responsiveness, check breathing and ensure that the airway is open. Use the jaw thrust without head tilt. Start artifical respiration if breathing stops.

- apply a cervical collar.

- assess the level of consciousness.

- if blood or fluid flows from the ear canal, apply a sterile dressing and secure lightly in position to allow fluids to drain.

- protect areas of depression, lumps, bumps or, scalp wounds where an underlying skull fracture is suspected, with thick, compressible, soft dressings bandaged in place. Avoid pressure on the fracture site.

- warn the casualty not to blow his nose if it is discharging blood or fluid. Do not restrict blood flow. Hold dressings at the nose to absorb the blood to prevent it from entering the mouth and interfering with breathing.

- do not leave the casualty unattended, transport to medical aid.

Give first aid for fractures of the facial bones and jaw as follows:

- maintain an open airway, ensuring that there is no obstruction in the mouth. Remove knocked-out teeth or dentures and maintain a drainage route for blood and saliva, using a finger to keep the airway open if the face is severely injured.

- control bleeding with direct pressure.

- support the jaw with a soft pad held in place by hand, not by a bandage.

- place the conscious casualty in a sitting position with head well forward to allow any secretions to drain freely.

● place the severely injured, but conscious casualty, in the recovery position if there is displacement of the chin or if there is soft tissue damage.

● place the unconscious casualty in the recovery position and keep the jaw well forward to allow free drainage of secretions. If the casualty vomits, support the jaw with the palm of your hand and turn the head to the uninjured side.

Conscious casualities with severe facial injuries should be transported sitting, if possible, with the head forward and supported. If movement by stretcher is required, ensure good drainage from the mouth and nose so that breathing will not be impaired.

CONCUSSION AND COMPRESSION

Concussion is a condition of widespread but temporary disturbance of brain function associated with injuries to the head. A person who "sees stars" after a head injury is suffering from a concussion. He may recover rapidly or his condition may deteriorate.

Signs of Concussion

The following signs may be present:

● partial or complete loss of consciousness, usually of short duration;

● shallow breathing;

● cold, clammy and pale skin;

● rapid, weak pulse;

● nausea and vomiting upon recovery;

● loss of memory of events immediately preceding and following the injury.

Compression is a condition of pressure on some part of the brain by fluids within the skull or by a depressed fracture of the skull itself. The condition may directly follow concussion with no return to consciousness, but it may also develop many hours after apparent recovery from concussion as a result of a gradual pressure build-up. It is very important to monitor the casualty's vital signs and the reaction of the eyes to light for hours after a concussion to look for signs of compression.

Signs of Compression

The following signs may be present:

- unconsciousness from the onset, particularly if actual damage to brain tissue has occurred.

- twitching of the limbs or even convulsions in the early stages, caused by pressure on the brain.

- irregular and noisy breathing, and slowing of the pulse.

- raised body temperature and flushed face.

- pupils of the eyes unequal in size; one or both pupils may be dilated and may not respond to light (see Fig. 25-2). Changes observed in the pupils of the eyes should be recorded for the physician.

- weakness or irregular movement. Twitching, convulsions, weak movement or paralysis should be recorded for the physician.

FIRST AID – CONCUSSION AND COMPRESSION

First aid for concussion and compression is the same as for unconsciousness (see chap. 11). In the case of concussion, watch carefully for signs of compression. Transport the casualty to a medical facility for further observation and treatment.

SPINAL INJURIES

The spine may be fractured anywhere along its length from the base of the skull to the coccyx. Injury to the spine threatens the spinal cord that runs through it and to the nerves that branch out from the cord. Damage to the spinal cord or nerves can result in complete loss of feeling and paralysis below the point of injury. Injury to the cord at the lower spine may affect only the legs, but damage to the cord in the upper spine could result in paralysis of the muscles that control chest movement in breathing. Blood pressure is often affected as the diameter of blood vessels increases, allowing blood to pool, depriving vital tissues of oxygen. This results in shock.

Therefore, the aims of first aid for any suspected spinal injury are to prevent damage to the spinal cord, to care for other life-threatening conditions and to slow down the progress of shock.

INJURIES OF THE CERVICAL SPINE

Injuries caused by violent flexion of the neck, as in motor vehicle accidents, frequently result in a fracture of the cervical spine. Special precautions must be taken if a fracture of the cervical spine is suspected. Movement may result in further severe damage to the spinal cord and nerves, causing paralysis.

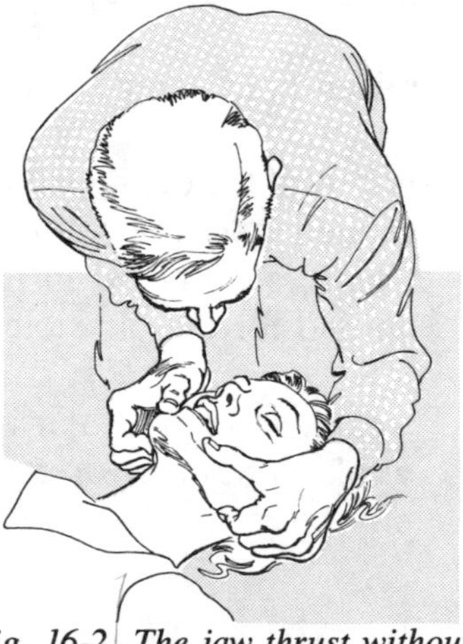

Fig. 16-2. *The jaw thrust without head tilt.*

Breathing must be closely and continuously monitored. If breathing ceases, open the airway and give artificial respiration. The jaw thrust without head tilt is the safest technique for opening the airway of a casualty with suspected neck injury (see chap. 7).

FIRST AID — CERVICAL SPINE INJURIES

First aid for a suspected neck injury is to steady and support the head and neck to prevent rotation (side to side movement) or flexion/extension (the head dropping forward or back). Immobilize the head and neck in the position found unless it is necessary to realign the head to clear the airway. If the head must be straightened, apply gentle traction during realignment.

A satisfactory head support can be made from two rolled towels, blankets, or padded weights. Place one of these on each side of the head and hold them in position by bandages tied to the spine board.

A sitting casualty with suspected neck injury should have the neck and upper body immobilized as a unit before being moved. Support the person's head and apply a **cervical collar.** Such a collar can be improvised with triangular bandages as follows:

- lay out a triangular bandage as a whole cloth on a flat surface;

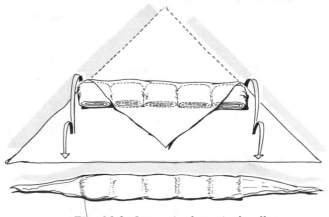

Fig. 16-3. Improvised cervical collar.

- place firm bulky material on a line about one-third the distance from the point to the base. Five folded triangular bandages, several pairs of folded socks, several folded scarves, or a piece of a blanket make suitable padding for this purpose.

● fold the point toward the base to enclose the line of padding. Roll the padding and bandage toward the base to form a collar about 8 to 10 cm (3 to 4 in.) in diameter with ties on each end for securing around the neck.

While maintaing support of the head and neck, place the center of the improvised collar under the chin and ease the ends under the neck in opposite directions. Carefully draw the ends to take up the slack and tie them off in the front on the padding. Maintain support of the head and neck until they can be immobilized to the spine board.

Slide a board or other rigid material behind the casualty with as little movement of the head, neck and back as possible. Secure the casualty's head and body to the board with straps designed for this purpose or with improvised bandages (see chap. 28). Tie off on the edge of the board if possible.

Fig. 16-4 (a). Applying a short spine board.

Fig. 16-4 (b). Immobilized head and neck.

THORACIC AND LUMBAR SPINE INJURIES

Fractures and dislocations of the thoracic spine or lumbar spine (see Fig. 2-11) are very serious. Incorrect handling can cause paralysis. Such fractures of the spine are caused by:

Fig. 16-5. Fracture of the spine.

- direct force, as from the dropping of a heavy weight on the casualty's back, from a long fall onto the back, or from the impact of a vehicle accident;

- indirect force, as from a long fall on to the feet or buttocks, or from a fall on the head.

Signs and Symptoms

The signs and symptoms of thoracic and lumbar spine injury may include a loss of sensation (numbness or tingling) in the extremities, particularly the lower limbs.

The conscious casualty will be aware of pain and may be able to direct attention to the area of injury. Movement that causes pain should be avoided. Loss of function can be determined by asking the casualty to move fingers and toes. Loss of sensation may be determined by gently touching the extremities and asking the casualty if the sensations of touch or pain can be felt.

If the casualty is unconscious, those important signs are not available to you and assessment is more difficult. The circumstances of the accident that caused the injury and information from witnesses are then most important.

FIRST AID FOR SPINAL INJURIES

If medical aid is readily available, do only what is necessary to prevent body movement and to slow the progress of shock. Instruct two bystanders to steady and support the casualty to prevent movement of the head, neck and trunk.

One bystander supports the head and neck by kneeling at the head and gently placing his hands on either side of the head. Instruct him to maintain head alignment and to prevent the head from turning from side to side and from dropping forward. Tell him to monitor breathing and call out if breathing problems occur.

Maintain an open airway and assist with breathing if necessary. Because the casualty may be immobilized on his back, it may be necessary to use suction to keep the airway free of fluids and mucus. A commercial aspirator or a suction bulb, such as a domestic baster, may be used. Do not use a glass baster that may break if the teeth are clenched.

The second bystander supports the ankles and feet to prevent rotation of the legs and trunk. He kneels at the feet and places one hand under the casualty's ankles to grasp the ankle joint on one side. He brings the other hand over the instep to grasp the ankle joint on the opposite side. Instruct him to maintain body alignment and to prevent rotation.

Warn the casualty not to move. Provide coverings to keep the casualty warm to slow the progress of shock.

If medical aid is not readily available, or if it is necessary to move the casualty, the following are required to ensure safe handling:

* a minimum of four, but preferably more bearers;

- a spine board prepared or improvised from a door or other suitably firm object, long and wide but not so large that it will not clear passageways through which the casualty must be carried;

- padding sufficient to fill the hollows between the legs, and to fill the spaces along the spine board at the natural hollows of the body, such as under the neck, the small of the back, the knees and the ankles;

- bandages sufficient to immobilize the joints at the hips, knees, legs, ankles and feet, and to secure the casualty to the spine board;

- a suction bulb (or a baster from the kitchen) to clear the casualty's airway during movement.

When the required equipment and bearers are ready, immobilize the casualty as follows:

- maintain support at the head and feet while you apply a cervical collar and place pads of soft material between the legs, knees and ankles.

- secure the ankles and feet together with a bandage in a figure-8. Maintain support before, during and after the ankles are secured.

- apply broad bandages around the thighs, knees and legs to immobilize the joints. All bandages should be eased under the casualty without moving his body. Use the natural hollows of the body whenever possible.

- gently secure the casualty's wrists together across the chest to prevent the arms from falling and causing unnecessary movement.

Use the logroll manoeuvre to place the casualty on the spine board.

The Logroll Manoeuvre

When the casualty is immobilized, prepare a spine board alongside the casualty with padding in positions corresponding to the natural hollows of the body at the neck, the small of the back, the knees and the ankles. Take care that padding will not put pressure on the fracture site. Position and instruct the rescue team as follows:

● instruct the two rescuers at the head and feet to maintain body traction throughout the procedure and to rotate the head and feet in unison with the roll of the body to prevent twisting of the head and spine. Caution the rescuer at the head to be especially careful not to allow the head to bend forward.

● tell one or more rescuers to take positions along the casualty's side away from the spine board at the hips and lower legs. They should reach over the casualty to grasp clothing to enable them to roll the casualty toward them onto her side when directed to do so.

● have one rescuer control the spine board and move it into position when the casualty is rolled over onto her side. He should make the final padding adjustment before the casualty is rolled back onto the board and help to slide the casualty over the centre of the board.

● if you are the First Aider, take the position at the shoulders so that you can control the rescue team and pay particular attention to the neck and upper back during the manoeuvre.

When you are satisfied that everyone is in position and ready, direct the team to roll the casualty gently onto her side. Ensure that the spine board is in proper position and direct the bearers to roll the casualty back onto the board.

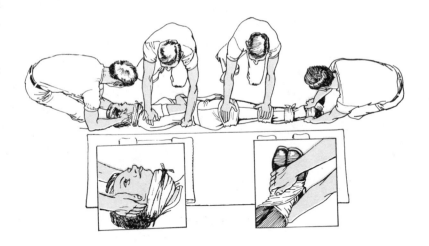

Fig. 16-6. Logroll onto a prepared spine board.

Cover the casualty with a blanket and secure her to the board with bandages or straps before the board is carried. Immobilize the head to the spine board to prevent movement during transportation. Monitor breathing and transport to medical care as smoothly as possible.

REMOVAL TO HOSPITAL

It is important that casualties with spinal injuries be transported urgently. However, more harm is likely to result from a fast and rough ride than from a slow and smooth one.

Notes

CHAPTER 17

MUSCLE, LIGAMENT AND JOINT INJURIES

Injuries to the musculoskeletal systems are common and are often preventable. Injuries to muscles and joints are called strains, sprains and dislocations. Sprains and dislocations may cause fractures at a joint and threaten blood vessels and nerves that pass through the joint. These injuries can be serious and, in most cases, should receive medical attention. This is especially true of children under the age of 14 years, whose ligaments and tendons are stronger than their bones. Strains and sprains in children are more likely to fracture the length of the bone or the growth plate at the ends of long bones. If a fracture cannot be ruled out in a strain or a sprain, treat the injury as a fracture.

PREVENTION

Strains, sprains and dislocations are caused by sudden excessive pulling or twisting of a muscle or joint. Strains or sprains are often the result of using poor body mechanics or of inadequate conditioning of the body for a particular sport or physical activity. Dislocations are usually caused by violent movement.

Most lower back injuries can be prevented by getting help to lift or lower heavy objects and by using proper body mechanics in such activities. When lifting:

- stand close to the object to be lifted;

- bend your knees — do not stoop;

- tilt the object so that you can put one hand under the near edge or corner;

- place your other hand diagonally opposite, getting a grip on the object;

- lift, using the thigh and leg muscles and keeping the back straight.

- when turning, follow the feet — do not twist the body.

Fig. 17-1. Lifting technique.

When lowering a heavy object, reverse the procedure. Remember that poor body mechanics can exert extreme pressures on the spine, intervertebral discs and supporting muscles, causing muscle and disc injuries.

STRAINS

When muscles are stretched beyond their normal limits, the injury is called a strain. Signs and symptoms of a strain may be delayed for some time until there is a reaction in the surrounding tissue and the following signs and symptoms appear.

Signs and Symptoms

Strains can usually be recognized by:

- sudden sharp pain in the affected muscle;

- swelling of the muscles causing severe cramps (charley horse);

- discolouration and stiffness.

FIRST AID FOR STRAINS

First aid for strains is limited and consists of the following:

- place the casualty in the position of greatest comfort;

- apply cold to help relax muscle spasms and prevent further tissue swelling. Ice packs should be applied—15 minutes on, 15 minutes off.

SPRAINS

A sprain is a stretching or tearing of the ligaments that support a joint. A sprain occurs when the bones at a joint are forced beyond their normal range of movement, stretching and tearing the supporting ligaments.

Signs and Symptoms

The signs and symptoms of sprains are:

- pain that may be severe and increase on movement;

- loss of function;

- swelling and discolouration.

FIRST AID FOR SPRAINS

Sprains may not be distinguishable from fractures and most should be treated as fractures, with the following additional procedures:

- apply gentle pressure with bandages (compression) to decrease swelling. Loosen these if circulation below the bandages is restricted, or, if they cause the casualty pain;

- immobilize and elevate the injured joint if possible.

- apply ice packs (15 minutes on, 15 minutes off) to the joint to reduce the pain and control swelling.

The mnemonic ICE may be helpful in remembering the three first aid steps in the care of sprains — **I**ce, **C**ompression, **E**levation.

DISLOCATIONS

When the abutting bone surfaces at a joint are no longer in proper contact, the joint is said to be dislocated. A dislocation stretches and tears the fibrous capsule that holds the joint together.

A dislocation can be caused by a severe twist of a joint or by indirect force. The joints most frequently dislocated are those of the shoulder, elbow, thumb, finger, lower jaw and knee. A shoulder, for example, may be dislocated by a fall on the elbow or on the extended arm. Occasionally, sudden muscular contraction will cause a dislocation. The lower jaw may be dislocated by yawning.

Signs and Symptoms

The signs and symptoms of a dislocation are not unlike those of a fracture and may include:

- deformity or abnormal appearance;

- pain and tenderness aggravated by movement;

- loss of normal function;

● swelling of the joint.

FIRST AID FOR DISLOCATIONS

Since many dislocations are complicated by a fracture, they should be treated as fractures if there is any doubt, with the following additional procedures:

● make no attempt to return bones to their normal position.

● immobilize and support the joint in the position of greatest comfort. Use padding and a sling if appropriate to support the limb. Chapter 12 describes the use of a collar and cuff sling for dislocations of the shoulder and elbow.

● apply cold in the form of ice packs or cold packs (15 minutes on, 15 minutes off) to limit pain and swelling.

● check circulation frequently by feeling the pulse or by watching for changes in temperature and colour of the extremity (see chap. 12).

● seek medical aid urgently if the circulation is impaired.

Notes

CHAPTER 18

EYE INJURIES

ANATOMY

The eye is one of a pair of organs of vision. Its functions are so complex and its structure is so delicate that it can be injured by as little as a speck of dust. Further injury can also be caused by improper first aid. First Aiders should know the basic structure of the eye and the precautions necessary to avoid aggravating existing injuries while giving first aid.

The main part of the eye is a fluid-filled globe called the **eyeball.** Within the structure of the eyeball, at the front, is "the window" of the eye. This consists of the cornea, the iris, the pupil, and the lens. The **cornea** is a delicate, transparent covering of the front of the eyeball. The **iris** is a coloured, circular muscle with a centre opening called the **pupil.** The pupil changes its size to control the amount of light that enters the eye through the lens. The **lens** focusses the light onto the **retina** a light-sensitive layer on the inside of the eyeball. The retina helps the brain to convert light rays into images.

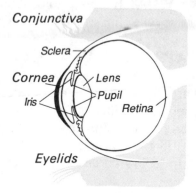

Fig. 18-1. The eye.

The external parts, consisting of the sclera, the conjunctiva and the eyelids, serve to protect the eye. The **sclera** is the tough white outer coat of the eyeball. The **conjunctiva** is the smooth membrane that covers the inside of the eyelids and parts of the sclera. The upper and lower **eyelids** are layers of skin controlled by muscles to provide a protective outer covering for the eyes.

PREVENTION OF EYE INJURIES

Avoid eye injuries by following basic safety and accident prevention practices. Consider the consequences of eye injury — impairment of vision or blindness — that could result from a momentary lapse in safety and ask yourself:

• WHAT IF eye goggles are not worn when grinding, drilling, cutting or chipping hard, brittle materials?

• WHAT IF eye shields are not worn during hazardous sports?

• WHAT IF corrosive chemicals are kept on a high shelf? What if face shields are not worn and the chemical should splash?

• WHAT IF eye shields are not worn when spraying pesticides and fertilizers?

• WHAT IF eyes are not shielded from arc welding flashes or if an eclipse of the sun is viewed without eye protection?

PARTICLES IN THE EYE

Particles of sand, grit or loose eyelashes may lodge on the eyeball or under the eyelids causing discomfort and inflammation of the conjunctiva. Inflammation from particles under the eyelid gives the eye a characteristic pink or reddish colour. Tears help to loosen and wash away such particles.

Do not attempt to remove a particle from the eye when:

• it is on the cornea;

• it is embedded in or is adhering to the eyeball;

• it cannot be seen — even though the eye is inflamed and painful.

When the above conditions exist, give first aid as follows:

- warn the person not to rub the eye because that may cause pain and irritation of the conjunctiva.

- wash your hands before starting first aid.

- close the person's eyelids and cover the affected eye with an eye or gauze pad. Extend the covering to the forehead and cheek to avoid pressurc on the eye. Secure lightly in position with a bandage or adhesive strips.

- obtain medical aid.

REMOVING A PARTICLE FROM THE UPPER EYELID

If the particle is under the upper lid, ask the person to pull the upper lid down over the lower lid. The lashes of the lower lid may dislodge the particle and brush it out

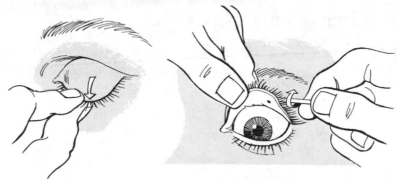

Fig. 18-2. Removal of a particle body from the upper lid.

Fig. 18-3. Turning back the upper lid.

It may be necessary to expose the inner surface of the eyelid to locate and remove a loose particle under the eyelid. Use the following procedures to expose the upper eyelid and remove a particle from it:

- wash your hands thoroughly.

- seat the person facing a good light. Stand beside the person. Steady the head and ask the person to look down.

- place an applicator stick or a matchstick at the base of the upper lid and press the lid gently backwards.

- grasp the upper eyelashes between the thumb and index finger. Draw the lid away from the eye, up and over the applicator stick and roll the applicator back. That will turn the eyelid outward and expose the underside.

- if the particle can be seen and it is not on the cornea or adhering to the eyeball remove it with the moist corner of a facial tissue or clean cloth.

- gently replace the upper eyelid in its proper position.

- if pain persists after removal, obtain medical aid.

REMOVING A PARTICLE FROM THE LOWER EYELID

Use the following procedures to expose the lower eyelid and remove a loose particle from it:

- wash your hands thoroughly.

- place the person facing a light.

- stand in front and gently draw the lower eyelid downwards and away from the eyeball while the person rolls the eye upward. This may expose the particle. Wipe it away with the moist corner of a facial tissue or clean cloth.

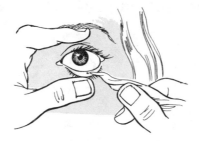

Fig. 18-4. Removal of a particle from the lower lid.

REMOVING A PARTICLE FROM THE EYEBALL

To locate particles on the eyeball, shine a light across the eye, not directly into it. The light will often cast a shadow of the particle, showing its location. If the particle is loose and it is not on the cornea, remove it with the moist corner of a facial tissue or clean cloth.

EMBEDDED OBJECTS

Foreign bodies that become embedded in the eye or in the soft tissue near the eye should be removed only by a physician. Give first aid as follows:

- lay the casualty down and support the head to reduce movement.

- place a dressing around the embedded object and cover with a paper cup or cone to prevent movement and to keep it from being driven further into the eye.

- secure the cup, cone or dressings with tape, ensuring that there is no pressure on the embedded object.

- Immobilize the head to prevent movement.

- transport the person on a stretcher to medical aid.

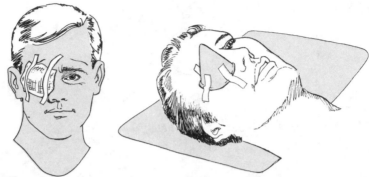

Fig. 18-5. Eye dressing.   Fig. 18-6. Protecting an eye with
                                          an embedded object.

LACERATIONS AND CONTUSIONS

Lacerations of the eyelids and soft tissue surrounding the eye are serious because there may be injury to the eyeball. If the eyeball is not damaged, vision should not be impaired, but lacerations of the eyeball frequently cause damage to eyesight.

Blows from blunt objects may cause contusions (bruises) and damage the bones that surround and protect the eyes. Such blows may also rupture blood vessels of the eye and damage internal structures, causing loss of vision.

Wounds from sharp objects penetrating the eyeball are serious because of the internal damage they may cause and the infection they may produce.

Lacerated eyelids usually bleed profusely because of their rich blood supply. A dressing on the area will usually control bleeding. Never apply pressure to the eyeball. This may force fluid out of the eyeball and cause irreparable damage to the eye.

Give first aid for all lacerations and contusions as follows:

- lay the person down and support the head.

- close the eyelid and cover the eye with an eye or gauze pad, secured lightly with a bandage or adhesive strips.

- immobilize the head to prevent unnecessary movement.

- obtain medical aid or transport the casualty on a stretcher.

EXTRUDED EYEBALL

A severe injury may thrust the eyeball out of its socket. Do not replace the eye in its socket. Cover the eye gently with a moist dressing and a protective cone. Place the casualty face up on a stretcher with the head immobilized for transportation to medical aid. Serious injury could result if the person is not kept quiet and is not moved carefully by stretcher.

CHEMICAL BURNS

The eyes can be injured by corrosive chemicals (acids or alkalies) in either liquid or solid form. Casualties normally suffer intense pain and an intolerance to light. Medical aid is required urgently.

The aim of first aid is to eliminate and dilute the chemical immediately by flooding the eye with water. A chemical powder, such as lime, should be brushed away, and then the corrosive solids flushed out of the eye for a period of at least 10 minutes.

Proper eye irrigation equipment should be kept near at hand when there is a high risk of eye injury from chemicals. Workers in these areas should practise locating these facilities blindfolded. If such equipment is not available, use one of the following methods:

- sit or lay the person down with the head tilted back and turned slightly toward the injured side. Cover the uninjured eye. Flush the injured eye with tepid or cool water. Since pain may make it difficult for the person to keep the eye open, you should gently force the lids apart so that the substance can be washed out. Milk may be used if water is not available.

- hold the person's head under gently running water. In an emergency, a drinking fountain, a garden hose or a shower can be used for eye irrigation.

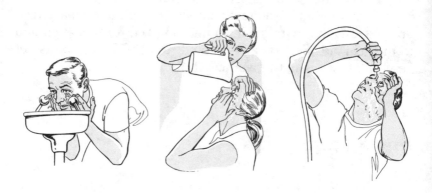

Fig. 18-7. Emergency methods of irrigating the eye.

After flushing, cover the injured eye with dressings and arrange for immediate medical aid. If both eyes are injured, cover the eye that is more seriously injured. If the casualty is more comfortable with both eyes coverd, cover both eyes.

It is recommended to only cover the more seriously injured eye to avoid the psychological stress that the casualty suffers when blinded by covering both eyes. If both eyes must be covered due to serious injury in both eyes, (e.g. intense light burn from arc welding, see next page) reassure the casualty often by explaining what is being done.

THERMAL BURNS

When a person suffers burns of the face from a fire, the eyes usually close rapidly because of the heat. This is a natural reflex that protects the eyes. However, the eyelids remain exposed and may be burned. Burned eyelids requires special care. As a first aid measure, cover the eyelids with moist, cool dressings and transport the person to medical aid immediately.

BURNS FROM INTENSE LIGHT

Direct or reflected sunlight, arc welders flash, infrared rays or laser beams can injure the retina, the light-sensitive portion of the eye. These injuries may not be painful at first, but may become very painful 3 to 5 hours after exposure. Permanent damage to vision may result.

If the casualty complains of a burning sensation in the eyes caused by an earlier exposure to bright light, cover both eyes with thick, moist pads and tape them in place to exclude light and cool the eyes. Reassure the casualty as he is now blinded by the pads and the bandages. Transport the casualty to medical aid.

Notes

CHAPTER 19

COLD EXPOSURE AND INJURIES

Exposure to cold can injure the surface of the body by causing local tissue damage. It can also cause generalized body-cooling called hypothermia, which can be fatal. Factors contributing to cold injury are:

● temperature of the environment;

● velocity of the wind;

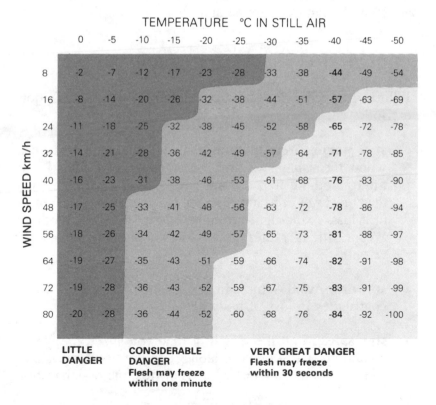

TEMPERATURE °C IN STILL AIR

WIND SPEED km/h	0	-5	-10	-15	-20	-25	-30	-35	-40	-45	-50
8	-2	-7	-12	-17	-23	-28	-33	-38	**-44**	-49	-54
16	-8	-14	-20	-26	-32	-38	-44	-51	**-57**	-63	-69
24	-11	-18	-25	-32	-38	-45	-52	-58	**-65**	-72	-78
32	-14	-21	-28	-36	-42	-49	-57	-64	**-71**	-78	-85
40	-16	-23	-31	-38	-46	-53	-61	-68	**-76**	-83	-90
48	-17	-25	-33	-41	48	-56	-63	-72	**-78**	-86	-94
56	-18	-26	-34	-42	-49	-57	-65	-73	**-81**	-88	-97
64	-19	-27	-35	-43	-51	-59	-66	-74	**-82**	-91	-98
72	-19	-28	-36	-43	-52	-59	-67	-75	**-83**	-91	-99
80	-20	-28	-36	-44	-52	-60	-68	-76	**-84**	-92	-100

LITTLE DANGER

CONSIDERABLE DANGER
Flesh may freeze within one minute

VERY GREAT DANGER
Flesh may freeze within 30 seconds

Fig. 19-1. Windchill.

- age and physical condition of the person;

- degree of protection by clothing or covering.

Windchill index is the result of the wind on still-air temperature that magnifies its cooling effect on exposed human skin. For example, a still-air temperature of − 10°C (+ 14°F) poses little danger, but the same temperature in a wind of 48 kilometres per hour produces a chilling effect of − 33°C (− 27°F) ! It can be seen on the chart that this poses considerable danger of freezing.

When the body is exposed to dangerously low temperatures, cold injuries such as hypothermia and frostbite may occur. Repeated exposure to even mildly cold, damp conditions can result in chilblain and immersion foot.

PREVENTION OF COLD INJURIES

Injuries from cold need not occur if simple safety precautions are followed:

- **stay warm.** Wear clothing that will maintain body heat without causing sweating. Several layers of light loose-fitting clothing trap air and have greater protective value than one layer of heavy clothing. Cover your head to reduce heat loss. Avoid tight-fitting jewellery, shoes and clothing. Wear mittens rather than gloves for maximum finger warmth.

- **stay dry.** Avoid wetness from sweating, rain or snow which contributes to loss of body heat.

- **stay safe.** Limit the length of time you spend in extreme conditions and do not go alone. Use the "buddy system" and check one another for signs of frostbite or exhaustion.

- **avoid fatigue.** Rest periodically in sheltered areas.

- **eat high-energy foods.** Take easily converted high energy food, such as raisins and nuts, to maintain your energy level.

- **avoid tobacco and alcohol.** Nicotine affects blood vessels and alcohol will give a false impression of rewarming — both contributing to cold injury.

GENERAL RULES OF FIRST AID FOR COLD INJURIES

Observe the following general rules of first aid for cold injuries:

- shelter the casualty from the cold and provide warmth and hot drinks;

- loosen tight clothing and remove tight boots as well as tight gloves, and rings;

- remove wet clothing and replace with dry, warm clothing.

- protect the face, hands or feet with warm dry coverings or by applying heat from your own body;

- when it is necessary to bandage frozen areas or blisters, ensure that the bandages are placed lightly in position;

- obtain medical aid as quickly as possible.

There are precautions which should be observed in the care of cold injuries:

- do not thaw a frozen limb unless the casualty can remain warm and medical aid is not available.

- do not apply direct heat.

- do not apply snow or cold water to the frozen area.

- do not rub a frozen area because frozen tissue cells contain ice crystals that can cut or destroy the tissue.

- do not rub the extremities or cause the casualty to un-necessarily move. This will cause cold blood from the extremities to flow to the inner body, further reducing core temperature.

- do not aggravate the injury — treat injured parts very gently to prevent further tissue damage.

If thawing a frozen part is necessary, use warm water baths at a temperature of 40°C (104°F). Warmer water will cause extreme pain.

HYPOTHERMIA

Hypothermia is body temperature below normal that most frequently develops from exposure to abnormally low temperatures. During early exposure, the body will attempt to conserve heat by drawing it away from the extremities to the body core to protect the vital organs. Shivering is the body's effort to generate heat to replace that which has been lost at the body surfaces. Continued exposure eventually drops core temperature below normal and threatens life. Even though a person has been taken out of a cold environment, core temperature will continue to drop until cooling is stopped and body heat is replaced.

Hypothermia can develop as the result of:

- immersion in cold water or exposure to cool air in water-soaked clothing. The severity of hypothermia will depend on factors such as the water and air temperature, the length of exposure and the circumstances of the accident.

- prolonged exposure to low environmental temperatures, even indoors in poorly heated houses. The elderly and infants are particularly susceptible. Persons who are injured or are in ill health are at high risk. Susceptibility is increased, even in the young healthy person, by fatigue and the use of drugs and alcohol.

As hypothermia progresses, it causes increased loss of consciousness, and a slowing of the pulse and respiration. The stages of hypothermia can be recognized by these signs, as illustrated in Fig. 19-2. Hypothermia may be accompanied by frostbite if the temperature is below freezing.

Signs and Symptoms

The signs and symptoms of hypothermia are progressive, going through states of mild, moderate and severe, indicating decreasing levels of core temperature. These stages are not clear-cut, but they may be recognized by changing signs and symptoms. Hypothermia in the initial stages can be reversed if first aid is given promptly. In the advanced stages first aid becomes more difficult and may, in some cases, be dangerous. Severe hypothermia can be fatal. Recognize these early signs:

- pulse in the normal range;

- respirations in the normal range;

- appearance and behaviour — shivering and slurred speech;

- level of consciousness — conscious, but withdrawn.

As core temperature drops to below 32°C (90°F), signs progressively deteriorate;

- pulse becomes slow and weak;

- respirations become slow and shallow;

- appearance and behaviour — casualty lacks coordination, stumbles and shivers violently,

- level of consciousness — casualty may be irrational, confused and sleepy.

A further drop of core temperature to below 27°C (81°F) causes:

- pulse to be weak, irregular or absent;

- respirations to be slow or absent;

- shivering to stop, and loss of consciousness — coma.

SIGNS AND SYMPTOMS	PROGRESSIVE STAGES OF HYPOTHERMIA		
	MILD	MODERATE	SEVERE
Body core temperature	35°C to 32°C	32°C to 27°C	below 27°C
Pulse	normal range	slow and weak	weak, irregular or absent
Respirations	normal range	slow and shallow	slow or absent
Appearance and behaviour	shivering, slurred speech	stumbling, violent shivering	shivering stops
State of consciousness	conscious, but withdrawn	sleepy, confused, irrational	unconsciousness

Fig. 19-2. Signs and symptoms of hypothermia.

FIRST AID FOR HYPOTHERMIA

The aims of first aid for hypothermia are to:

- prevent further loss of body heat;

- improve the body heat and circulation.

Depending on the circumstances in which the person is found, the distance from medical aid and the length and extent of exposure, all or some of the following actions should be taken:

- handle the casualty gently;

- remove the casualty from cold water, snow or a poorly-heated dwelling;

- provide shelter from wind, snow or rain, and protection from the cold or wet ground;

- replace wet clothing with dry clothing;

- provide warmth to prevent further body cooling.

Reflected heat from a campfire, wrapping the casualty in a warmed sleeping bag, applying a rescuer's body heat by huddling are recommended. Skin-to-skin contact in the area of the chest, neck, armpits and groin is a most effective way of supplying warmth. Application of direct heat, such as hot-water bottles or hot baths is not recommended.

If the person is conscious, give warm, sweet drinks to help maintain the blood sugar level to provide energy.

When heat loss has been rapid, as in water immersion, or exposure to cold has been prolonged, body temperature will drop from its normal value of 37°C (98.6°F) to 32°C (89.6°F) or lower. Shivering may be violent, indicating moderate hypothermia. Every effort must be made to prevent further loss of body heat and to move the casualty to a medical facility for controlled rewarming and professional care. Handle this casualty as gently as possible to avoid disturbing heart rhythm.

The casualty in severe hypothermia will have stopped shivering, probably be unconscious, show no signs of breathing and have no detectable pulse. Do not assume that this casualty is dead. Victims of hypothermia have been successfully revived after long periods with no apparent breathing or pulse.

Artificial Respiration – Hypothermia

If there are no signs of breathing, start artificial respiration by a direct method and ventilate at a rate appropriate for the age of the casualty. Indirect methods require physical movement of the casualty and, if at all possible, should not be used because this may seriously affect heart rhythm.

Check the carotid pulse carefully for up to two minutes to detect what may be a very slow, weak pulse. Any sign of a pulse, no matter how weak, indicates that the heart is beating — do not start CPR.

Cardiopulmonary Resuscitation – Hypothermia

If a pulse cannot be detected and CPR rescuers are available, you must decide whether or not to begin chest compressions in addition to lung ventilations. Remember that CPR, once started, must be continued without interruption until hand over to medical aid. Consider the following factors in making your decision:

1. Are the rescuers themselves in a mild state of hypothermia or at risk of hypothermia?

2. Are the rescuers physically able to carry out CPR for the length of time required to reach medical aid?

3. Is the estimated time until medical aid is reached so long (more than one hour) that CPR cannot reasonably be maintained?

If it appears that CPR cannot be continued uninterrupted, it should not be started. Get the casualty to medical aid quickly, being as gentle as possible, while continuing lung ventilations. If CPR can be maintained until hand over to medical aid, give ventilations and chest compressions at an appropriate rate for the age of the casualty.

FROSTBITE AND FREEZING

Frostbite may be superficial, when only the skin and tissues just beneath the skin are affected, or it may be deep, when deep tissues are frozen and may be destroyed.

Frostbite is progressive. If superficial frostbite is identified early, tissues may not be damaged and gradual warming of the frozen part of the body may prevent more serious injury.

SUPERFICIAL FROSTBITE

Superficial frostbite usually affects the ears, face, fingers or toes. It appears as a sudden whiteness. In early stages, it is painless and may not be noticed by the person affected. As freezing progresses, the skin takes on a white, waxy appearance and is numb and firm to the touch, but the tissues beneath it are soft and resilient.

If frostbite is more severe and affects tissues beneath the outer layer of skin, there may be enough tissue damage and fluid seepage to cause blistering.

Gradual rewarming is the recommended first aid for superficial frostbite. It can be accomplished by the firm steady pressure of a warm hand, by breathing on the frostbitten part, or by placing the frostbitten area in close contact with a warm area of your own body, such as the armpit or the groin. This treatment may be all that is required.

DEEP FROSTBITE

Deep frostbite is a serious injury, usually affecting the hands and feet. The frozen part appears white and waxy, and is cold and hard to the touch. The person with deep frostbite requires immediate medical attention. If the feet are affected, transport on a stretcher. However, walking a reasonable distance on frostbitten feet to get medical aid is not likely to cause much harm provided that the feet have not been thawed.

CHILBLAIN

Chilblain results from repeated exposure to cold temperatures for prolonged periods. This cold injury results in a red, swollen and itchy area, usually on the fingers or toes. This may recur in the same area during cold weather. There is no first aid for chilblain, except to prevent recurrence by protecting the injured area when exposure to cold is unavoidable.

IMMERSION FOOT

Immersion foot is caused by the wet cooling of the feet, over an extended period, at temperatures above freezing. It is most prevalent in persons who spend long periods with their feet in cool water and mud.

Immersion foot can be prevented by keeping the feet dry. Carrying spare wool socks in a warm dry place, such as inside the jacket, and changing them often will help prevent the condition.

Initially, the feet are cold, swollen and waxy, and may be numb. After warming, they may become red, swollen and hot, and blisters may occur. In advanced stages of immersion foot, gangrene may develop.

First aid consists of removing wet footwear, warming the cold extremities and preventing infection. Medical aid is required.

Notes

CHAPTER 20

HEAT EXPOSURE AND ILLNESSES

TEMPERATURE CONTROL

Normal body temperature is 37°C (98.6°F). A healthy person, acclimatized to his environment, can maintain a normal temperature by conserving heat in the cold and by dissipating heat when it is hot. When a person is in poor health or is exposed to extreme heat, maintaining a temperature balance stresses the body. Prolonged exposure to extremes of heat may cause one or more of the following heat illnesses — heat cramps, heat exhaustion and heat stroke. While each of these heat disorders is different and has different effects on the body, the rules for their prevention are much the same.

PREVENTION

A healthy, fit person adapts more readily to a hot climate than a person who is unfit or in poor health, but each needs to moderate physical activities, maintain body fluids and guard against overexposure to avoid heat disorders.

Replace fluids lost by sweating to prevent heat cramps. Drinking water containing a small amount of salt is recommended. Mix 5 mL of table salt (about 1 level teaspoon) to a litre of water to make a 0.5% salt solution. Keeping fit and adjusting gradually to a hot climate helps to avoid heat exhaustion. Avoiding overexposure to extremely hot sun and wearing head protection in such an environment prevents heatstroke.

HEAT CRAMPS

Heat cramps are painful muscle spasms, usually of the legs and abdominal muscles, that occur with vigorous exercise and profuse sweating in a hot environment. This condition is not serious and is usually reversed by first aid measures.

Signs and symptoms

The most notable signs and symptoms of a person in heat cramps are excessive sweating and muscular spasms of the extremities and the abdomen.

FIRST AID

Remove the casualty with cramps from the hot environment and place him at rest in a cool place. Give the conscious casualty slightly salted water to drink. One glass (250 mL) of 0.5% saline solution is recommended (5 mL of salt to 1 L of water = 1 tsp of salt to 1 quart of water = 0.5%). A second glass may be given after ten minutes if cramps persist. If cramps are not relieved, do not give more water to drink. There may be a more serious condition and medical aid is needed.

HEAT EXHAUSTION

Heat exhaustion, also called heat prostration, occurs when excessive sweating causes a depletion of body fluids and when conditions prevent the evaporation of sweat to cool the body. Strenuous work in an area of high humidity and wearing heavy clothing in a warm climate are common causes.

Signs and symptoms

A casualty of heat exhaustion may show some or all of the following signs and symptoms:

- **temperature** may range from slightly below to slightly above normal (the skin may feel cool or slightly warm to the touch);

- **pulse,** weak and rapid;

- **respirations,** rapid and shallow;

- **consciousness** — casualty may complain of blurred vision, dizziness and headache and lose consciousness;

- **appearance** — pale, skin cold and clammy;

- **muscular reaction** — cramps of the extremities and abdomen, nausea and vomiting.

FIRST AID

First aid for heat exhaustion is a combination of procedures for the care of heat cramps and shock:

- place the person at rest, lying down in a cool place with the feet and legs elevated.

- loosen tight clothing at the neck and waist — remove excessive clothing.

- give the fully conscious casualty slightly salted water (0.5% salt solution) to drink to replace body fluids. Give as much as the casualty will take.

- place the unconscious person in the recovery position.

- monitor breathing closely.

- transport to medical aid.

HEATSTROKE

Prolonged exposure in a hot, humid, poorly ventilated environment puts excessive stress on the body as it attempts to cool itself. **Classic heatstroke** occurs when the body's temperature control mechanism fails; sweating ceases and body temperature rises rapidly. **Exertional heatstroke** occurs as a result of heavy physical exertion in high temperatures; sweating continues, but again, body temperature rises rapidly. Heatstroke can result in permanent damage or death if first aid is not given immediately. Medical aid is needed urgently.

Signs and symptoms

The heatstroke casualty will show the following signs and symptoms:

● **temperature** markedly elevated, reaching 42°C to 44°C (108°F to 110°F);

● **pulse** rapid and full becomes weaker;

● **respiration** noisy;

● **consciousness** — headache, dizziness, restlessness, convulsions, progressing to unconsciousness and coma;

● **appearance** — skin flushed, hot and either dry or wet;

● **muscular reaction** — convulsions, nausea and vomiting.

Body temperature and the appearance of the skin are the two signs that will distinguish heatstroke from heat exhaustion. Body temperature in heat exhaustion is near normal and the skin is moist and cold. The extremely high body temperatures and flushed, hot skin (may be dry or wet) in heatstroke indicate the need for immediate first aid to prevent brain damage and to save the person's life.

	HEAT CRAMPS	HEAT EXHAUSTION	HEATSTROKE
Temperature	Normal	May be above or below normal	Elevated – as high as 44°C (111°F)
Pulse	Weak and regular	Weak and rapid	Rapid and full becoming weaker
Respiration	Normal	Rapid and shallow	Noisy
Consciousness	Conscious	Headache, blurred vision, dizziness and loss of consciousness	Headache, dizziness, restlessness, unconsciousness and coma.
Skin Appearance	Excessive sweating	Pale, cold and clammy	Flushed, hot and either dry or wet
Muscular Reaction	Spasms – extremities and abdomen	Spasms – extremities and abdomen	Convulsions, nausea and vomiting

Fig. 20-1. Heat illnesses – signs and symptoms.

FIRST AID

Lowering body temperature is the most urgent first aid for heatstroke. The casualty's life depends on how quickly this can be done. Proceed as follows:

- remove the person to a cool, shaded place.

- remove any excess clothing.

- place the person in a cool bath or sponge with cold water, particularly the armpits, neck, head and groin area. As an alternative, the casualty may be covered with wet sheets over which cool air from a fan is directed.

- place the person in the recovery position after body temperature has been reduced.

- monitor body temperature closely after it has been lowered.

- monitor breathing.

- transport to medical aid in a car or ambulance in which the air has been cooled.

CHAPTER 21

BURNS

Burns are injuries to the skin and other tissues caused by heat, radiation and chemicals. Scalds are burns caused by moist heat, such as hot liquids and steam. Burns are a leading cause of injury in the home, particularly of the elderly and the very young. The extreme pain and intense suffering caused by burns should be sufficient to ensure that all safety precautions are taken to prevent a burn accident.

PREVENTION

Consider what may happen to members of your family if conditions in your home are unsafe. Think of the consequences and take steps to prevent accidental burns. WHAT IF . . .

- water tank thermostats are set higher than 54°C (129°F) and the hot water tap is accidentally opened?

- hot water is run first in a bathtub before cold water is added?

- pot handles extend over the edge of the stove where children may reach them?

- a teething child is allowed to chew on an electric cord?

- children or elderly persons wear clothing of flammable materials, such as brushed cotton or rayon?

- an elderly person wears loose-fitting clothing near open flames?

- members of your family smoke in bed?

- smoke alarms are not installed or are not in operating condition?

- a fire evacuation plan for your home has not been prepared or practised?

EFFECTS OF BURNS

The skin protects the body from bacterial invasion, helps to control body temperature and retains body fluids (see chap. 2). Injury to the skin from burns and scalds can cause the loss of these functions and is considered to be a serious injury if damage is extensive.

The effects of burns and scalds depend on several important factors which can be determined by:

- the **amount of the body surface** that is burned.

- **the location of the burn.** For example, burns about the face may interfere with breathing and those of the groin area can result in serious infection.

- the **degree** of the burn, that is, the depth to which the skin and tissues have been injured;

- the **age, physical and medical condition** of the casualty. Even small burns may be critical in elderly or infirm persons and in small children.

Four major types of burns are:

- **thermal,** caused by fire, contact with hot objects, or steam;

- **corrosive,** caused by strong chemicals, such as acids or alkalies;

- **electrical,** caused by electric current or lightning;

- **radiation,** caused by excessive exposure to the sun, X-ray radiation, or radioactive material.

For first aid purposes, burns may be classified according to their depth, as follows:

- **first degree** burns are limited to the most superficial layer of the skin and cause reddening of the skin;

- **second degree** burns extend to the deeper layers of the skin and cause blisters with redness;

- **third degree** burns destroy the entire depth of the skin down to the fatty tissue, resulting in pale, dry and white skin, or brown and charred skin. There is less pain because the nerve endings in the skin have been destroyed, but a greater risk of infection because the skin has been destroyed.

Other more severe burns involve destruction through all the structures including the bone.

COMPLICATIONS OF BURNS

Burns are frequently complicated by conditions that result from the destruction of body tissue. These conditions are:

- **shock,** caused by pain and the loss of whole blood or plasma to surrounding tissue.

- **infection,** a serious threat when the skin is burned and underlying tissues are exposed.

- **breathing problems,** common in casualties with severe facial burns, who may have inhaled hot smoke or fumes, damaging the airway and lungs.

- **swelling,** particularly if the burned area is constricted by tight clothing or jewellery.

FIRST AID FOR THERMAL BURNS

For surface burns, first aid is to:

- **immerse the burned part** immediately in ice water to relieve pain and to reduce swelling and blistering. Place cold packs, ice or wet cloths on the burned area if immersion is not possible.

- **remove anything that is constrictive,** such as rings, bracelets or footwear, before swelling begins.

- **cover the burn** with a clean, preferably sterile, lint-free dressing, such as facial tissue.

Take particular care when giving first aid for burns to avoid causing further injury and contaminating the wound. Therefore:

- do not apply lotions, ointments or oily dressings;

- do not break blisters;

- do not breathe, cough over or touch the burned area;

- do not remove clothing that is stuck to the burned area.

For more serious burns, arrange for medical aid and give additional first aid as follows:

- monitor breathing and give artificial respiration if needed (see chap. 7);

- cover the burned area lightly with a clean, preferably sterile, lint-free dressing or facial tissue;

- take care of other immediate life-threatening injuries;

- treat for shock (see chap. 10);

- arrange for immediate transportation to a medical facility.

FIRST AID FOR CHEMICAL BURNS

Burns from corrosive chemicals, such as strong acids or alkalies, are always serious. Corrosive chemicals will continue to burn as long as they remain on the skin. To minimize injury, remove the chemical immediately. First aid for chemical burns is to:

- immediately flush liquid chemicals with water. Do not wait for clothing to be removed. Flood the area while removing clothing, and continue flooding until the chemical has been completely washed away. If it is a dry chemical such as lime, brush it off before flushing with water.

- continue first aid as for a thermal burn after the chemical has been washed away. Cover the burn with a clean dressing and obtain medical aid.

Do not use chemical neutralizers such as vinegar, soda or alcohol in first aid for any chemical burn unless advised to do so by a physician.

First aid procedures for injuries from specific chemicals, such as liquid sulfur, may vary from these general rules and are beyond the scope of this manual. You must familiarize yourself with the chemicals in use in your work environment and learn the recommended first aid for injuries which they might cause.

First aid for chemical burns to the eyes is decribed in chapter 18.

FIRST AID FOR ELECTRIC BURNS

Burns from electric current may be more serious than they appear because of the life-threatening injuries that may accompany them. Electric current passing through the body frequently disrupts heart action and breathing. A person who receives a serious electric shock may be thrown violently resulting in fractures and dislocations.

Shut off the current or remove the casualty from danger. Then proceed quickly with first aid as follows:

● check for breathing and give artificial respiration if needed. Check circulation and give cardiopulmonary resuscitation if a pulse cannot be felt and if you are trained in CPR (see chaps. 7 and 8).

When breathing is restored:

● give first aid for the entry and exit burns by covering them with a dry, clean dressing;

● immobilize fractures and dislocations;

● obtain medical aid.

RADIATION BURNS

Although there is no specific first aid for radiation burns from X-rays or radioactive material, you can treat minor sunburn. Cover the burn area with a wet towel, using a solution of 10mL of salt to a litre of water (a tablespoon of salt to a quart of water). This soothes and cools the skin. Commercial ointments and creams may also be used. If blisters are broken, there is a grave risk of infection and the casualty should be seen by a physician.

CHAPTER 22

POISONS, BITES AND STINGS

POISONS

A poison is any substance that can cause illness or death when it is absorbed into the body. An antidote is a substance that acts against a poison to offset its effects.

PREVENTION

Most accidental poisonings can be prevented if the presence of poisons is recognized and proper care is taken in their use and storage. The average household has as many as 250 poisonous substances[1] used in medicines, in cleaning products, for plant care, or for hobbies and crafts. By law, all consumer products must be labelled to show their chemical content, precautions for use and storage, and specific first aid in case of accidental poisoning. Workplace Hazardous Materials Information System (WHMIS) regulations require that hazardous chemicals in the workplace be identified and that Material Safety Data Sheets (MSDS) describe the precautions in their use and the first aid to be given for accidental overexposure *(see chap. 1 – Principles and Practices of Safety Oriented First Aid)*.

To prevent accidental poisoning:

- keep household and drug products in their original containers for identification, so that instructions will be available each time they are used, and so that label information will be at hand in case of poisoning.

---

[1]*How to Poison-Proof Your Home*. Health and Welfare Canada, Ottawa, 1984.

- read label instructions on containers before using, and follow the directions carefully. Read, understand and follow MSDS instructions for industrial chemicals.

- do not put harmful products in food or drink containers.

- destroy foods which you believe may be contaminated.

- flush unused portion of medicines down the toilet and dispose of empty containers.

- ventilate areas where toxic chemicals are used—open windows and doors so tht fumes do not become concentrated.

- operate gas combustion engines where there is good ventilation, preferably outdoors.

- prevent medication errors by carefully checking the five *RIGHTS* for giving medicines—the *RIGHT MEDICINE*, the *RIGHT PERSON*, the *RIGHT DOSE*, the *RIGHT TIME*, the *RIGHT METHOD*.

- keep all harmful products out of the reach of children. Do not leave medications in a purse or on a night table where children can get at them.

- do not take medicines in front of children, because they may imitate you.

- when children need medicine, call it medicine and not candy.

- learn to identify poisonous plants, and warn children that plants may be poisonous.

- call the Poison Information Centre for prevention and first aid information in advance of going to an isolated area where you will be more than one hour away from a telephone.

HISTORY, SIGNS AND SYMPTOMS

Accidental poisoning may occur despite all reasonable precautions and when it does, act quickly but do not panic. Four basic facts should be known to give appropriate first aid for poisoning:

- **identify the poisonous substance.** Look for bottles, pills, containers or remnants of poisonous material, even vomitus, that can be used to identify the toxic agent.

- **determine the quantity taken.** Estimate, from the container's size, the number of pills or amount of chemical available and, from the remaining chemical or pills, how much of the poisonous substance may have been taken.

- **determine the route of entry into the body.** First aid will vary according to whether the substance was ingested into the stomach, inhaled into the lungs, absorbed through the skin, injected into the bloodstream, or taken by a combination of two or more of these.

- **determine the time elapsed** since the poisoning occurred.

Signs and symptoms may appear quickly or they may be delayed. If the history of the accident does not provide the information needed to identify the substance or the route of entry, look for signs and symptoms that may help in determining the route of entry:

- **ingested** poisons may cause nausea, abdominal cramps, vomiting and other gastrointestinal distress. They may discolour the lips and mouth, cause burns, or leave a distinctive odour on the breath.

- **inhaled** poisons usually affect the respiratory system and may affect the circulatory and central nervous systems. Early respiratory symptoms may include coughing, chest pain and rapid or difficult breathing. Carbon monoxide and

hydrogen sulphide poisoning will cause dizziness and headache in the early stages. Continued exposure to inhaled
poisons can lead to collapse and unconsciousness and eventually to respiratory and cardiac arrest.

● **absorbed** poisons may irritate the skin in the areas of
contact. They may have an immediate or delayed effect on
the central nervous system and subsequently on the respiratory and circulatory systems.

● **injected** poisons may irritate the skin at the point of entry,
but they are usually faster acting and have more widespread
effects on the central nervous system, with impairment of
the respiratory and circulatory systems.

FIRST AID FOR POISONING

You must act quickly. Do not waste time if the poison cannot
be readily identified. Call a Poison Information Centre or a
doctor and follow their advice on treatment. You should have
the telephone number of the local Poison Information Centre
readily available. If there is no centre in your area, call the
Ottawa centre anytime at 1-800-267-6351.

If a doctor or a Poison Information Centre cannot be reached
quickly, give first aid to eliminate the poison or reduce its
effects. Give first aid for the effects of the poison, but do not
delay getting the casualty to medical aid.

Eliminate the Poison or Reduce its Effects

Swallowed poisons should not be diluted. If the casualty is
conscious, wipe the casualty's face to remove any poison/cor-
rosive residue and rinse or wipe out the mouth, particularly if
a solid or powdered corrosive/poison is involved.

Never induce vomiting except on the advice of the Poison Information Centre or the physician. Corrosives will cause more burns when they are vomited and petroleum products may be aspirated into the lungs and cause severe chemical pneumonia.

Vomiting can be induced by giving syrup of ipecac under the direction of a physician or a Poison Information Centre. Sealed, one-dose bottles (14 mL) of syrup of ipecac are available at most pharmacies. At least two bottles should be kept in the home, but out of reach of children, for use in emergencies. You will usually be instructed to give a quantity of clear fluids to drink—water or juices (not milk)—following the administration of syrup of ipecac. Milk prevents the emetic action of ipecac and it should not be given to the casualty.

If you do not have ipecac, the Poison Information Centre may instruct you to induce vomiting by giving the conscious casualty 30-45 mL (2-3 tablespoons) of liquid dish detergent in 250 mL (8 oz.) of water to drink. Vomiting caused by gagging is usually ineffective. Never use salt or mustard to induce vomiting.

Inhaled poisons, such as gases, should be cleared from the lungs as quickly as possible. Move the casualty to fresh air and away from the source of the poison. Artificial respiration may be needed to get oxygen to the lungs if the casualty is not breathing.

Absorbable poisons, such as liquid or powdered chemicals (e.g. insecticides), must be removed from the skin as quickly as possible by flushing the affected area with large amounts of tepid water and then washing it with soap and water. Pay careful attention to hidden areas such as under the fingernails and in the hair.

Injected poisons should be contained near the injection site. Keep the casualty at rest and keep the affected limb at heart level to delay absorption. Flush the entry site to eliminate any surface poison.

First aid for the effects of poisoning should not delay transportation to medical aid. While awaiting transportation or en route to medical aid:

● monitor breathing, and administer mouth-to-mouth artificial respiration if needed. If poisonous/corrosive residue is in or around the mouth, an alternative method of artifical respiration should be used.

● ensure that the unconscious casualty is kept in the recovery position (see chap. 11);

● prevent further injury if the casualty develops convulsions;

● give first aid for shock (see chap. 10).

ANIMAL BITES

The bite of an animal usually causes a puncture wound or a laceration. These wounds should always be considered dangerous because infected saliva may have been carried into the wound.

Rabies

Rabies, a viral disease that can kill both animals and humans, is of particular concern here. The rabies virus can be transmitted by being bitten by a rabid animal, by handling a diseased animal or through a wound that has been infected with rabies.

Make sure to take all necessary precautions against infection when giving first aid to anyone who may have been exposed to rabies and in handling the live or dead animal involved. Scrub your hands thoroughly after contact and be especially careful if you have breaks in the skin—cuts or chapped hands. If an animal must be touched, wear gloves.

If the animal can be captured without risk, it should be kept for examination. If it must be killed, keep the head intact so that the brain can be examined to determine the presence of rabies.

Even if a person has been exposed to rabies, the disease can be prevented by immediate immunization. The immunization now being used for rabies consists of inoculations given in the muscle of the arm or leg and these are no more painful than a pinprick. This new method of immunization is much less painful than the previous one and there are fewer complications.

FIRST AID FOR ANIMAL BITES

The aims of first aid for animal bites are to remove as much of the contamination as possible from the wound area, to control bleeding and to get medical aid. Give first aid as follows:

- allow the wound to bleed. Some bleeding helps to cleanse the wound. Control bleeding if it is severe.

- wash the wound with antiseptic soap or detergent and rinse with running water as hot as the person can bear, or apply a salt solution.

- apply a dressing and bandage and transport to medical aid.

SNAKEBITE

The rattlesnake is the only poisonous snake found in the wild in Canada. Varieties of this snake are found in parts of British Columbia, Alberta, Saskatchewan, and Ontario. They are not numerous, and snakebites are not common. A rattlesnake bite leaves two puncture holes in the skin, and a burning sensation is felt in the area. This is followed by swelling and discolouration, severe pain, weakness, sweating, nausea, vomiting and chills. Breathing may be affected.

The aim of first aid is to prevent absorption of the venom and obtain medical aid as quickly as possible. Therefore:

- place the casualty at rest and steady and support the affected limb. Movement stimulates circulation and spreads poison through the body more quickly.

- calm and reassure the casualty; fear and apprehension may increase shock.

- flush the affected area with soapy water; do not cool or use ice packs.

- apply a constricting band (see below) and immobilize the limb.

- keep the limb level with the heart.

- transport to medical aid as quickly as possible.

Do not give alcohol to a snakebite casualty; it could make his condition worse. Do not attempt to suck out the venom with your mouth; it will be absorbed into your bloodstream through the mucous membrane of your mouth and you could become another casualty. Do not make cuts at the puncture site; they cause unnecessary tissue damage and infection.

CONSTRICTION FOR BITES AND STINGS

When a serious bite or sting occurs on a limb, a constricting band should be placed on the limb between the bite and the heart to slow the spread of the poison through the casualty's body. The recommended material for a constricting band is soft rubber tubing, however, a narrow triangular or elastic bandage may be used.

Place the constricting band 5 to 10 cm (2 to 4 in.) above the wound. **Do not tie the band too tight.** You should be able to slip two fingers under the band. If you see signs of loss of circulation below the band, the band must be loosened. Swelling will occur with this type of injury; therefore you must adjust the constricting band so it does not become too tight. Constricting bands should not be placed around a joint, or around the head, neck or trunk.

INSECT BITES AND STINGS

In most persons, an insect bite or sting causes only a painful swelling with redness and itching. Bee and wasp stings, however, may cause a severe allergic reaction in some people. Look for hives, swelling around the eyes and mouth, nausea and vomiting, and breathing difficulties. When these signs occur, obtain medical aid urgently.

Do not delay transporting the casualty to medical aid. If time permits, give first aid as follows:

● ask the person if they have medication which they take for such a reaction and help them to take prescribed medication if it is available.

● if the insect bite or sting is on a limb, place a constricting band above the bite site and keep the limb at heart level. Place the casualty in the recovery position or any position that makes breathing easier.

Provide first aid to the site of a bite or sting as follows:

● apply rubbing alcohol, a weak ammonia solution or a paste of bicarbonate of soda *(baking soda)* and water. Alcohol and ammonia should not be used near the eyes.

● when the stinger remains in the skin, remove it by carefully scraping it and its attached poison sac from the skin. Do not use tweezers or anything that may squeeze more poison into the body.

● if the sting is in the mouth, give the person a mouthwash of one teaspoonful of bicarbonate of soda to a glass of water or give him a piece of ice to suck. If there is swelling in the mouth, or if there is difficulty breathing, monitor the person closely. Get medical aid.

OTHER BITES

Leeches are found in swamps, ponds, lakes and stagnant water. Some feed on the warm blood of animals or humans. They make a tiny lesion in the skin, which may not be felt at the time. Once a leech has attached itself, attempts to remove it by force may not be successful and may increase the risk of infection.

First aid for lesions from leeches consists of:

- removing the leech by applying salt, a heated pin, a lighted match, a hot cigarette, kerosene, turpentine or oil to its body. This will cause the leech to detach itself from the skin and to fall off intact. Do not pull or scrape them off the skin.

- cleansing the area and relieving irritation with a solution of bicarbonate of soda or ammonia.

Ticks are found in abundance throughout the forests in some parts of Canada. They drop from the foliage onto animals and humans, biting through the skin and anchoring themselves to the tissue with barbed mouth parts. Poison from the tick may be harmful and the tick should be removed. If one tick is found, check your body and clothing thoroughly for others.

First aid for bites from ticks consists of:

- removing the embedded tick by grasping it as close to the casualty's skin as possible and pulling away from the skin with even, steady pressure. It is preferable to use tweezers for this manoeuvre. If fingers must be used, they should be covered with gloves or tissue paper. Keep the dislodged tick for later identification.

- cleansing the area to prevent infection. Following this, wash your hands.

- seeking medical aid because of the risk of disease transmission by the tick. The dislodged tick should be given to medical personnel for identification.

CHAPTER 23

WATER ACCIDENTS

Water accidents are always serious because they may result in drowning. Frequently they are complicated by other injuries such as fractures, wounds and hypothermia. Water accidents present special hazards to rescuers and First Aiders who must take care not to become casualties themselves.

PREVENTION

Most water accidents that occur during swimming, diving, boating, waterskiing and wind surfing can be prevented by observing the following water safety rules:

● learn to swim, swim only in safe or guarded areas, and do not swim alone;

● supervise others who are swimming, and fence off swimming pools to prevent unsupervised swimming;

● dive only in water where the depth, the bottom, and the current are known; avoid hyperventilation to increase the time under water because it will decrease the level of carbon dioxide in the blood, and could cause a blackout.

● do not swim to rescue a drowning person unless you are a good swimmer and are proficient in rescue techniques;

● wear a personal flotation device when boating and waterskiing; avoid the use of air mattresses, inner tubes, and inflatable water toys in deep water.

- do not stand in small boats and do not overload a boat;

- avoid the use of alcohol which may affect judgement and make water sports and other activities on the water more dangerous.

DROWNING

Drowning is defined as death by suffocation in water. In some drownings, the larynx goes into spasm, sealing the airway from the passages of the mouth and nose and the person stops breathing. The term "near-drowning" is used when there is survival after temporary suffocation by water.

RESCUE

Survival of a near-drowning casualty depends on speedy rescue and immediate first aid. The rescuer must use reasonable caution, to avoid becoming another drowning casualty. Some basic rules of water rescue are summed up in the words THROW, TOW, ROW and GO in that order:

- **THROW** flotation gear to the drowning person, using an inflated tire, a life jacket or even an oar to support the casualty.

- **TOW** the drowning person to land by rope or cable;

- **ROW** to the drowning person by boat, on a surfboard, on a plank or by using other flotation gear.

- **GO** to the drowning person by swimming, if you are qualified to do so. Only persons properly trained should attempt a swimming rescue.

FIRST AID FOR NEAR-DROWNING

First aid for near-drowning must not be delayed until the casualty is out of the water and on land. It must be started as soon as the casualty's face is clear of the water. Restore breathing immediately. This is the most important single requirement in the first aid for drowning. Trained rescuers should be able to start the following procedures while the person is still in the water:

- clear the airway of any obvious foreign matter;

- start direct artificial respiration if breathing does not return spontaneously (see chap. 7);

- treat the casualty as if there were a spinal injury, if there has been a diving, waterskiing, or boating accident, or if there are any other indications of neck or back injury (see chap. 16).

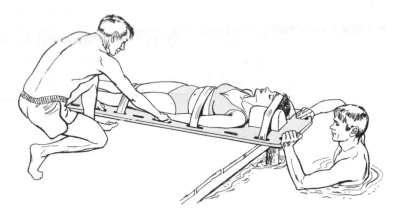

Fig. 23-1. Spine board or other flotation device.

A swimmer with a spinal injury is often found face down in the water. You must clear the face from the water as carefully as possible to avoid twisting the neck. The head and neck must be supported at all times while a flotation device is secured. Begin and maintain artificial respiration while the person is being taken from the water and until medical aid is obtained.

As soon as the casualty is on a firm surface, check for circulation by feeling for the carotid pulse (see chap. 5). If there is no pulse, begin cardiopulmonary resuscitation, if you are qualified to do so (see chap. 8). Artificial respiration or CPR must be administered continuously until the casualty recovers or is handed over to medical care.

Give first aid for hypothermia if needed (see chap. 19).

DIVING ACCIDENTS

An underwater diver may drown or suffer from hypothermia and the first aid is no different than for any victim of water accidents. However, the diver is exposed to other hazards in the water, related to pressure changes.

When a diver descends or ascends in water, the body is subjected to a wide range of pressure changes. These pressure changes act on air and other gases enclosed in body cavities such as the lungs, the middle ear and the sinuses. If the diver is in good health and dives with care, the body can adjust to the pressure changes. However, if the diver has a head cold or other respiratory problem, or if he makes his descent or ascent improperly, the trapped gases will contract or expand, and cause varying degrees of internal injury.

SIGNS AND SYMPTOMS

While you may not be able to evaluate diving injuries completely, it is important that you recognize when a diver is injured and take appropriate action. An injured diver may show some of these signs and symptoms:

● blotchy and itchy skin;

- froth, often bloody, from the mouth and nose;

- pain in the muscles and joints;

- severe toothache;

- breathing difficulties;

- dizziness, vomiting and inability to speak or see properly;

- paralysis and unconsciousness.

FIRST AID

Failure to recognize severe injuries that require immediate medical care can be dangerous. First aid is to:

- reassure;

- care for asphyxia (see chap. 7);

- care for shock (see chap. 10);

- obtain medical aid.

Diving partners, diving equipment and air tanks should accompany the casualty to the medical facility for evaluation.

Notes

CHAPTER 24

EMERGENCY CHILDBIRTH

An incident of emergency childbirth usually occurs when there is a sudden premature delivery or when the mother is prevented from getting to hospital for a full-term delivery. The aims of first aid for an emergency childbirth are to assist the mother in delivering the baby and to protect the mother and child until they can be transported to medical aid.

ANATOMY

A basic knowledge of the female reproductive system and its relationship to the unborn child will help you to give the assistance and protection required during an emergency delivery.

The **fetus** (unborn child) develops inside a fluid-filled membrane called the **amniotic sac.** This sac is contained within the **uterus,** the female organ in which the development of the fetus takes place. During its development, the fetus receives blood, oxygen and nourishment from the mother through the **placenta** and **umbilical cord.** The placenta is a large flat, spongy organ that is attached to the wall of the uterus and the umbilical cord connects it to the unborn child. Both of these organs are delivered along with the baby at birth. The **cervix** (neck of the uterus) is the opening through which the fetus will pass into the **vagina** (birth canal) as it is born.

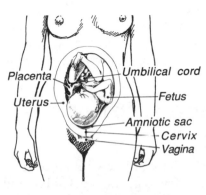

Fig. 24-1. Female reproductive system.

LABOUR – SIGNS AND SYMPTOMS

Labour is the process through which the body prepares itself to deliver a baby. Normally, the beginning of labour gives sufficient warning for the mother to be transported to a medical facility for delivery. The process of labour is in three stages and the first can be recognized by:

- contractions of the uterus, usually accompanied by pain;

- breaking of the amniotic sac and release of the fluid through the vagina;

- "bloody show" consisting of blood and mucus from the vagina.

Transport the mother to a medical facility during the early stages to avoid an incident of emergency childbirth.

IMMINENT DELIVERY – SIGNS AND SYMPTOMS

Contractions of the uterus become stronger, last longer and are more frequent as the time for delivery approaches. The mother may express a desire to move her bowels or she may know, from previous experience, that birth is imminent. The vaginal opening becomes distended and the baby's scalp will appear (crowning). These signs indicate the beginning of the second stage of labour.

ASSISTANCE TO THE MOTHER BEFORE DELIVERY

When the second stage of labour begins, there will not be time to transport the mother to hospital. Try to get medical aid or find another person to assist you, preferably a woman. Wash your hands thoroughly and gather the materials you will need to provide protection for the mother and child. Look for such articles as:

- clean towels to drape the mother and to receive and dry the newborn. Clean sheets, preferably flannel, may be used.

- a soft blanket in which to wrap the newborn;

- sanitary pads or other absorbent material to absorb vaginal bleeding after delivery;

- plastic bag with ties to hold the placenta and umbilical cord;

- soap, water and towels to wash your hands;

- sterile, narrow roller bandage or tape in case it is needed to tie off the cord.

Some of these items, such as diapers and receiving blankets, may be found in the materials that the mother had packed for the hospital.

Preparing the Mother for Delivery

During labour, the mother should have been placed in the position she found most comfortable, usually on her left side. When birth is imminent, place the mother on her back with knees bent and her head supported on pillows.

Cover the mother with sheets or towels so that she is not exposed unnecessarily and provide as much privacy as possible. Reassure the mother and try to appear calm and unhurried.

Draping the Birth Area

Place clean towels or a sheet under the mother's buttocks, extending between her thighs. Place a clean towel between the mother's legs on which to lay the newborn.

ASSISTING IN THE DELIVERY

The role of the First Aider in an emergency childbirth is to assist the mother in her efforts to deliver the baby and to protect the baby during and after delivery. Ensure safe handling of the newborn, but do not interfere with the natural birth process during the last stage of labour.

Normal Delivery

In a normal delivery, the baby's head will be presented first and it will turn to one side to allow passage of the shoulders through the vaginal opening. The baby's head can be injured if it is allowed to emerge too rapidly. Prevent rapid expulsion of the head by asking the mother to control her expulsion efforts while you gently restrain the baby's head with your hands. Allow the head to be expelled slowly. Once the head is delivered, the mother should be encouraged to continue her expulsion efforts.

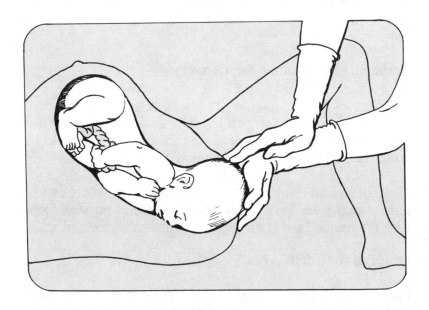

Fig. 24-2. Preventing rapid expulsion of the head.

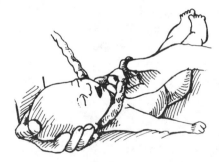

Fig. 24-3. Easing the cord from around the infant neck.

Gently support the head and body as the baby is delivered. If the cord is around the baby's neck ease it away either by passing it over the head or shoulders. Do not pull or exert force on the cord. There should be enough slack to allow you to clear the cord gently.

Breech Delivery

A breech presentation is when the baby's buttocks, knees or feet are presented first instead of the head. This is an infrequent but dangerous situation, even in ideal hospital surroundings. If the mother cannot be transported to medical aid, support the presenting part and encourage the mother's efforts to deliver the extremities, abdomen and thorax. At this point, but not before, apply gentle but firm traction while lifting (rotating) the baby towards the mother's abdomen. This will usually allow the baby's mouth and nose to come clear of the vagina.

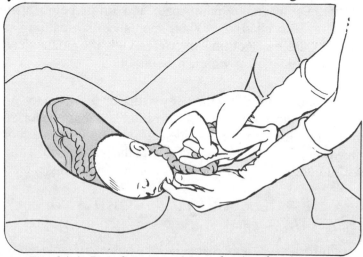

Fig. 24.4. Breech presentation – clearing the airway.

You may find the umbilical cord wrapped around the baby's neck. Gently ease it over the baby's head or allow it to slip over the baby's shoulders during delivery. If possible, note and record the time of birth.

Clearing the Airway

Wipe the baby's face with a clean cloth or tissue to clear the nose and mouth. All babies have fluid in the nose and throat. This must be drained immediately after delivery. One way of doing this is to position the baby with the lower body and feet slightly elevated. Newborns are covered with a slippery material called **vernix** that makes them difficult to hold. Use both hands with extreme care to hold the baby firmly but gently. Use the left hand to hold the feet with the index finger between the ankles, the thumb around one ankle, and the remaining fingers around the other. Support the back of the baby's head, neck and shoulders with the other hand. Lift the baby's legs and back slightly, just enough to allow drainage from the nose and mouth. Keep the baby at the same level as the mother's vagina.

Most babies will cry right away; the face becomes pink as they expand their lungs and begin breathing. If the baby does not start to breathe and remains pale and limp, begin artificial respiration (see chap. 7). When spontaneous breathing is restored, ensure that nothing interferes with the infant's airway, such as the blanket in which it is wrapped.

Keep the baby warm. Dry the baby with a clean warm towel and wrap in another warm towel or suitable clean material for warmth. Lay the baby on its side across the mother's abdomen facing away from the mother's face with the head down. This will assist drainage and allow you to monitor breathing.

CARE OF THE UMBILICAL CORD AND PLACENTA

The umbilical cord, which attaches the baby to the placenta, is a delicate organ with veins and arteries. The placenta is normally expelled from the mother within twenty minutes of the baby's birth. Gentle massage of the abdomen will hasten delivery of the placenta. However, there should not be any cause for alarm if the placenta is not expelled for some time. **Do not, under any circumstances, attempt to force delivery by pulling on the cord.** Care must be taken not to pull or put pressure on the umbilical cord at any time.

Let the placenta be delivered into a clean towel and protect it in a clean plastic bag. Ensure that all parts of the placenta and membranes are saved and taken to the medical facility with the mother.

Usually, the cord should not be tied or cut. However, if there is obvious bleeding from the placenta, tie the cord with a clean tape or heavy string 15 to 30cm (6 to 12 in.) from the baby's abdomen. Ordinary string or thread may cut the cord and should not be used.

Keep the placenta at the same level as the newborn. It may be enclosed in the newborn's blanket covering.

If medical aid will be delayed for more than 12 hours and the mother and baby are well, the umbilical cord can be tied and cut. First, check the cord for a pulse. If there is a pulse, do not cut the cord; wait for the pulsations to stop. When pulsations have stopped, tie or clamp the cord in two place approximately 7 cm (3 in.) apart positioned 15 to 30 cm (6 to 12 in.) from the baby's body. Cut the cord between the two clamps with a pair of scissors or a knife that has been sterilized. Check the end of the cord for bleeding periodically and control any bleeding that occurs.

CARE OF THE MOTHER

Some bleeding from the mother following expulsion of the placenta is normal. This can usually be controlled by firm massage of the uterus, which can be felt as a hard, round mass in the lower abdomen. Examine the skin between the anus and the vagina for lacerations and apply pressure to any bleeding tears. Apply sanitary pads to absorb bleeding. If bleeding is not controlled, elevate her feet and legs and transport to medical aid immediately.

Transfer the mother and child to medical aid as soon as possible with the mother on her back and the baby securely wrapped in the mother's arms. If there is likely to be some delay in moving the mother to a hospital, let the baby suck from the mother's breasts. This provides the baby with the first secretion of the breasts, which has a high proportion of immunizing antibodies.

Sucking also helps, by stimulation of the breasts, to tighten up the womb and prevent bleeding.

If bleeding from the vagina does not stop, continue to massage the abdomen and place the mother in the shock position (see chap. 10). Keep the mother and the baby warm to help prevent shock from worsening and transport to medical aid urgently.

REMEMBER

(1) Support the infant gently but firmly during the birth process.

(2) Ensure that the infant breathes and that an open airway is maintained.

(3) Dry the infant quickly and wrap for warmth.

(4) Do not cut the cord, nor pull on it. If there is bleeding from the cord or placenta, tie the cord with clean tape or heavy string 15 to 30cm (6 to 12 in.) from the infant's abdomen.

(5) Keep the mother and infant warm and comfortable. Place the infant next to the mother's skin.

(6) Transfer to medical aid as soon as possible.

CHAPTER 25

HEART DISEASE AND STROKE

HEART DISEASE

The heart receives its own blood supply, containing oxygen, through the coronary arteries. If these arteries become narrow or blocked, that part of the heart muscle supplied by them will stop functioning properly. The heart can usually continue to pump blood, even though part of its muscle does not function. However, if too much muscle function is lost, the heart will not circulate enough blood to provide for the needs of the body, and the heart itself will fail. Slow muscle deterioration may cause long-term physical incapacity; rapid muscle deterioration will result in shock and death.

HEART ATTACK – PREVENTION

There are some factors, over which one has little control, that make a person more susceptible to heart attacks. If there is a family history of heart disease, if you have had a previous heart attack, or if you are a diabetic, you are at high risk. Other risk factors, however, are created by unhealthy life-styles. Knowing the risk factors, avoiding life-styles that contribute to coronary heart disease, and adopting positive health attitudes can prevent the disease or retard its progress to give many years of healthy living.

RISK FACTORS

Take positive steps to reduce the risk of heart attack by following proper health counselling and by changing those factors that contribute to heart disease, such as cigarette smoking, high blood pressure, elevated blood cholesterol, overweight and stress.

Cigarette Smoking. Cigarette smokers put themselves at much higher risk of heart disease than non-smokers. However, the conditions caused by cigarette smoking are reversible and people who stop smoking usually drop back to the risk level of non-smokers.

Hypertension. High blood pressure is linked to stroke, kidney failure and heart failure. Blood pressure can be controlled if it is diagnosed. Therefore, it is important to have blood pressure checks done regularly so that treatment for hypertension can be started early in its development.

Cholesterol. Elevated blood cholesterol, another important factor in the progress of coronary artery disease, can be controlled if it is detected. Periodic physical examinations should include tests for blood cholesterol. Schedule a physical examination at least once a year, preferably in your birth month so that you do not forget.

Contributing Risk Factors. Obesity, lack of exercise and stress are all considered to be factors that contribute to the progress of coronary artery disease. Make a determined effort to follow your physician's counsel regarding weight control, exercise programs and stress reduction.

TYPES OF HEART PROBLEMS

The three most common heart problems requiring first aid are **angina pectoris, heart attack,** and **heart failure**. Although the signs and symptoms of each may help to identify the particular condition, first aid for all heart conditions is virtually the same. Persons with heart disease often carry medical identification, such as Medic-Alert, that gives information on medication.

ANGINA PECTORIS

Angina pectoris is chest pain caused by a decrease of blood supply to the heart muscle. The inside diameter of the arteries carrying blood to the heart becomes too narrow for an adequate supply of oxygen to reach the heart muscle when the heart is working harder than usual. Stress or over-exertion may cause the heart to work harder and this may bring on chest pain, which often spreads to the neck, shoulders, arms, elbows and the fingers. It usually lasts only seconds to minutes, and should be relieved by rest and medication.

Many people with angina are able to live normal lives by taking medication to increase the blood flow to the heart muscle.

HEART ATTACK

Heart attack (myocardial infarction) occurs when the blood flow in a coronary artery or in one of its branches is decreased or blocked. The casualty may deny that he is having a heart attack, but some or all of the following signs and symptoms may be observed:

- pain that may force the person to sit down or to seek support;

- pain, typically behind the sternum, that is severe, vise-like or crushing, though it may be milder and is sometimes misinterpreted as indigestion; the pain which may radiate into the upper limbs, throat and jaw, resembles the pain of angina except that rest and medication do not relieve it;

- fear and apprehension;

- pallor;

- nausea and sometimes vomiting;

- profuse sweating;

- dizziness;

- shortness of breath;

- shock or unconsciousness;

- cardiac arrest.

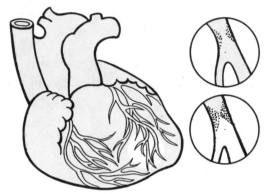

Fig. 25-1. Insufficient blood supply to the heart muscle.

HEART FAILURE

Heart failure occurs as a result of chronic heart disease, when the heart loses some of its ability to pump blood containing oxygen to the body. The signs and symptoms of heart failure are:

- inappropriate shortness of breath, especially when the person is exercising;

- shortness of breath when lying down flat;

- coughing bloodstained sputum;

- cyanosis (blueness around lips) nail beds, ears and other parts of the body;

- swelling of the ankles.

FIRST AID

First aid for all heart problems is aimed at reducing the work of the heart, preventing the person's condition from deteriorating and restoring circulation if necessary. Give first aid for a heart problem as follows:

- immediately call medical aid to the site or arrange for the person to be taken to the nearest medical facility;

- do not move the casualty unnecessarily;

- place him at rest in the most comfortable position, usually semisitting with the head and shoulders raised and supported;

- loosen tight clothing at the neck, chest and waist;

- reassure the person to lessen fear and anxiety;

- help the conscious casualty to take his prescribed medication;

- if breathing fails, begin artificial respiration immediately (see chap. 7); if the heart stops, give CPR if you are trained (see chap. 8).

The First Aider should search for medical identification that may give information about the person's condition.

STROKE

Stroke (cerebrovascular accident) is a condition in which a part of the brain ceases to function because of a shortage of oxygenated blood. A stroke may be caused by a ruptured blood vessel that is bleeding into the brain, or by a blockage in the circulation of blood to the brain.

A severe stroke may cause death; a less severe stroke may cause brain damage and impairment of certain body functions. Transient ischemic attacks (TIA) are strokes of a short duration (transient) during which blood flow to the brain is interrupted (ischemic) producing a sudden effect on the brain (attack). The person may experience some of the signs and symptoms of a stroke and recover without apparent ill-effects. Such attacks are a serious warning of more serious conditions that should receive medical attention to prevent a more severe stroke.

A stroke may occur at any age, but usually in middle-aged and elderly persons, and it may be associated with high blood pressure. A stroke can occur during sleep and may remain undetected initially.

It is sometimes difficult to determine whether a person has suffered a stroke; the age of the person and the suddenness of the attack may be the only factors to suggest that a stroke has occurred.

Signs and symptoms of strokes differ depending on the part of the brain involved. You should look for any of the following signs and symptoms:

● changes in the level of consciousness (see chap. 11);

● unequal size of the pupils of the eyes;

● paralysis or weakness of the facial muscles and difficulty in speaking and swallowing;

● numbness or paralysis of the extremities;

● mental confusion;

● loss of bladder and bowel control;

● convulsions.

*Fig. 25-2. Unequal size of pupils
may indicate stroke or head injury.*

FIRST AID

First aid for strokes is limited to protective and supportive measures until medical aid is obtained. While awaiting medical aid:

- make the person as comfortable as possible in a semisitting position if conscious;

- if the person becomes unconscious, place him in the recovery position, keeping the good side up, if there is paralysis, to make breathing easier;

- loosen tight clothing;

- give nothing by mouth if the person is unconscious; if the person requests it, moisten lips and tongue with a wet cloth;

- protect the person from injury when being lifted or moved or during convulsions;

- give reassurance and avoid excitement;

- do not apply heating pads or hot water bottles. If they are too hot, the person may not know it because of a loss of sensation.

Notes

CHAPTER 26

DIABETES, EPILEPSY, CONVULSIONS, HERNIA AND ALLERGIC REACTION

DIABETES

Diabetes is a condition in which body processes fail to maintain a proper balance of sugar. A certain amount of sugar is always found in a normal person's blood where it is used as a source of energy. The pancreas produces **insulin** to regulate the level of sugar in the blood. Too much or too little insulin results in a diabetic emergency.

A diabetic emergency can be either **insulin shock** resulting from too much insulin or **diabetic coma** resulting from too little insulin. Insulin is prescribed for diabetics in quantities that keep blood sugar at a normal level.

In diabetic emergencies, the casualty may know of his condition and, if conscious, should be encouraged to explain what is needed. Keep in mind that he may be confused. If the person has taken insulin but has not eaten or has exercised excessively, the condition is probably insulin shock. Such a person may require sugar. If insulin has not been taken, the condition is probably diabetic coma and the person may need insulin.

The unconscious casualty should be searched for medical information, such as a medical alert device, that may indicate a diabetic condition. The diabetic person should advise fellow workers of his condition so that they will be prepared to help in an emergency.

Signs and symptoms that help the First Aider to determine whether the casualty needs sugar or insulin are listed in the following table:

	INSULIN SHOCK (Needs Sugar)	DIABETIC COMA (Needs Insulin)
Pulse	Full, rapid	Weak, rapid
Respirations	Shallow	Deep, sighing
State of Consciousness	Faintness to unconsciousness developing quickly	Gradual onset of unconsciousness
Skin	Pale, sweating	Flushed, dry
Breath Odour	Odourless	Musty apple, nail polish (acetone)
Other Signs and Symptoms	– Headache and – Trembling – Confusion – Aggressive behaviour (sometimes)	

Fig 26-1. Diabetic emergencies.

FIRST AID

The objectives of first aid are to prevent the diabetic person's condition from deteriorating, and to obtain medical aid as quickly as possible. If there is doubt about whether insulin or sugar should be given, help the conscious diabetic to take a sweetened drink. A drink sweetened with two tablespoons of sugar or some other sweet substance will not harm the casualty and could be beneficial.

If there is no improvement, the casualty may lapse into unconsciousness. Treat the person as an unconscious casualty and place in the recovery position. When the casualty is in this state, the need for medical aid is urgent.

EPILEPSY

Epilepsy is a disorder of the nervous system characterized by seizures which may involve partial or complete loss of consciousness and perhaps convulsions. In most cases, this condition is controlled by medication. A minor seizure is called an "abscence" (formerly "petit mal") and a major seizure is called a "tonic-clonic" (formerly "grand mal").

During a minor seizure the person may become pale, with eyes fixed and staring, and although the eyes may be open, the person may be unconscious for a few seconds. The condition may resemble a fainting attack and should be treated as such (see chap. 11).

In a major epileptic seizure, the person may sense the seizure is about to occur because of a brief characteristic feeling or aura that may accompany the seizure. A typical seizure has two phases:

The "tonic" phase:

- a sudden loss of consciousness causing the person to fall. The person's body becomes rigid for a few seconds during which the face and neck may become cyanosed.

The "clonic" phase:

- convulsions occur, breathing is noisy, frothy saliva may apear around the mouth and the teeth may grind.

Once the seizure passes, gradual relaxing of the muscles follows along with a return to consciousness. A tonic-clonic seizure seldom lasts longer than 3 minutes. On regaining consciousness, the person may be unaware of recent events and may appear dazed and confused. This phase may be followed by exhaustion or sleepiness.

FIRST AID

The aim of first aid is to protect the epileptic person from injury during the period of convulsions. Clear the area of curious onlookers, and give the casualty as much privacy as possible. Give first aid as follows:

- guide but do not restrict movement;

- protect the person from injury;

- ensure an open airway and if possible put the person in the recovery position;

- do not insert anything between the teeth;

- maintain the person's privacy as much as possible, clear all nonessential persons away;

- do not leave the person unattended as a second seizure is quite possible. If a second tonic-clonic seizure occurs within a few minutes, call for medical aid.

CONVULSIONS IN CHILDREN

Children with a high temperature may go into convulsions, which can be recognized by contractions of the muscles of the face and extremities. The body may become rigid and arch backward. The child may hold his breath, causing congestion, and have froth at the mouth.

FIRST AID

The aim is to protect the child from injury and:

- gently attempt to maintain an open airway;

- loosen constrictive clothing;

- when convulsions cease, place the child in the recovery position with the head lowered and turned to one side;

- reassure the child's parents;

- obtain medical aid.

HERNIA

The condition commonly called **hernia** is a protrusion through the muscular wall of the abdomen causing a swelling or bulge in the abdominal area. It occurs most frequently in the groin and can be caused by lifting or strenuous exercise.

The condition may be painless or may be accompanied by pain and nausea. The First Aider should not press on the swelling. The casualty should be placed at rest lying in the faceup position with head and shoulders lowered. Lowering the head and shoulders may allow the hernia to reduce itself. If the casualty is nauseated or has breathing problems, place him in the recovery position and obtain medical aid.

ALLERGIC REACTION

An allergic reaction is the body's response to a substance to which it has become highly sensitive. This response tends to be violent and affects mainly respiration, circulation, digestion and the skin. The reaction will range from mildly annoying, such as an itch or sneezing, to severe and life-threatening, such as respiratory distress and shock (anaphylactic shock).

HISTORY

Almost anything in the environment can cause an allergic person to react — airborne pollens and dusts, food and drugs, chemicals and plants, toxin and venom from insect stings and snakebites, even sunlight. The cause of an allergic reaction is important information for the casualty's medical care, but it is more important that you recognize the onset of a reaction, remove the cause, and take the necessary steps to protect the casualty during transportation to medical aid.

SIGNS AND SYMPTOMS

Look for difficult breathing, for changes in circulation, for digestive disorders and for skin irritations. Some or all of the following signs and symptoms may be present:

● sneezing and coughing with complaints of pain and tightness in the chest. Breathing may become more difficult with wheezing on exhalation and may stop if swollen tissues obstruct the airway.

● the pulse may be weak and the casualty will show signs of low blood pressure — dizziness, pallor, unconsciousness.

● abdominal cramps, nausea, vomiting and diarrhea may occur, particularly if the substance was ingested.

● severe itching, especially where the skin is flushed or when hives (raised skin eruptions) are present.

● swelling of tissues about the face, mouth and throat.

● cyanosis (blueness of the lips).

FIRST AID

A severe allergic reaction can only be reversed by appropriate medical treatment. First aid is limited to providing care for shock (see chap. 10), maintaining breathing and circulation (see chaps. 7 & 8), and providing urgent transportation to a medical facility. The first aid for insect stings and snakebites is detailed in chapter 22.

Some people with known allergies wear a medical alert device and carry prescribed medication in the form of pills or injectable liquids. The liquids are usually carried in a prepared hypodermic syringe in an allergy kit. Do not administer these medications yourself, but give whatever assistance you can to a conscious casualty to administer his own medication.

Notes

CHAPTER 27

BEHAVIOURAL PROBLEMS

EMOTIONALLY DISTURBED CASUALTIES

The best possible preparation that a First Aider can have to cope effectively with another person's severe emotional stress is education and training. Education should include instruction about the causes of disaster, the types of reactions to be expected from disaster casualties, and the basic principles of psychological first aid.

Head injuries and a variety of medical conditions that can cause unusual behaviour are described elsewhere in this manual. This section is concerned with bizarre or abnormal behaviour that is specifically related to severe emotional shock, chemical (alcohol or drug) abuse, or mental illness.

Recognizing and relating a person's behaviour to its cause enables the First Aider to use appropriate psychological first aid. Proper care of such casualties can achieve positive results, preventing the behaviour from becoming more disruptive and protecting such persons from injuring themselves and others.

EMOTIONAL REACTIONS

Certain types of behaviour can result from severe emotional trauma and are categorized as follows:

- **normal reaction** to stress in which the individual may appear calm, although he may be trembling and perspiring, and he may be nauseated to the point of vomiting. Recovery, for most people, occurs fairly quickly with a return to near-normal function.

- **individual panic,** sometimes called blind-flight or hysteria, in which the individual cannot accept reality, runs about in useless physical activity, may weep hysterically and make unreasoned attempts to flee. Two or three persons in such a state can cause mass panic.

- **depressed reaction** is the opposite of panic. The person is unable to relate to his surroundings, stands about numbed and confused as though completely alone, and is unable to help himself or others.

- **overactive response** results in a flurry of activity that may seem purposeful to the person affected. This person may spread rumours, make unreasonable demands and behave with unrealistic confidence in his abilities. He may disrupt rescue efforts if not controlled.

- **grief reaction** is characterized by recurrent waves of physical distress, with choking, tightness of the throat, shortness of breath and intense mental anguish. A person suffering from grief reaction is restless, shows a lack of concern for others and may respond with anger and irritability to attempts to help.

- **physical reaction** (conversion hysteria) results in the loss of functions such as hearing, sight or the use of limbs. Such casualties have unconsciously transferred their great fears into a strong belief that some part of the body is disabled. The First Aider must recognize that such conditions are real to the casualty and are not the result of malingering.

PSYCHOLOGICAL FIRST AID

Although different behaviour will require a different approach, you should be aware that a casualty may show features of more than one reaction, simultaneously or at successive stages. The probability of other reactions is decreased, however, if the initial behaviour is controlled promptly.

First aid for psychological casualties is quite limited. You should concentrate on providing quiet, supportive, reassuring care while arranging for medical aid. When large numbers of casualties are involved, as in a disaster, try to restore as many casualties as possible to normal function so that they can look after themselves and help others. Exercise care in approaching persons who exhibit aggressive behaviour. The casualty may perceive help as a threat to his safety and react violently. Try to calm the person's fears with reassurances of your intentions.

If restraint is necessary for the safety of others, act quickly but humanely with whatever assistance is available. Do not attempt to restrain anyone unless enough help is available to ensure success. Whenever possible, seek police assistance.

Provide care to those exhibiting severe emotional stress in the following ways:

- persons showing a normal reaction usually respond to quiet reassurance, encouragement, and involvement with the care of others.

- persons showing individual panic should be isolated in the care of two or more persons who are emotionally stable and have been briefed on the situation. Isolating panic cases reduces the possibility of mass panic and also helps such persons to calm down.

- persons showing an apathetic or depressed reaction should be gathered in small groups and encouraged to help each other.

- overactive persons need physical activity, preferably activity that is supervised and away from other casualties. Working with equipment and supplies are ideal activities for overactive persons.

- persons with grief reaction may not respond to first aid and may need medical aid.

- persons with physical reaction should be encouraged to do whatever small tasks they can, despite their symptoms. This will help them to regain their composure while waiting for medical help.

All psychological casualties need comforting and attention to their physical needs — hunger, pain, or other physical complaints. If medical aid is delayed, provide whatever physical comforts are at your disposal. If the casualty can take fluids, give non-stimulating drink such as milk or hot chocolate. Warm drinks will help them to relax. Reassure and protect such persons from harm until medical aid can be obtained.

HYPERVENTILATION

Hyperventilation, a condition of "overbreathing", is brought on by acute anxiety or emotional stress, or is caused by drug withdrawal or aspirin poisoning. Stress related hyperventilation may be reversed by first aid, but drug related conditions must be seen by medical aid.

Signs and Symptoms

A hyperventilating person breathes faster than normal, but may have a feeling of shortness of breath. He may complain of pains in his chest, numbness, tingling, cold hands and feet and of feeling dizzy. Although breathing is rapid and the pulse is fast, the casualty's skin colour is good with no signs of cyanosis.

FIRST AID

The aim of first aid for hyperventilation is to calm the person and reassure him that this condition is not serious. In stress related hyperventilation, quiet reassurance and encouraging the person to slow the rate of respirations will provide relief and ease the symptoms. Drug related cases will not respond as readily because the rate of respirations is drug induced.

Casualties in hyperventilation should be taken to medical aid for evaluation and further care. Some serious medical conditions may give the appearance of hyperventilation and these need medical care.

ALCOHOL AND DRUG-INDUCED BEHAVIOUR

Persons involved in an accident may be under the influence of alcohol or drugs and may display abnormal behaviour. Be careful that a serious injury or a medical condition is not overlooked as a result of the casualty's behaviour or because signs and symptoms are masked by the effects of drugs or alcohol. In cases of head injury or diabetic coma, for example, the condition of the pupils of the eyes or the characteristic odour of the breath might be masked (see chaps. 25 & 26).

The behaviour of persons who are under the influence of alcohol or drugs may interfere with attempts to give first aid. You may need help to calm and reassure the casualty. Police assistance should be sought, but if that is not available, ask two or more bystanders to help provide firm but gentle restraint. Other forms of restraint, such as straps or blankets, must not be used. Once the casualty is calm, proceed with an evaluation of his signs and symptoms and give appropriate first aid.

MENTAL ILLNESS AND SUICIDE GESTURES

In the absence of any history of other causes, persistent abnormal behaviour may be assumed to result from some form of mental illness. The behaviour patterns may resemble those described for disaster casualties, except that they will be more persistent and the person may show suicidal tendencies. Ensure that the behaviour does not result from other causes such as head injury or diabetes and make arrangements to have the casualty taken to medical aid.

Casualties who have attempted suicide or have made suicide gestures should be protected from further attempts, treated for their injuries if any, and taken to medical aid. Report the suicide gesture or attempt to the medical facility.

CHAPTER 28

RESCUE AND TRANSPORTATION

Moving a casualty can be dangerous. Improper, hurried or rough handling can cause serious harm to a sick or injured person. Casualties should be moved only under the following circumstances:

- life-threatening hazards to yourself or the casualty make the move necessary e.g. danger from fire, explosion, gas or water;

- essential first aid for wounds or other conditions cannot be given in the casualty's present position or location;

- medical aid cannot come to the scene, so the casualty must be moved to a medical facility;

- the casualty's condition will permit the move without serious danger;

- support and immobilization can be provided during the move.

If the casualty must be moved, select the rescue method that will give maximum protection to the person's injuries and that will subject the rescuer to minimum risks. You can be of little help to accident victims if you injure yourself in their rescue.

First Aiders are exposed to a number of hazards at the scene of an accident. Some are described in chapter 1. A personal injury to which rescuers are most susceptible is muscle strain caused by using incorrect body mechanics in lifting or moving a casualty. Follow the techniques for lifting, outlined in chapter 17, to prevent such injuries.

RESCUE

Rescue is the process of moving a casualty the shortest possible distance for safety or for essential first aid. It may require a simple rescue carry, or immobilization and extrication of the casualty. Rescue is usually done under urgent and dangerous conditions and the casualty may have to be moved with less than ideal support for injuries. You must assess the risks to the casualty in each case and use your best judgement in deciding the best way to make the rescue.

EXTRICATION

In many accidents, victims are trapped or entangled and they cannot free themselves. The process of freeing them is called extrication. You should provide as much support as possible to the casualty during extrication. If possible, give essential first aid and immobilize the injuries before the casualty is moved. If neck or back injuries are suspected, the head, neck and trunk should be immobilized on a spine board (see chap. 16). If the casualty is sitting up, a short spine board may be used.

USE OF THE SHORT SPINE BOARD

Use of a short spine board requires at least two rescuers. One to support the casualty by holding the head and neck in a rigid position until immobilization is completed; the other to prepare the short spine board. Prepare a short spine board by threading broad bandages or straps through the strap holes along the sides of the board. The bandages or straps should be brought around the back of the board and secured temporarily on one edge.

While one First Aider holds the casualty firmly, the second positions the short spine board along the back of the casualty. The bottom edge of the board should be below the pelvis and the headpiece at least level with the top of the head. All natural hollows of the body must be padded, especially those at the neck to keep the head and neck in the position of injury. Pad both sides of the head to prevent rotation.

Secure the head to the board with one narrow bandage around the forehead. Position the casualty's arms at the sides. Secure the chest to the board with a prc-positioned strap or bandage. Secure the lower trunk to the board with a bandage or strap.

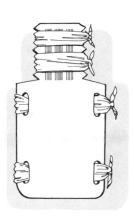

Fig. 28-1. Prepared short spine board.

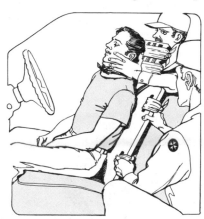

Fig. 28-2. Short spine board in position.

Now, ease the casualty out of the motor vehicle or other accident site. Do not use the strap holes on the spine board as hand holds to lift the casualty; that could seriously aggravate injuries. Bear the casualty's weight on your hands and arms as you lift him out so that the spine board is not disturbed.

URGENT EXTRICATION

If there is an immediate and grave danger and you are alone to move a casualty from a sitting position without a short spine board, proceed as follows:

- disentangle the person's feet from the wreckage and bring the feet toward the exit;

- ease your forearm under the person's armpit on the exit side, extending your hand to support the chin;

- ease the person's head gently backward to rest on your shoulder while maintaining the neck as rigid as possible;

- ease your other forearm under the armpit on the opposite side and grasp the wrist of the casualty's arm nearest the exit;

- establish a firm footing and pivot with the person, maintaining as much rigidity in the neck as possible.

- drag the casualty from the vehicle to a safe distance, with the least possible twisting or flexion of the vertebral column.

Fig. 28-3 (a). Providing support for extrication.

Fig. 28-3 (b). Drag carry from a sitting position.

Drag Carry

A drag carry, as the name implies, involves dragging the casualty while providing maximum protection to the head and neck.

Because there is a real risk of aggravating the casualties injuries, drag carries should be used only in the most extreme cases when there is an immediate threat to life.

Emergency extrication, outlined above, describes a drag carry for a casualty who is in the sitting position. The drag carry can also be applied to a casualty who is lying on his back.

Stand at the casualty's head facing his feet. Crouch down so that you can ease you hands under the casualty's shoulders to grasp the clothing on each side. Support the casualty's head between your forearms to prevent rotation (side-to-side turning) and flexion (dropping forward). Move backward carefully and drag the casualty only as far as necessary for his safety. If time

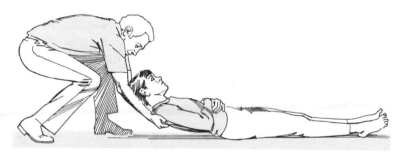

Fig. 28-4. Drag carry from a lying position.

permits, apply a cervical collar and secure the casualty's hands together across his chest before dragging. If the casualty must be dragged down stairs, grasp him under the arms, support his head and neck on your chest, and descend the stairs backwards on your knees.

THE RESCUE CARRY

A rescue carry is any one of various methods used in an emergency to move a casualty over a short distance to safety, to shelter, or to a better means of transportation. A rescue carry may be performed by one, two or three rescuers.

The Human Crutch

Fig. 28-5. The human crutch.

You may use your body as a crutch to help a casualty to walk. Take the weight of the casualty's injured side on your shoulders by grasping his wrist and bringing his arm over your shoulders and neck. Reach around the casualty's back and grasp his clothing or his belt at the waist. Instruct the casualty to step off with you, each using the inside foot. This lets you bear the weight of the injured foot for the casualty. A walking stick will help the casualty to provide additional support on the uninjured side.

The Pick-a-Back

The pick-a-back carry is used for a conscious casualty with lower limb injuries, provided she can use her arms.

The casualty must be able to help get into position on your back or she must be sitting at chair or table height. Crouch with your back between the casualty's knees. Ensure that the casualty can support her upper body by holding on with her arms around your neck. Cradle the casualty's legs on your forearms and lift, using the muscles of your thighs and lower legs to bring yourself into an upright position.

If the casualty is to be carried pick-a-back for a long distance, you can make a carrying seat. A large adjustable loop should be improvised from a strap or belts. Put your arms through the loop, arranging it comfortably behind your neck and down the front of your shoulders. This should leave the bottom half of the loop free at the back about the level of your buttocks. Pass the casualty's legs through the bottom end of the loop; one leg on each side. Position the loop under the casualty's buttocks so that it makes a seat. Adjust the length of the loop as necessary for a good carrying position and proper weight distribution. The casualty must still hold his arms around your neck, but your hands can be freed when necessary to cross rough terrain.

Fig. 28-6. The pick-a-back.

Fig. 28-7. The carrying seat.

The Cradle

Fig. 28-8 (a). Cradle carry — prepared to lift.

Fig. 28-8 (b). Cradle carry.

The cradle carry may be used for children and lightweight adults. Stoop and place the casualty's arm around your neck.

Pass your forearm under the casualty's knees and the other under the armpits. Ensure a solid footing and place the feet apart for good balance. Lift the casualty, using the leg and thigh muscles, but keep your back as straight as possible.

If the casualty is on the ground, lift in two stages. Kneel on one knee at the casualty's side near the head and shoulders. Place one arm under the armpits and the other under the casualty's legs at the knees and lift to rest on your raised knee. Using the muscles of both legs, rise to a standing position in one smooth motion.

Fireman's Carry

The fireman's carry is useful for casualties who are helpless and are not too heavy for the rescuer. The casualty can be lifted from ground level using the following procedure. Face the person and flex his knees to bring the heels up against his buttocks. Then, standing with your toes against the casualty's toes, grasp the wrists and pull the casualty upward and forward. Maintain a grip on one wrist as you turn and stoop to catch the casualty's upper body across your shoulders.

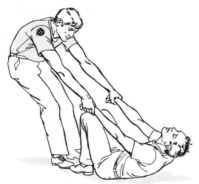

Fig. 28-9 (a). Fireman's carry — start position.   *Fig. 28-9 (b). Fireman's carry — lift position.*

The lifting manoeuvre is a continuous, smooth motion to bring the casualty through a sitting position to an upright position, finishing with the casualty draped over your shoulders.

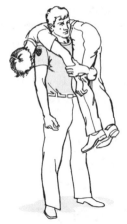

Next, stoop to adjust the weight across your shoulders, with the casualty's legs straddling your shoulder. Pass your arm between the casualty's legs and grasp his wrist. This will stabilize the casualty on your shoulders and leave your other hand free to help in extrication.

Fig. 28-9 (c). The fireman's carry.

TWO-RESCUER CARRIES

Whenever you call on bystanders to help move a casualty, the following principles must be observed:

● you remain responsible for the casualty;

● the bystander must be told exactly what to do and what precautions must be taken for the casualty's safety;

● you must coordinate the rescue activities with precise cautionary and executive commands. For example you give the cautionary command, "Prepare to lift." and when everyone is ready, give the executive command, "Lift!" These commands should be explained and may be practised before being carried out.

Four-Hand Seat

If the casualty is conscious and can help support his upper body, two rescuers can form a four-hand seat by joining their hands and wrists. Each rescuer grasps his own left wrist with his right hand, then grasps the right wrist of the other rescuer with his left hand to form a rigid four-hand seat.

Instruct the casualty to put his arms around the rescuers' shoulders and hoist up to permit the bearers to pass their hands under the buttocks to position them under the thighs at a point of balance. Instruct the casualty to hold onto the rescuers' shoulders to maintain balance and to support his upper body. The rescuers step off together, each using the inside foot.

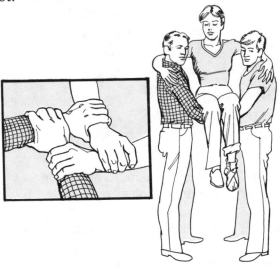

Fig. 28-10. The four-hand seat.

Two-Hand Seat

If the casualty is unable to support his upper body, two rescuers can provide support using a two-hand seat. The rescuers crouch on each side of the casualty. Place light padding or a folded handkerchief inside the bent fingers of the hands to be joined.

Fig. 28-11 (a). Hand grip for the two-hand seat.

Pass the hands under the casualty's buttocks and hook the fingers together to form a rigid two-hand seat. Cross the free hands at the casualty's back to grasp the clothing or belt at the casualty's waist. The rescuers lift, with backs held straight and the lifting force exerted by the leg and thigh muscles. The First Aider coordinates the lift with the commands, "Prepare to lift. Lift".

Fig. 28-11 (b). Two-hand seat — grip and lift.

Fig. 28-11 (c). Two hand seat.

Once in the standing position, adjust the hands and arms at the casualty's back. The bearers step off together, each on the inside foot.

The Chair-Carry

The chair-carry enables two rescuers to carry a conscious or an unconscious casualty through narrow passages and up and down stairs. If the casualty is unconscious or helpless, strap her upper body and arms to the back of a chair with a bandage.

If unconscious and lying on the ground, the casualty can be placed on the chair by sliding the back of the chair under her legs and buttocks, and along the lower back. After the casualty is secured, the chair can be raised on its back legs and placed upright.

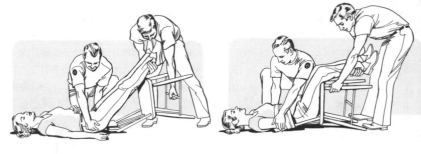

Fig. 28-12 (a). Chair lift —
positioning the chair.

Fig. 28-12 (b). The chair carry —
secure the casualty.

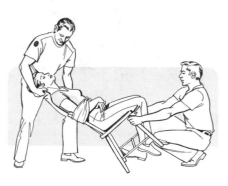

Fig. 28-12 (c). Chair carry —
upright position.

Fig. 28-12 (d). Chair carry.

The chair is carried by two rescuers, one at the chair back and one at the front, both facing forward. The rescuer at the back crouches and grasps the chair legs just below the seat. The rescuer at the front crouches with his back between the casualty's knees and grasps the front chair legs near the floor. The casualty is lifted on the command of the First Aider. The rescuers walk out-of-step for the chair carry.

The casualty should be carried downstairs facing forward. The rescuers adjust their grips on the chair back and the front legs so that the front rescuer faces the casualty. Because the front rescuer will be descending the stairs backwards, a third person should act as a guide and support the front rescuer in the event of a loss of footing.

Fig. 28-12 (e). Chair-carry — descending stairs.

The Extremities Carry

If a chair is not available and the casualty does not have fractures or serious injuries of the trunk, two rescuers can use the extremities carry (fore-and-aft carry). One rescuer passes his hands under the casualty's armpits and grasps his wrists, crossing them over his chest. The second rescuer crouches with his back between the casualty's knees and grasps each leg just above

Fig. 28-13. The extremities carry.

the knee. The two rescuers lift on command, and step off on opposite feet on the command, "Advance". Walking out-of-step is smoother for the casualty.

TRANSPORTATION

There may be times when medical aid cannot be contacted or for other reasons cannot come to the casualty. In these circumstances, it may be necessary to transport the casualty to the medical facility. If the casualty is unable to walk or if the injury or illness allows only the most gentle movement, a stretcher should be used.

STRETCHERS

Stretchers are either commercially made or improvised. The most common of the commercial stretchers is the rigid-pole, canvas stretcher. It has hinged bracing bars at right angles between the rigid poles at either end that must be locked in the extended position before the stretcher is used.

Improvised Stretchers

Stretchers can be improvised from tabletops, doors or two rigid poles and a blanket. If a door is being used, make sure it will clear all intervening passageways and doorways. Test whatever stretcher is used to make sure that it will bear the casualty's weight.

Fig. 28-14. The rigid-pole, canvas stretcher.

A stretcher can be improvised by using a blanket and two poles. Place a pole across the width of blanket, one-third the distance from one end. Fold the shorter end of the blanket over the pole. Place the second pole parallel to the first so that it is on the doubled part of the blanket and about 15 cm (6 inches) from the

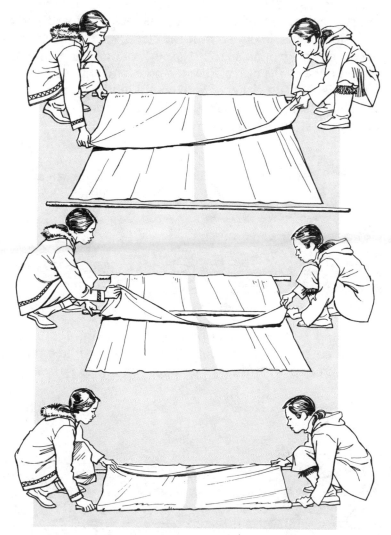

Fig. 28-15. Improvised blanket stretcher.

doubled edge. Bring the remaining end of the blanket over to cover both poles. The casualty's weight on the blanket will make the folds secure to provide a non-rigid stretcher. This stretcher is not recommended for casualties with suspected back and neck injuries.

A non-rigid stretcher can also be improvised from two jackets and two poles. Button and zipper the jackets closed and turn their sleeves inside out so that the sleeves are inside. Lay the jackets on the ground so that top edge of one jacket meets the bottom edge of the other. Pass the poles through the sleeves of the two jackets on either side to complete the stretcher. If the casualty is tall, prepare another jacket as before and add it, top edge first, to the stretcher.

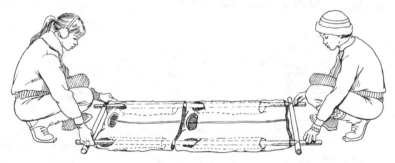

Fig. 28-16. Improvised jacket stretcher.

Sacks and poles may also be used. Make small holes in the bottom corners of two grain or potato sacks. Place the sacks on the ground with their open ends touching. Pass the poles

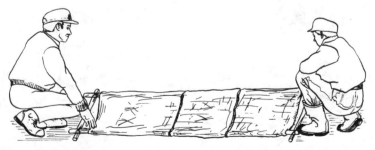

Fig. 28-17. Improvised sack stretcher.

through the corner holes on either side to complete the stretcher. A third sack, open end first, may be added for taller casualties.

If time and materials are available, use two sticks of suitable length to hold the poles apart to the width of the stretcher. Tie these sticks securely to each pole at either end.

Test all improvised stretchers with someone of equal weight to the casualty, or heavier, to ensure that it will hold. This will not only reassure the casualty, it will prevent an accident that may cause more harm. Non-rigid stretchers are not recommended for casualties with suspected back and neck injuries.

BLANKETING A STRETCHER

A casualty can be wrapped on a stretcher using one or two blankets. These two methods provide maximum warmth with minimum weight on the patient. They also permit easy access to the casualty's wounds if that is necessary during transportation. If extra blankets are available, one blanket folded to the width of the stretcher can be used as an underpad before blanketing, and another can be folded in half and laid loosely over the casualty for warmth after initial blanketing.

One-Blanket Method

To wrap a casualty on a stretcher with the **one-blanket method,** place the blanket diagonally on the length of the stretcher and fold the overhanging edges to either side of the stretcher bed to keep them off the ground. After the casualty has been centred on the stretcher, bring the bottom corner of the blanket (1 in the figure) over the feet and tuck it in between the ankles. Bring the corner at the head (2), around the head and neck to the chest.

Unfold one side of the blanket (3) and cover the casualty. Tuck the end around the body on the opposite side. Unfold the other side (4) and wrap it around the casualty to finish the procedure.

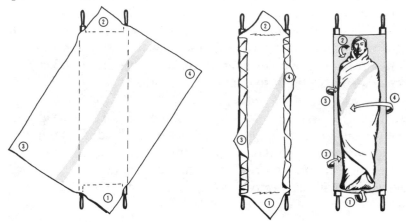

Fig. 28-18. Preparing a stretcher with one blanket.

Two-Blanket Method

To prepare a stretcher using the **two-blanket method,** spread the first blanket with its length across the width of the stretcher and off centre. Bring the upper edge high enough on the stretcher to provide a good cover for the casualty's head. Cover half to three-quarters of the length of the stretcher handles to give sufficient blanket for a head cover.

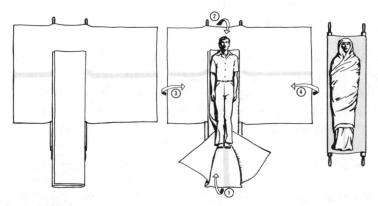

Fig. 28-19. Preparing a stretcher with two blankets.

Fold the second blanket in thirds along its length and position it along the length of stretcher. Leave enough blanket at the foot to provide good cover for the casualty's feet. Open out the folds of the second blanket at the foot of the stretcher to a length of about 60cm (24 in.).

Fold the overhanging edges of the first blanket (3 and 4) to the edges of the stretcher bed, ready to receive the casualty. When the casualty has been positioned on the stretcher, cover the feet, using the opened-out folds (1), and tuck some of the blanket between the ankles.

Bring the upper edge of the first blanket (2) around the casualty's head and shoulders. Carry the shorter end (3) over the body and upper legs, tucking it in against the body. Bring the long end of the blanket (4) over the body and tuck it in to complete the procedure.

PLACING A CASUALTY ON A STRETCHER

A casualty can be placed onto a stretcher by four or three bearers. The basic principles for lifting and positioning a casualty on a stretcher are:

● all essential first aid and immobilization should be completed before moving the casualty to a stretcher;

● bring the blanketed and padded stretcher to the casualty, rather than moving the casualty to the stretcher;

● as the First Aider in charge, take the position that will permit you to observe and control the most sensitive area of the body, usually at the head and shoulders;

● instruct the bearers carefully in what each is expected to do. If the move is difficult and time permits, a practice with a simulated casualty is advisable. That reduces risks and reassures the conscious casualty.

- control all manoeuvres with cautionary and executive commands to ensure smooth, coordinated movements.

Blanket Lift with Four Bearers

Four bearers can lift a casualty onto a stretcher using a blanket or rug as follows:

- roll the blanket or rug lengthwise for half its width and place the roll along the casualty's side.

- two bearers maintain firm control of the head and feet while you and one bearer gently roll the casualty toward you onto his side (logroll), keeping him rigid. Alignment of the body must be maintained without bending or twisting the neck or trunk.

- move the blanket roll up to the casualty's back.

- turn the casualty over the blanket roll toward the opposite side.

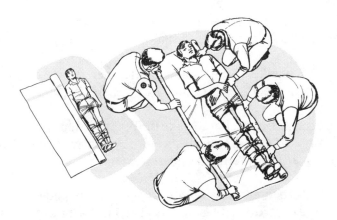

Fig. 28-20 (a). Placing the casualty on a blanket.

● unroll the blanket.

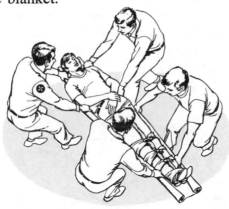

Fig. 28-20 (b). The blanket lift with four bearers.

Roll the edges of the blanket up to each side of the casualty and all bearers grip the rolls at points along the body at the head and shoulders and at the hip and lower legs. The blanket is kept taut by the bearers as the casualty is lifted and the stretcher is brought into place.

Four-Bearer Method – No Blanket

If a blanket or rug is not available, place a stretcher in line with the casualty, either at the head or at the feet. You and the three bearers take positions on your left knees on both sides of the casualty. As the First Aider, you take the position at the head and shoulders, bearer 2 takes a position along your side and opposite the casualty's hips. Bearer 3 kneels next to the lower legs on the same side. Bearer 4 assumes a position on the opposite side at the trunk and hips. Bearer 4, who will link his hands with you and bearer 2, is also required to position the stretcher under the casualty when you direct him to do so.

Tell the three bearers where they are to place their hands and forearms, and caution them on the care of the casualty's injuries. The hand grip, as for the two-man seat, should be demonstrated over the casualty before the procedure is started.

Pass one hand under the casualty's neck and grip the opposite shoulder. Ease your other hand under the casualty's back to join the hand of bearer 4, opposite. Bearer 2 eases one hand under the small of the casualty's back to join bearer 4, and places his other hand under the thighs. Bearer 3 eases his hands under the casualty's thighs and lower legs.

Fig. 28-21 (a). The four-bearer method: lift position.

When you are assured that each bearer has a firm hold on the casualty, give the cautionary "Prepare to lift" followed by the command "Lift". The casualty should be lifted smoothly to the height of the raised knees. On the command "Rest", the casualty is gently laid on your knee and the raised knees of bearers 2 and 3. Direct bearer 4 to position the stretcher against the bearers' toes and to resume his position as bearer 4, linking his hands with yours and bearer 2.

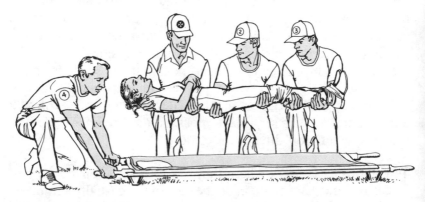

Fig. 28-21 (b). The four-bearer method: rest position.

When all are ready, give the commands "Prepare to lift. Lift" and the casualty's weight is raised from the knees. This is followed by the commands, "Prepare to lower. Lower", and the casualty is gently laid on the stretcher.

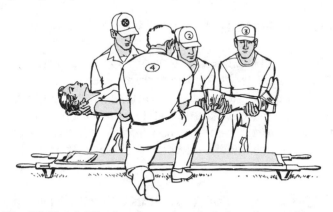

Fig. 28-21 (c). The four-bearer method: lowering position.

Three-Bearer Method, No Blanket

The three-bearer method is essentially the same as the four-bearer method, except that the First Aider and one bearer must share the weight on one side of the casualty. The third bearer links hands with the First Aider from the opposite side to take up the weight of the head and trunk. The casualty is lifted and rested

Fig. 28-22. Three-bearer lift.

on the bearers' knees while the stretcher is positioned and bearer 3 links hands again with the First Aider to help lower the casualty to the stretcher.

CARRYING THE STRETCHER

Stretchers may be carried by four or by two bearers. As the First Aider in charge, decide on the carrying method and instruct the bearers accordingly. You assume a position that will permit you to observe the casualty continuously as well as direct the bearers during transport. If there are enough bearers to carry the stretcher, walk beside the stretcher to observe the patient and the route.

Although stretcher casualties are usually carried feetfirst, certain conditions and circumstances require a headfirst carry. These are:

- lower limb injuries during a long downhill carry or when descending stairs. A headfirst carry decreases pressure on the lower limbs and minimizes discomfort.

- uphill carries and ascending stairs if there are no injuries of the lower extremities. A headfirst carry decreases blood flow to the casualty's head and is more comfortable.

- loading an ambulance or transferring the casualty to a bed. Headfirst ambulance loading is done for safety and to make observation easier.

Four Bearers

After the casualty has been strapped to the stretcher, you assume a position at the casualty's head and assign the remaining three bearers to respective corners of the stretcher. When the bearers have a firm footing and a good grip on the stretcher, give the commands, "Prepare to lift. Lift". On the command, "Advance", all bearers step off on the foot nearest the stretcher and try to keep in step. When it is necessary to stop, give the commands "Halt", "Prepare to lower", Lower".

Fig. 28-23. Stretcher carry: four bearers.

Two Bearers

The bearers crouch between the carrying handles of the stretcher, facing in the direction of travel. Assume whatever position will permit you to observe the patient. The bearers grasp the handles in each hand. Coordinate the lift by commands as in the four-bearer carry. Two bearers step off on

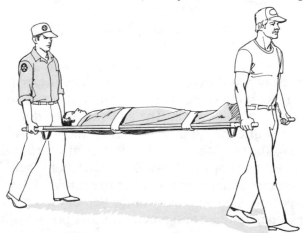

Fig. 28-24. Stretcher carry: two bearers.

opposite feet and walk out-of-step. This provides smoother transportation for the casualty.

Obstacles

When crossing uneven ground, the stretcher should be carried by four bearers and kept as level as possible. The bearers must adjust the height of the stretcher to compensate for dips and rises in the terrain. If the distance is short, the four bearers should face inwards to allow for smooth adjustments.

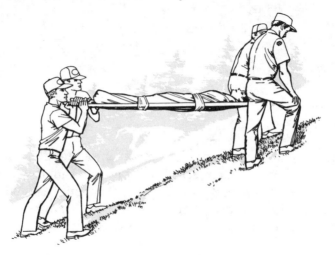

Fig. 28-25. Crossing uneven ground.

Avoid **crossing a wall,** even if it means a longer carry. If a wall must be crossed, the stretcher is lifted onto the wall so that the front runners are just over it. The stretcher is held level by the rear bearers while the front bearers cross the wall. All bearers then lift together and the stretcher is moved forward until the rear runners are resting on the wall. The stretcher is held level by the front bearers until the rear bearers have crossed the wall and assumed positions on both sides at the rear of the stretcher. The stretcher is then lowered and previous bearer positions resumed to continue the journey.

INDEX

(Illustrated pages in bold)

First Aid

We Can Help
An inexpensive course in first aid and safety awareness for children between the ages of 7 and 10. Ideal for integration with the junior school curriculum.

School Programme
Adapted from the Emergency and Standard First Aid courses, with lessons grouped into units to form a flexible time schedule suitable for any timetable requirements.

The Lifesaver
An introductory (2 ½ hour) first aid course for busy people. Students learn the essential first aid which may be required to save a life. Modules may be added to this course for special groups such as drivers or sports coaches.

Emergency First Aid Modular Course
A 6 ½ hour course comprised of 5 compulsory modules and 16 elective modules supported by audio-visual segments. This course, because of its flexibility, allows customization of course content to meet the first aid requirements of industry, business, government and schools.

Standard First Aid Modular Course
A 13 hour comprehensive programme comprised of 5 compulsory modules and 18 elective modules and supported by 16 audio-visual segments. CPR certification to the Heart Saver level is offered within the framework of this flexible programme. This course can be customized to meet the requirements of any person in industry, business, government or education.

Advanced First Aid - Level I
A one week (35 hour) programme that teaches the theory and practice of more advanced first aid procedures. This course is recommended for those who have specific first aid responsibilities.

Advanced First Aid - Level II
A two week (70 hour) comprehensive programme designed to train the Industrial First Aid Attendant.

National Instructor Training and Development Programme (NITDP)
One week (30 hour) course to develop and practice first aid and CPR teaching skills.

St. John Ambulance

St. John Ambulance Courses

CPR*

Level A (Heart Saver)
A 6 hour course that teaches one-rescuer CPR and choking manoeuvres for an adult casualty. This is the ideal CPR course for the lay person.

Level B (Heart Saver Plus)
An 8 hour course including Level A material and CPR and choking manoeuvres for an infant or a child casualty.

Level C (Basic Rescuer)
A 12 hour comprehensive course including one and two-rescuer CPR and choking manoeuvres for infant, child and adult casualties. This course is designed for those with specific health care responsibilities such as nurses and professional rescuers.

Level D (Child and Infant)
An 8 hour course designed for parents and day care providers which teaches CPR and choking manoeuvres for infant and child casualties.

Level E
Customized courses to provide CPR training to specific populations such as the physically challenged.

* All St. John Ambulance CPR courses are taught to the standards of the Heart and Stroke Foundation of Canada's Emergency Cardiac Care Committee.

Health Care

Family Health Care
A course designed to teach how to care for a sick or convalescent relative at home.

What Every Babysitter Should Know
A course on how to babysit infants, toddlers, and preschoolers. The emphasis is on safety, coping in emergency situations, and babysitting responsibilities.

Child Care in the Home
This course teaches the care of children from infancy to pre-school age, including information on common childhood ailments. This course is of particular interest to parents and day care providers.

Healthy Aging
A relaxed and informal health care course designed to provide older people with the skills to continue living healthy and productive lives.

Caring for the Aging
Teaches the basic nursing skills needed to look after an elderly person at home. This course is of interest to family members, homemakers, and other caregivers of the elderly.

National Health Care Instructor Training Programme
This course teaches the principles of learning and teaching as they apply to health care course instruction.

Serve your community in an important and unique way.

- learn invaluable first aid and health care skills
- apply your first aid skills to real life situations
- help and care for others
- meet new people
- develop new and lasting friendships

Brigade members serve others in their community at almost every kind of event, from rock concerts to rodeos, and from conferences for the disabled to hockey and football games. You too can improve the quality of life in your community by making it a better and safer place to live. You'll be rewarded with the personal satisfaction of knowing that you've made a contribution. There's a place for you in the Brigade. Ask your instructor for details or call your local St. John Office today.

...Join the Brigade

St. John Ambulance
Provincial Councils

Northwest Territories
P.O. Box 2640
Yellowknife, X1A 2P9
(403) 873-5658

British Columbia
6111 Cambie Street
Vancouver, V5Z 3B2
(604) 321-2651

Alberta
10975-124 Street
Edmonton, T5M 0H9
(403) 452-6565

Saskatchewan
2625-3rd Avenue
Regina, S4T 0C8
(306) 522-7226

Federal District
30 Driveway
Ottawa, K2P 1C9
(613) 236-3626

Quebec
405 de Maisonneuve Blvd. East
Montreal, H2L 4J5
(514) 842-4801

Manitoba
535 Doreen Street
Winnipeg, R3G 3H5
(204) 774-1851

Ontario
46 Wellesley Street East
Toronto, M4Y 1G5
(416) 923-8411

New Brunswick
P.O. Box 3599, Station"B"
Fredericton, E3A 5J8
(506) 458-9129

Nova Scotia
88 Slayter Street
Dartmouth, B3A 2A6
(902) 463-5646

Prince Edward Island
P.O. box 1235
Charlottetown, C1A 7M8
(902) 368-1235

Newfoundland
P.O. Box 5489
St. John's, A1C 5W4
(709) 726-4200

St. John Ambulance

PLEASE TELL US WHAT YOU THINK

St. John Ambulance training materials, including this first aid manual, are constantly being updated as new first aid techniques are developed and as the first aid marketplace changes.

At National Headquarters, we value the observations, thoughts and opinions of our clientele. If you have any comments regarding this first aid manual, or any of our manuals, materials, courses or services, please use the space below to tell us what you think.

_____

_____

_____

_____

_____

_____

_____

_____

_____

_____

_____

_____

_____

_____

_____

_____

_____

_____

FOLD AND MAIL

St. John Ambulance National Headquarters
Attention: Publications Officer
312 Laurier Avenue East
Box 388, Terminal A
Ottawa, Ontario
K1N 8V4